100 Letters

that Changed the World

JANUARY 1, 2018

Dear Sisters,

In Solidarity

---

right at the top of a ha... bush, the ...ches are quite ...ed with chickens. Those at ... farm go up a ... wall into a ... The farmer

a beautiful fat pig. He is a funny old man. He feeds the cal... every morning, he ...tles the spoon on the tin pail to ... them breakfast is ready, but ... won't always come. then there is a ... like a German band. I remain ... aff. Beatrice Potter.

Coniston 26 May.

THE WHITE HOUSE
WASHINGTON

Dear Churchill

Wendell Willkie will give you this - He is truly helping to keep politics out over here.

I think this verse applies to your people as it does to us:

"Sail on, Oh Ship of State!
Sail on Oh Union strong and great!
Humanity with all its fears,
With all the hopes of future years
Is hanging breathless on thy fate."

As ever yours
Franklin D Roosevelt

COMBINED OPERATIONS HEADQUARTERS,
1a, RICHMOND TERRACE,
WHITEHALL, S.W.1.

Telephone
Whitehall 9777

21st April
1943.

Dear Admiral of the Fleet,

I promised V.C.I.G.S. that Major Martin would arrange with you for the onward transmission of a letter he has with him for General Alexander. It is very urgent and very "hot" and as there are some remarks in it that could not be seen by others in the War Office, it could not go by signal. I feel sure that you will see that it gets on safely and without delay.

I think you will find Martin the man you want. He is quiet and shy at first, but he really knows his stuff. He was more accurate than some of us about the probable run of events at Dieppe and he has been well in on the experiments with the latest barges, and equipment which took place up in Scotland.

Let me have him back, please, as soon as the assault is over. He might bring some sardines with him - they are "on points" here!

Yours sincerely,
Louis Mountbatten

Admiral of the Fleet Sir A.B. Cunningham, G.C.B., D.S.O.,
Commander in Chief Mediterranean,
Allied Force H.Q.,
Algiers.

JAMES W. McCORD, JR.
7 WINDER COURT
ROCKVILLE, MARYLAND 20852

March 19, 1973

TO: JUDGE SIRICA

Certain questions have been posed to me from your Honor through the probation officer, dealing with details of the case, motivations, intent and mitigating circumstances.

In endeavoring to respond to these questions, I am whipsawed in a variety of legalities. First, I may be called before a Senate Committee investigating this matter. Secondly, I may be involved in a civil suit, and thirdly there may be a new trial at some future date. Fourthly, the probation officer may be called before the Senate Committee to present testimony regarding what may otherwise be a privileged communication between defendant and Judge, as I understand it; if I answered certain questions to the probation officer, it is possible such answers could become a matter of record in the Senate and there from available for use in the above considerations. By answers would, it would seem to me, in violate my fifth amendment rights, and possibly my 6th amendment right to counsel and possibly others.

On the other hand, to fail to answer your questions may appear to be non-cooperation, and I can therefore expect a much more severe sentence.

There are further considerations which are not to be lightly taken. Several members of my family have expressed fear for my life if I disclose knowledge of the facts in this matter, either publicly for to any government representative. Whereas I do not share their concerns to the same degree, nevertheless, I do believe that retaliatory measures will be taken against me, my family, and my friends should I disclose such facts. Such retaliation could destroy careers, incomes, and reputations of persons who are innocent of any guilt whatever.

So that as it may, in the interests of justice, and in the interests of restoring faith in the criminal justice system, which faith has been severely damaged in this case, I will state the following to you at this time which I hope may be of help to you in meting out justice in this case:

1. There was political pressure applied to the defendants to plead guilty and remain silent.

2. Perjury occurred during the trial in matters highly material to the very structure, orientation, and impact of the government's case, and to the motivation and intent of the defendants.

3. Others involved in the Watergate operation were not identified during the trial, when they could have been by those testifying.

1. ...

The point to be of such importance that I would urge you to consider the statement, and make your meaning perfectly clear and unmistakable.

Yours very sincerely,
Alexander Graham Bell

WASHINGTON, D.C., January 21, 1892.

Miss A.M. SULLIVAN, Teacher of Helen Keller, Boston, Mass.

Perkins Institution for the Blind, South Boston, Mass.

DEAR MISS SULLIVAN—Allow me to thank you for the privilege of reading your account of how you taught Helen Keller, which you have prepared for the second edition of the Souvenir issued by the Volta Bureau. Your paper is full of interest to teachers of the deaf, and it contains many valuable and important suggestions.

---

we shall stick it out
to the End but we
are getting weaker of
course and the end
cannot be far.

It seems a pity but
I do not think I can
write more —

R. Scott

Last Entry

For Gods sake look
after our people

February 3, 1976

An Open Letter to Hobbyists

To me, the most critical thing in the hobby market right now is the lack of good software courses, books and software itself. Without good software and an owner who understands programming, a hobby computer is wasted. Will quality software be written for the hobby market?

Almost a year ago, Paul Allen and myself, expecting the hobby market to expand, hired Monte Davidoff and developed Altair BASIC. Though the initial work took only two months, the three of us have spent most of the last year documenting, improving and adding features to BASIC. Now we have 4K, 8K, EXTENDED, ROM and DISK BASIC. The value of the computer time we have used exceeds $40,000.

The feedback we have gotten from the hundreds of people who say they are using BASIC has all been positive. Two surprising things are apparent, however. 1) Most of these "users" never bought BASIC (less than 10% of all Altair owners have bought BASIC), and 2) The amount of royalties we have received from sales to hobbyists makes the time spent of Altair BASIC worth less than $2 an hour.

Why is this? As the majority of hobbyists must be aware, most of you steal your software. Hardware must be paid for, but software is something to share. Who cares if the people who worked on it get paid?

Is this fair? One thing you don't do by stealing software is get back at MITS for some problem you may have had. MITS doesn't make money selling software. The royalty paid to us, the manual, the tape and the overhead make it a break-even operation. One thing you do do is prevent good software from being written. Who can afford to do professional work for nothing? What hobbyist can put 3-man years into programming, finding all bugs, documenting his product and distribute for free? The fact is, no one besides us has invested a lot of money in hobby software. We have written 6800 BASIC, and are writing 8080 APL and 6800 APL, but there is very little incentive to make this software available to hobbyists. Most directly, the thing you do is theft.

What about the guys who re-sell Altair BASIC, aren't they making money on hobby software? Yes, but those who have been reported to us may lose in the end. They are the ones who give hobbyists a bad name, and should be kicked out of any club meeting they show up at.

I would appreciate letters from any one who wants to pay up, or has a suggestion or comment. Just write me at 1180 Alvarado SE, #114, Albuquerque, New Mexico, 87108. Nothing would please me more than being able to hire ten programmers and deluge the hobby market with good software.

Bill Gates
General Partner, Micro-Soft

Chock full o'Nuts
425 LEXINGTON AVENUE
NEW YORK 17, N.Y.

THE WHITE HOUSE
May 14 11 36 AM '58
RECEIVED

May 13, 1958

The President
The White House
Washington, D.C.

My dear Mr. President:

I was sitting in the audience at the Summit Meeting of Negro Leaders yesterday when you said we must have patience. On hearing you say this, I felt like standing up and saying, "Oh no! Not again."

I respectfully remind you sir, that we have been the most patient of all people. When you said we must have self-respect, I wondered how we could have self-respect and remain patient considering the treatment accorded us through the years.

17 million Negroes cannot do as you suggest and wait for the hearts of men to change. We want to enjoy now the rights that we feel we are entitled to as Americans. This we cannot do unless we pursue aggressively goals which all other Americans achieved over 150 years ago.

As the chief executive of our nation, I respectfully suggest...

---

9 P.M.

Time Received

United States Military Telegraph,
War Department.

Head Quarters A.P.O. 9 P.M.
October 25th 1862.

His Excellency
The President

In reply to your telegram of this date I have the honor to state, from the time this army left Washington on the 17th of September my Cavalry has been constantly Employed in making reconnaissances, Scouting & picketing. Since the battle of Antietam six Regiments have made a trip of two hundred...

Albert Einstein
Old Grove Rd.
Nassau Point
Peconic, Long Is.

August 2nd, 1939

F.D. Roosevelt,
President of the United States,
White House
Washington, D.C.

Sir:

Some recent work by E.Fermi and L. Szilard, which has been communicated to me in manuscript, leads me to expect that the element uranium may be turned into a new and important source of energy in the immediate future. Certain aspects of the situation which has arisen...

IMMEDIATE RELEASE   October 27, 1962
Office of the White House Press Secretary

THE WHITE HOUSE

TEXT OF A LETTER BY THE PRESIDENT
ADDRESSED TO THE CHAIRMAN OF THE
PRESIDIUM OF THE USSR SUPREME
SOVIET, NIKITA KHRUSHCHEV

October 27, 1962

Dear Mr. Chairman:

I have read your letter of October 26th with great care and welcomed the statement of your desire to seek a prompt solution to the problem. The first thing that needs to be done, however, is for work to cease on offensive missile bases in Cuba and for all weapon systems in Cuba capable of offensive use to be rendered inoperable, under effective United Nations arrangements.

Assuming that is done promptly, I have given my representatives in New York instructions that will permit them to work out with weekend — in cooperation with the Acting Secretary General and your representatives — an arrangement for a permanent solution to the Cuban problem along the lines suggested in your letter of October 26th. As I read your letter, the key elements of your proposals — which seem generally acceptable as I understand them — are as follows:

1) You would agree to remove these weapons systems from Cuba under appropriate United Nations observation and supervision; and undertake, with suitable safeguards, to halt the further introduction of such weapons systems into Cuba.

2) We, on our part, would agree — upon the establishment of adequate arrangements through the United Nations to ensure the carrying out and continuation of these commitments — (a) to remove promptly the quarantine measures now in effect and (b) to give assurances against an invasion of Cuba. I am confident that other nations of the Western Hemisphere would be prepared to do likewise.

If you will give your representative similar instructions, there is no reason why we should not be able to complete these arrangements and announce them to the world within a couple of days. The effect of such a settlement on easing world tensions would enable us to work toward a more general arrangement regarding "other armaments", as proposed in your second letter which you made public. I would like to say again that the United States is very much interested in reducing tensions and halting the arms race; and if your letter signifies that you are prepared to discuss a detente affecting NATO and the Warsaw Pact, we are quite prepared to consider with our allies any useful proposals.

But the first [illegible], let me emphasize, is the cessation of work on missile sites in Cuba and measures to render such weapons inoperable, under effective international guarantees. The continuation of this threat, or a prolonging of this discussion concerning Cuba by linking these problems to the broader questions of European and world security, would surely lead to an intensification of the Cuban crisis and a grave risk to the peace of the world. For this reason I hope we can quickly agree along the lines outlined in this letter and in your letter of October 26th.

*****

(s) John F. Kennedy

Martin Luther King, Jr.
Birmingham City Jail
April 16, 1963

Bishop C. C. J. Carpenter
Bishop Joseph A. Durick
Rabbi Milton L. Grafman
Bishop Paul Hardin
Bishop Nolan B. Harmon
The Rev. George M. Murray
The Rev. Edward V. Ramage
The Rev. Earl Stallings

My dear Fellow Clergymen,

While confined here in the Birmingham City Jail, I came across your recent statement calling my present activities "unwise and untimely." Seldom, if ever, do I pause to answer criticism of my work and ideas. If I sought to answer all of the criticisms that cross my desk, my secretaries would be engaged in little else in the course of the day, and I would have no time for constructive work. But since I feel that you are men of genuine goodwill and your criticisms are sincerely set forth, I would like to answer your statement in what I hope will be patient and reasonable terms.

HISTORICAL

OFFICE FOR EMERGENCY MANAGEMENT
OFFICE OF SCIENTIFIC RESEARCH AND DEVELOPMENT
1530 P STREET NW
WASHINGTON, D.C.

February 25, 1943

Dr. J. R. Oppenheimer
University of California
Berkeley, California

Dear Dr. Oppenheimer:

We are addressing this letter to you as Scientific Director of the special laboratory in New Mexico in order to confirm our many conversations on the matters of organization and responsibility. You are at liberty to show this letter to those with whom you are discussing the desirability of their joining the project with you; many of course realizing their connection to secrecy, including the details of organization and personnel.

I. The laboratory will be concerned with the development and final manufacture of an instrument of war, which we may designate as projectile S-1-W. To this end, the laboratory will be concerned with

A. Certain experimental studies in science, engineering and ordnance; and

B. At a later date large-scale experiments

On board R.M.S. Titanic
Sunday afternoon

My dear ones all,

As you see it is Sunday afternoon and we are resting in the Library after luncheon. I was very bad all day yesterday, could not eat or drink & sick all the while, but today I have got over it. This morning Eva & I went to church & she was so interested...

First published in the United States of America in 2019 by
Universe Publishing, A Division of
Rizzoli International Publications, Inc.
300 Park Avenue South
New York, NY 10010
www.rizzoliusa.com

Originally published in the United Kingdom in 2019 by Batsford,
an imprint of Pavilion Books Group Limited

Printed in Singapore

2019 2020 2021 2022 / 10 9 8 7 6 5 4 3 2 1

ISBN: 978-0-7893-3684-2
Library of Congress Control Number: 2019940138

Visit us online:
Facebook.com/RizzoliNewYork
Twitter: @Rizzoli_Books
Instagram.com/RizzoliBooks
Pinterest.com/RizzoliBooks
Youtube.com/user/RizzoliNY

OVERLEAF: A montage of many of the letters included in this book

100 Letters

that Changed the World

Colin Salter

UNIVERSE

Contents

Introduction

Ever since the spoken word evolved into its written form, letters have played a significant part in history. Some have played a pivotal role and shaped the fate of nations, others have recorded momentous events, while many have simply given us an insight into what it was like to live in times past.

On board R·M·S "Titanic."

Sunday afternoon

My Dear ones all,

As you see it is Sunday afternoon & we are resting in the Library after Luncheon I was very bad all day yesterday could not eat or drink, & sick all the while, but today I have got over it, This morning Eva & I went to church & she was so pleased they sang oh God our help in ages past, that is her Hymn she sang so nicely, so she sang out loud, she is very bonny. she has had a Nice Ball & a box of Toffee

ABOVE: Letters from the ill-fated transatlantic liner RMS Titanic have often turned up at auctions and commanded high prices. Ironically RMS is short for Royal Mail Ship.

OPPOSITE: One of the most critical letters from history, sent by Russian leader Nikita Khrushchev to John F. Kennedy during the 1962 Cuban Missile Crisis.

Edinburgh,
Scotland
2019,

Dear Reader,

I thought it was a good time to write you a short letter. This book is all about letters from history—letters from figures great and small. Within these pages you will find private letters, public letters, and open letters; letters to be obeyed, disobedient letters; first letters, chain letters, last letters, lost letters, telegrams, and a couple of important messages sent on the eve of battle.

They may or may not have changed history, but all have historical significance. Pliny the Younger's eye witness account of the 79 AD eruptions of Vesuvius didn't change history, but his letters to Tacitus describing the event have provided archaeologists with a vivid insight for the excavations at Pompeii and Herculaneum. His uncle, Pliny the Elder, died during the catastrophe, and his report was so accurate that his name is remembered by modern vulcanologists when they speak of Plinian eruptions.

Other letters are much more intimate in their contents. Here you will find an example of Henry VIII's courtly letters to the latest love of his life, Anne Boleyn; letters that curiously ended up in the Vatican in Rome. They also include Pierre Curie's first attempt to make his partnership with his future wife Maria (later, Marie) more than merely a scientific collaboration. After her spell as a student in Paris she returned home to her native Poland to continue her work there. He wrote her an impassioned letter and she came back to Paris.

Marie Curie is not the only scientist to have received a letter which ultimately led to world-changing scientific breakthroughs. The routine letter which advised a young Charles Darwin that there was a place as Naturalist on the surveying vessel HMS *Beagle* was an ordinary piece of correspondence, but as a result of that five-year trip he developed his theory of Natural Selection. There are letters from technological pioneers, including one from Galileo in 1609 describing the moons of Jupiter which he had just seen through his telescope; and the telegram from the Wright Brothers immediately after their historic first flight. Leonardo da Vinci's 1480 résumé and cover letter to the Duke of Milan includes career highlights you won't find on any other cv.

Elsewhere you can read the letter which gave J. Robert Oppenheimer the go-ahead to develop the atomic bomb, which is interesting for the fact that it doesn't mention the atomic bomb. If that was Oppenheimer's beginning, his end was the letter from William Borden which accused him of being a Communist spy. And the consequences of his work, nuclear weapons, nearly brought the world to extinction, averted only by the correspondence between Nikita Khrushchev and President Kennedy to resolve the 1962 Cuban Missile Crisis.

Oppenheimer wasn't a spy; but espionage is a theme that runs through much of the book. You can read about the scandal of letters secretly passed to Ben Franklin which revealed the true opinion of Britain's governor of the Massachusetts colony; and you can read the letter from George Washington commissioning America's first spy ring. The book also contains the letter suggesting that one of Britain's most notorious spies, Guy Burgess, had passed through his Communism phase, as if it were a childhood illness.

Britain's own spy network was well established by the sixteenth century when it uncovered letters of collusion between Mary, Queen of Scots and a group plotting to assassinate Queen Elizabeth I of England. There's also the story of the Bletchley Park codebreakers who wrote directly to Winston Churchill begging for more resources to help break the Germans' Enigma code, work which would eventually turn the tide in favor of the Allies in World War II.

Wars are history's ugly landmarks—the milestones through time which change the lives of millions. The first letter in the book is an impertinent reply to an ancient Greek army demanding the surrender of its enemy Sparta. Elsewhere there are letters between allies (for example Roosevelt and Churchill, Hitler and Mussolini) and enemies (Napoleon of France declaring war on Alexander I of Russia), and between

DEPARTMENT OF STATE
DIVISION OF LANGUAGE SERVICES

(TRANSLATION)

LS NO. 45989
T-85/T-94
Russian

[Embossed Seal of the USSR]

Moscow, October 23, 1962

Mr. President:

I have just received your letter, and have also acquainted myself with the text of your speech of October 22 regarding Cuba.

I must say frankly that the measures indicated in your statement constitute a serious threat to peace and to the security of nations. The United States has openly taken the path of grossly violating the United Nations Charter, the path of violating international norms of freedom of navigation on the high seas, the path of aggressive actions both against Cuba and against the Soviet Union.

The statement by the Government of the United States of America can only be regarded as undisguised interference in the internal affairs of the Republic of Cuba, the Soviet Union and other states. The United Nations Charter and international norms give no right to any state to institute in international waters the inspection of vessels bound for the shores of the Republic of Cuba.

And naturally, neither can we recognize the right of the United States to establish control over armaments which are necessary for the Republic of Cuba to strengthen its defense capability.

We reaffirm that the armaments which are in Cuba, regardless of the classification to which they may belong, are intended solely for defensive purposes in order to secure the Republic of Cuba against the attack of an aggressor.

His Excellency
John Kennedy,
President of the United States of America

winners and losers. General Sherman's letter to the citizens of Atlanta during the Civil War is a very human acknowledgment of the necessary horrors of war, while the telegram reporting the bombing of Pearl Harbor is stark in its brevity.

There are more personal accounts of war, too. Sullivan Ballou's loving letter to his wife Sarah was found among his possessions after his death at the First Battle of Bull Run in 1861. Poet Siegfried Sassoon's outspoken letter to his commanding officer during World War I may have helped him to survive the conflict. John F. Kennedy's celebrated letter-on-a-coconut certainly saved his life when he was stranded on a Pacific Island after his patrol boat was sunk.

Modern espionage is as likely to be corporate or political as military. James McCord admitted the extent of his involvement in the Watergate Affair in a confessional letter which blew the scandal wide open. The whistleblower is a modern phenomenon and this book includes letters from those who exposed malpractice at institutions as diverse as Enron and the National Security Agency. Often at personal risk, these individuals have always brought about change and a new transparency which benefits us all.

In Britain, weapons inspector David Kelly admitted in a letter to the Ministry of Defence that he had expressed misgivings about the veracity of a "dodgy dossier" assembled to aid Tony Blair's call to arms for the Iraq war. Once the news of that letter was in the public domain he was hounded by press and politicians alike. The fallout tainted the careers of all involved

and drove him to take his own life. Suicide notes can be grimly fascinating, and we have included Virginia Woolf's achingly sad last letter to her husband; and what was meant to be the last letter from French poet Baudelaire to his mistress. Despite stabbing himself in the chest he managed to miss any vital organs and survived to write his best work.

Other arts are represented in the book. The roots of Beatrix Potter's popular Peter Rabbit books are in a letter she wrote to a young friend; Vincent van Gogh tried to explain his art to his brother Theo in a letter; and a letter from Mozart to his wife illustrates the frenzy of his final days of urgent composition. Pop music has largely replaced the classical repertoire in the public's hearts. It's incredible to think that the Beatles received a

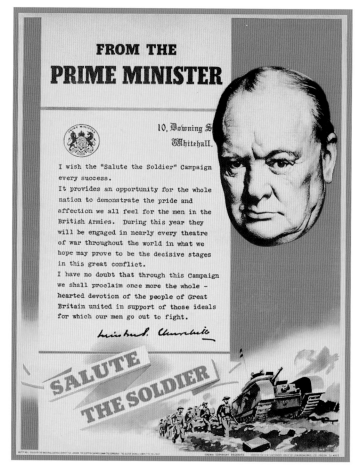

RIGHT: Better known for his rousing speeches than his letters, during World War II Churchill wrote a letter to support the Salute the Soldier campaign to raise funds for military equipment.

rejection letter from Britain's leading record company at the start of their career.

Oscar Wilde is here too, but not for a letter with a string of witty *bon mots*. He wrote a celebrated letter from Reading Gaol where he was forced to reflect on his wild living. Martin Luther King Jr. also found time in prison to write a long letter, in defense of the crime of civil disobedience for which he had been locked up. Nadezhda Tolokonnikova, a member of the feminist Russian punk group Pussy Riot, wrote philosophical letters during her detention for hooliganism which consider the vital role of public protest.

King and another famous prisoner, Nelson Mandela, wrote letters as part of the centuries-long fight for civil rights for Africans and African-Americans. We have also included letters from Abraham Lincoln, George Washington Williams, and Eleanor Roosevelt which take stands on the subject. Addressing another aspect of social injustice, the book includes the Time's Up letter of 2018, signed by three hundred women from the world of entertainment, which called for equality of the sexes and an end to male abuse wherever it occurs. We can only hope this brings about more change than the letter from Abigail Adams to her husband John in 1776, asking him to enshrine the rights of women in the American Constitution which he was about to help write. He thought she was joking.

There's something about all these letters. They are a very direct link between us and those who wrote and received them, and the times when they were written. The paper and the ink and the writing are often tangible elements which bring their history alive.

I like a letter, sealed in an envelope, with a postmarked stamp, and delivered not to a virtual mailbox, but to a real one. Everyone writes emails these days and the letter seems to be on its way out. But however personal their contents, emails are never really personal, or private.

They're not hand-written; no one has chosen the writing paper; and they can be read by anyone from your email provider to your national security agency. Emails all look the same; and they can be deleted by the accidental touch of a keyboard. They are never scented! There's nothing to hold on to, nothing to keep, nothing to take out of your wallet or purse and re-read in a quiet moment; nothing to treasure.

Well, that's that. I hope you like the book. If you do, why not send me a letter?

With very best wishes,
Colin Salter

ABOVE: *The neat handwriting of Queen Anne Boleyn, writing to thank Cardinal Wolsey for promoting her marriage to Henry VIII.*

The Spartans respond to a letter from Philip II of Macedon

(c. 346 BC)

A laconic phrase is the embodiment of verbal cool: a short, blunt, pithy, witty remark that deflates or dismisses a grander, more verbose person or idea. It was invented by the ancient Greek city-state of Sparta and named after their region of Greece, Laconia.

The Spartans had a fearsome reputation. Male Spartans began their military service at the age of seven with basic training. They were also educated in the arts, including the art of the reply: there were special punishments for "unlaconic" answers to questions. From the ages of twenty to thirty they were pressed into national military service, and remained on call as reservists until they were sixty. If a Spartan man were called on to go to war, it was a tradition for his wife to formally present him with his shield and say, "With this, or on it"—in other words, come back victorious or be carried back dead.

In nearby Macedon, King Philip II was the youngest of three brothers, whose father had unified Macedon (called Macedonia today) into a recognizable and powerful state. Warfare with neighboring states was a family business. Although his father had lived to a ripe old age, none of his sons were so fortunate. It was only after a series of early deaths by assassination or in battle that Philip found his way to the top, when he deposed his nephew in 359 BC.

Despite his unorthodox rise, Philip proved to be an effective ruler. He reinvigorated the Macedonian army and set about restoring and expanding the country's borders through military conquest. As Macedon's reputation grew, sometimes the mere threat of invasion was enough to secure the surrender of a neighboring state. In around 346 BC Philip wrote a letter to the leaders of Sparta, giving them the chance to give up without a fight. "You are advised to submit without further delay, for if I bring my army into your land, I will destroy your farms, slay your people, and raze your city."

It was a cheeky offer; Sparta had been the dominant fighting force in the ancient Greek world for three hundred years. Since a defeat by Thebes in 371 BC, Sparta had been further rocked by internal slave revolts, and Philip may have sensed Spartan weakness and instability. But his letter is chiefly remembered today for the reply that he received from the Spartans.

Sparta replied simply: "If."

Philip is reputed to have approached the Spartans on another occasion, writing: "Should I enter your lands as a friend or as a foe?" This time the reply was just as terse: "Neither."

Philip II was assassinated in 336 BC at the wedding of his daughter to a neighboring ruler. He was succeeded by his son Alexander III, Alexander the Great. Although Alexander's conquests extended to the subcontinent of India, the Macedonian army never did invade Sparta.

LEFT: A Spartan hoplite, or citizen-soldier. The red cloak was part of the characteristic Spartan uniform, but it was discarded in battle.

ABOVE: The Philippeion at Olympia in Greece. This monument was erected to celebrate Philip's complete victory at the Battle of Chaeronea in 338 BC. His Macedonian forces routed the forces of Thebes and Athens and left him in command of all Greece … with the exception of Sparta …

100 Letters That Changed the World_____15

Letter from Decimus Brutus to Marcus Brutus and Cassius

… Being in these straits, I decided to demand for myself and our other friends an honorary ambassadorship, so as to discover some decent pretext for leaving Rome. This Hirtius has promised to obtain for me, and yet I have no confidence that he will so do, so insolent are these men, and so set on persecuting us. And even if they grant our request, it will not, I fancy, prevent us being declared public enemies or banned as outlaws in the near future.

"What then," you say, "have you to suggest?" Well, we must bow to fortune; I think we must get out of Italy and migrate to Rhodes, or somewhere or other; if there is a change for the better, we shall return to Rome; if there is no great change, we shall live on in exile; if it comes to the worst, we shall have recourse to the last means of defending ourselves.

It will perhaps occur to someone among you at this point to ask why we should wait for that last stage rather than make some strong effort at once? Because we have no center to rally around, except indeed Sextus Pompeius and Caecilius Bassus, who, it seems to me, are likely to be more firmly established when they have this news about Caesar. It will be time enough for us to join them when we have found out what their strength really is. On behalf of you and Cassius, I will make any engagement you wish me to make; in fact Hirtius insists upon my doing so.

I must ask you both to reply to my letter as soon as possible—because I have no doubt that Hirtius will inform me about these matters before the fourth hour—and let me know in your reply at what place we can meet, where you would like me to come.

Since my last conversation with Hirtius I have determined to ask for permission, while we are at Rome, to have a bodyguard at the public expense; but I do not expect they will grant us that privilege, because we shall raise a storm of unpopularity against them. Still I thought I should not refrain from demanding anything that I consider to be reasonable. …

Caesar's murderers correspond to work out their next move

(March 22, 44 BC)

Scattered across various collections, there are twenty-seven letters from a remarkable correspondence between members of the conspiracy to assassinate Julius Caesar. These letters were written more than 2,000 years ago, and somehow, their contents have survived.

Julius Caesar, everyone's favorite ancient Roman, was a brilliant military commander and a skilled politician. As a maverick general he fought unsanctioned wars, and after his move into populist politics he steered the Roman Republic toward dictatorship, with himself at the top.

Rome was ruled by a senate. While some senators showered honors and titles on Caesar, others were concerned that he was undermining the democracy of the Republic. Senator Cassius and his brother-in-law, Brutus, hatched a plot to remove the tyrannical leader. In 44 BC, on March 15 (the Ides of March, when traditionally debts had to be paid), Julius Caesar was stabbed twenty-three times on the pavement outside the Theater of Pompey.

Assassinations don't just plan themselves. The conspirators met in one anothers' houses and naturally didn't put much in writing before the event. Afterward, however, all hell broke loose, and in a letter from Brutus to Cassius, written only a few days after the murder, he considered the conspirators' options.

The fact that they had not been rounded up and executed already says something about the times. Caesar's assassination was not entirely unpopular. Nor had it extended to killing his closest ally, Mark Antony: the conspirators' only aim was the removal of a tyrant, not regime change.

However, Brutus noted that "it was not safe for any of us to be in Rome." Someone loyal to Caesar might easily seek revenge, and "I have determined to ask for permission, while we are at Rome, to have a bodyguard at the public expense; but I do not expect they will grant us that privilege, because we shall raise a storm of unpopularity against them."

Meanwhile Brutus was trying to make a deal with Mark Antony that would get them out of the capital. He seems to have asked Mark Antony for a governorship, but "he said that he could not possibly give me my province." So "I decided to demand for myself and our other friends an honorary ambassadorship, so as to discover some decent pretext for leaving Rome." He is resigned to living in exile, at least for a time: "If there is a change for the better, we shall return to Rome; if there is no great change, we shall live on in exile."

If Mark Antony hoped to step into Caesar's shoes as leader, he was to be disappointed. Caesar had named his great nephew Octavian as his successor; and Caesar had already concentrated such power in his own hands that a return to the more democratic Roman Republic was impossible. Dictatorship-by-emperor was the future for the new Roman Empire.

Octavian's first act was to declare the conspirators to be murderers. Civil war broke out between supporters of Julius and Octavian and their opponents. Brutus and Cassius fled to Greece, where they raised an army. But after they were defeated by the joint forces of Octavian and Mark Antony at the Battle of Philippi, both men committed suicide.

OPPOSITE: Vincenzo Camuccini's 1844 painting of the murder of Julius Caesar held by the Galleria Nazionale d'Arte Moderna in Rome.

First Letter of Paul to the Corinthians

Chapter 13

1 Though I speak with the tongues of men and of angels, and have not charity, I have become as sounding brass, or a tinkling cymbal.

2 And though I have the gift of prophecy, and understand all mysteries, and all knowledge; and though I have all faith, so that I could remove mountains, and have not charity, I am nothing.

3 And though I bestow all my goods to feed the poor, and though I give my body to be burned, and have not charity, it profiteth me nothing.

4 Charity suffereth long, and is kind; charity envieth not; charity vaunteth not itself, is not puffed up,

5 Doth not behave itself unseemly, seeketh not her own, is not easily provoked, thinketh no evil;

6 Rejoiceth not in iniquity, but rejoiceth in the truth;

7 Beareth all things, believeth all things, hopeth all things, endureth all things.

8 Charity never faileth: but whether there be prophecies, they shall fail; whether there be tongues, they shall cease; whether there be knowledge, it shall vanish away.

Paul's Letter to the Romans

Chapter 13

1 Let every soul be subject unto the higher powers. For there is no power but of God: the powers that be are ordained of God.

2 Whosoever therefore resisteth the power, resisteth the ordinance of God: and they that resist shall receive to themselves damnation.

3 For rulers are not a terror to good works, but to the evil. Wilt thou then not be afraid of the power? Do that which is good, and thou shalt have praise of the same:

4 For he is the minister of God to thee for good. But if thou do that which is evil, be afraid; for he beareth not the sword in vain: for he is the minister of God, a revenger to execute wrath upon him that doeth evil.

5 Wherefore ye must needs be subject, not only for wrath, but also for conscience sake.

6 For this cause pay ye tribute also: for they are God's ministers, attending continually upon this very thing.

7 Render therefore to all their dues: tribute to whom tribute is due; custom to whom custom; fear to whom fear; honour to whom honour.

LEFT: A painting of St. Paul writing his epistles, attributed to the French painter Valentin de Boulogne and dated to c. 1618 to c. 1620.

St. Paul guides the principles of Christianity through his letters

(c. 50 AD)

Letters (or epistles) attributed to Paul the Apostle make up almost half the New Testament of the Bible—thirteen of its twenty-seven books. It's a large body of work, and it built the Christian Church on the foundations of the four Gospels.

Paul was born during Jesus's lifetime; in fact, the two men were of similar age. But Paul, then known as Saul, was a devout Jew, a Pharisee dedicated to the persecution of Christ's followers. On the road to Damascus to arrest some Christians, not many years after Jesus Christ's crucifixion, Paul was confronted by a vision of Christ who asked him, "Saul, Saul, why do you persecute me?" Saul replied, "Who are you, Lord?" and Christ said, "I am Jesus whom you persecute."

Paul was temporarily blinded by the experience, which is related in the New Testament book Acts of the Apostles. When he recovered his sight three days later, he converted at once to Christianity and traveled widely, spreading the Gospel and encouraging local Christians to form groups or churches together. His letters to these churches were intended to support and strengthen their faith. Paul's advice, and his clarifications on matters of theology, have been guiding principles of Christianity ever since.

Paul's theology focuses on Man's redemption through Christ's crucifixion—the idea that Christ died for our sins. Followers of Jesus were assured forgiveness and salvation at the end of time with Christ's Second Coming. "For he who has died has been freed from sin," he wrote in his Letter to the Romans, "for sin shall not have dominion over you, for you are not under law but under grace."

In the hope of this heavenly promise, Christians had a duty to set themselves apart from the sinful ways of the world. Paul argued that a higher moral standard and faith in Jesus were more important than blindly obeying the laws of the land. "We walk by faith, not by sight," he told the Christians at Corinth. "Do not be conformed to this world," he advised the Roman church, "but be transformed by the renewing of your minds."

These are aspects of Christianity that we take for granted now, but it was Paul's letters that defined them for the earliest Christians. Whether or not you count yourself a Christian, many of the principles that Paul laid out are universal. Behind many of them are a generosity of spirit and a simple love for one's fellow man. In another letter to the Corinthians, Paul explains it beautifully:

"Love is patient, love is kind, and is not jealous; love does not brag and is not arrogant, does not act unbecomingly; it does not seek its own [will], is not provoked, does not take into account a wrong suffered, does not rejoice in unrighteousness, but rejoices with the truth; bears all things, believes all things, hopes all things, endures all things."

BELOW: The Chester Beatty Library in Dublin holds this Egyptian find, an early copy of St. Paul's Letter to the Romans.

Tablets reveal details of life at the edge of the Roman Empire

(C. 100 AD)

In the 1970s, hundreds of letters were unearthed during an archaeological dig at Vindolanda, a Roman fort in the north of England. They were written in the last decade of the first century AD, and at the time they were the oldest examples of handwriting ever found in the United Kingdom.

Vindolanda was an uncomfortable posting for any Roman soldier. "Vindo" comes from the same root as the modern English word "winter." One of the most northerly outposts of the Roman Empire, it could be bitterly cold, and the high average rainfall of the region was compounded by the location of the fort on wet ground. To give themselves some insulation from the elements, the Romans took to covering the packed-earth floors of their barracks with a crude carpet of straw and moss.

Dropped items were easily lost in this tangle of fibers, which was frequently topped with fresh layers. It's thanks to this damp environment that so many items have been preserved. The letters are written in ink on thin sheets of wood about the size of a postcard. All are in Latin: some are written in a previously unknown script, which has now been deciphered, and some are in a form of shorthand that has yet to be understood. Some are letters received at Vindolanda and others are drafts of letters sent out from there to other forts in the area and farther south in Roman Britain.

Around 750 letters have so far been transcribed, and they paint a vivid and previously unseen picture of daily life in this little corner of Rome. The sheer volume indicates that literacy was much more widespread than had been assumed; the letters are by members of all ranks, not just the officer class, and indeed not only by members of the army. There are messages from shoemakers and plasterers as well as wagon mechanics and men in charge of the bathhouse.

One must have accompanied a parcel: it reads in part, "… I have sent (?) you … pairs of socks from Sattua, two pairs of sandals and two pairs of underpants." Another, from the wife of an officer in a neighboring fort to the wife of one at Vindolanda, is an invitation to a birthday party:

> "Claudia Severa to her Lepidina, greetings. On 11 September, sister, for the day of the celebration of my birthday, I give you a warm invitation to make sure that you come to us, to make the day more enjoyable for me by your arrival, if you are present. Give my greetings to your Cerialis. My Aelius and my little son send him their greetings."

Most of the letter has been dictated to a scribe, but Claudia Severa adds in her own hand at the end: "I shall expect you, sister. Farewell, sister, my dearest soul, as I hope to prosper and hail."

It is one of the earliest pieces of Latin known to have been written by a woman.

OPPOSITE TOP: Over 750 wooden tablets have been found at Vindolanda and more continue to be unearthed. They provide intimate details of everyday life in a Roman garrison, including the confirmation that Roman soldiers wore underpants (subligaria).

LEFT: Vindolanda was a Roman auxiliary fort close to Hadrian's Wall and occupied between 85 AD and around 370 AD. Two towers have been reconstructed at the site near the village of Bardon Mill in Northumberland.

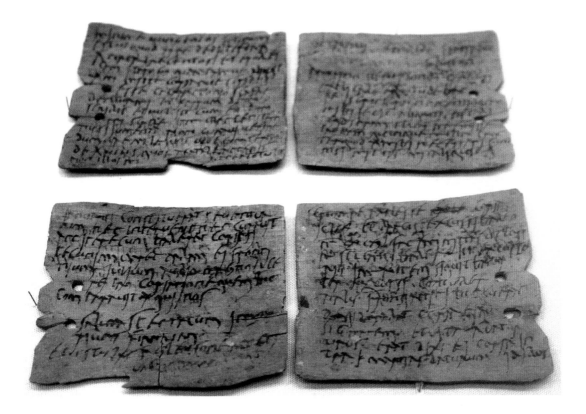

Birthday invitation from Claudia Severa to Sulpicia Lepidina

Claudia Severa to her Lepidina greetings. On 11 September, sister, for the day of the celebration of my birthday, I give you a warm invitation to make sure that you come to us, to make the day more enjoyable for me by your arrival, if you are present. Give my greetings to your Cerialis. My Aelius and my little son send him their greetings. (2nd hand) I shall expect you, sister. Farewell, sister, my dearest soul, as I hope to prosper, and hail. (Back, 1st hand)
To Sulpicia Lepidina, wife of Cerialis, from Severa.

Memorandum on fighting characteristics of Britons

... the Britons are unprotected by armour. There are very many cavalry. The cavalry do not use swords nor do the wretched Britons mount in order to throw javelins. ...

Letter from Pliny the Younger to Tacitus

… It is with extreme willingness, therefore, that I execute your commands; and should indeed have claimed the task if you had not enjoined it. He was at that time with the fleet under his command at Misenum. On the 24th of August, about one in the afternoon, my mother desired him to observe a cloud which appeared of a very unusual size and shape. He had just taken a turn in the sun and, after bathing himself in cold water, and making a light luncheon, gone back to his books: he immediately arose and went out upon a rising ground from whence he might get a better sight of this very uncommon appearance. A cloud, from which mountain was uncertain, at this distance (but it was found afterwards to come from Mount Vesuvius), was ascending, the appearance of which I cannot give you a more exact description of than by likening it to that of a pine tree, for it shot up to a great height in the form of a very tall trunk, which spread itself out at the top into a sort of branches; occasioned, I imagine, either by a sudden gust of air that impelled it, the force of which decreased as it advanced upwards, or the cloud itself being pressed back again by its own weight, expanded in the manner I have mentioned; it appeared sometimes bright and sometimes dark and spotted, according as it was either more or less impregnated with earth and cinders. This phenomenon seemed to a man of such learning and research as my uncle extraordinary and worth further looking into. He ordered a light vessel to be got ready, and gave me leave, if I liked, to accompany him. I said I had rather go on with my work; and it so happened, he had himself given me something to write out. As he was coming out of the house, he received a note from Rectina, the wife of Bassus, who was in the utmost alarm at the imminent danger which threatened her; for her villa lying at the foot of Mount Vesuvius, there was no way of escape but by sea; she earnestly entreated him therefore to come to her assistance. He accordingly changed his first intention, and what he had begun from a philosophical, he now carries out in a noble and generous spirit. He ordered the galleys to be put to sea, and went himself on board with an intention of assisting not only Rectina, but the several other towns which lay thickly strewn along that beautiful coast. Hastening then to the place from whence others fled with the utmost terror, he steered his course direct to the point of danger, and with so much calmness and presence of mind as to be able to make and dictate his observations upon the motion and all the phenomena of that dreadful scene. …

LEFT: A classic engraving of the eruption of Vesuvius in 79 AD. Pliny the Younger survived; his uncle, Pliny the Elder, perished.

Pliny the Younger describes the eruption at Pompeii to Tacitus

(c. 106/107 AD)

Pliny the Younger (61–c107 AD) was a Roman lawyer and magistrate. Pliny the Elder was his uncle and a celebrated author. Both men experienced the eruption of Vesuvius, which buried Pompeii in 79 AD, and the nephew's letters describing the events are history's earliest eyewitness accounts.

How many letters must Roman lawyer Pliny the Younger have written in his life, for as many as 247 of them to have survived? He was a prolific correspondent, and historians value his insights into the life of imperial Rome. His letters to and from the emperor Trajan about the legal position of early Roman Christians are fascinating documents of their time.

Pliny the Younger's father died when he was a boy, and he was raised in Rome by his uncle, whom he greatly admired. Pliny the Elder had a post in charge of the Roman naval fleet at Misenum, west of Naples. While the nephew and his mother were visiting the uncle in 79 AD, Mount Vesuvius on the other side of the Bay of Naples, began to erupt.

When Pliny the Elder heard that people were in danger, he set sail from Misenum with a fleet of light ships to rescue them from the shore below Vesuvius. Faced with the fear and panic of those around him when he arrived, he tried to soothe them by appearing unconcerned—coolly taking a bath, a meal, and a nap. This delay to his return to Misenum was fatal. Almost trapped in his bedroom by falling debris, he escaped to the shore but was overcome by noxious fumes and fell down dead.

Twenty-five years later the Roman historian Tacitus wrote to the younger Pliny to ask about his experiences of the eruption. In two replies, Pliny gave such detailed and accurate descriptions of the unfolding disaster that today volcanologists describe similar volcanic events as "Plinian eruptions."

As so often with history, it is the little moments affecting ordinary people that make Pliny's recollections leap off the page. He notes the flight of people from their houses, which are shaking from the earthquakes, to the fields where "the calcined stones and cinders fell in large showers, and threatened destruction. They went out," Pliny recalls, "having pillows tied upon their heads with napkins; and this was their whole defense against the storm of stones that fell round them."

The terror of the population is palpable. "You might hear the shrieks of women, the screams of children and the shouts of men; some calling for their children, others for their parents, others for their husbands … some wishing to die, from the very fear of dying; some lifting their hands to the gods; but the greater part now convinced that there were no gods at all and that the final endless night of which we had heard had come upon the world."

Of his uncle's relaxed approach to rescue, he paints a very human picture. "It is most certain that he was

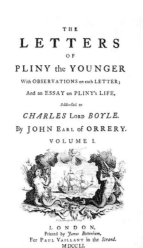

THE
LETTERS
OF
PLINY the YOUNGER
With OBSERVATIONS on each LETTER;
And an ESSAY on PLINY's LIFE,
Addressed to
CHARLES Lord *BOYLE.*
By JOHN EARL of ORRERY.
VOLUME I.

LONDON,
Printed by *James Bettenham,*
For PAUL VAILLANT in the *Strand.*
MDCCLI.

so little disquieted as to fall into a sound sleep; for his breathing, which on account of his corpulence was rather heavy and sonorous, was heard by the attendants outside." Pliny the Elder is, for a moment, no longer a natural historian of repute but a fat man snoring.

Of the letters themselves, he tells Tacitus: "You will pick out whatever is most important; for a letter is one thing, a history quite another. It is one thing writing to a friend, another thing writing to the public." But in fact, such is the quality of Pliny's writing that he has done both.

Romano Britons plead for help from Rome as the empire fails

(c. 450 AD)

In the declining twilight years of the Roman Empire, Rome gradually withdrew from its outlying provinces, including Britannia—Roman Britain. The well-ordered society fostered by the Roman presence collapsed into chaos. The Dark Ages were descending ...

By the time the last Roman soldiers left Britain in 407 AD, the land we now call England was under attack on all sides by Picts, Scots, and Saxon marauders. Even while Roman troops still remained in Britain, the Romano Britons had felt it necessary to appeal to Rome to send reinforcements. In 368 AD the neglected garrison of Rome's remotest outpost, Hadrian's Wall, had revolted over conditions there and joined forces with the barbarians. Rome sent an expeditionary force, which crushed the rebellion, but in the 390s the Britons asked for further help to hold back the tide of Pictish raids from the north. "Owing to inroads of these tribes and the consequent dreadful prostration," they wrote, "Britannia sends an embassy to Rome, entreating in tearful appeals an armed force to avenge her."

Rome again sent a legion, which dealt with the immediate problem. But as soon as it returned to Rome, the raids resumed, this time by Scots and Saxons from across the North Sea. The Brits wrote another letter. "Again supplicant messengers are sent with rent clothes and heads covered with dust. Crouching like timid fowls under the trusty wings of the parent birds, they ask help of the Romans, lest the country in its wretchedness be completely swept away."

Rome reluctantly obliged, but it had problems of its own; elsewhere in the empire the Vandals and Visigoths were overrunning Europe, and troops were dispatched from all parts of the empire, including in 407 AD all those remaining in Britannia, to fight them off. In fury at being abandoned the Britons threw out the Roman civil administration in 409 AD, giving Emperor Honorius the excuse he needed in 410 to wash his hands of troublesome Britannia altogether.

Without any support from Europe, Britannia was now defenseless. Raiding parties from Ireland attacked Wales and the southwest; the Picts reasserted themselves in the northeast; and by the 440s there were Saxon settlements along England's eastern shores. In around 450, Britons made another desperate appeal to Rome for help. They wrote to Flavius Aetius, the leading Roman general of his day, and in a letter headed "The Groans of the Britons," they spelled out their plight. "The barbarians drive us to the sea, the sea drives us to the barbarians; between these two means of death, we are either killed or drowned." This time, there was no reply from Rome.

As a last resort a British king called Vortigern hired mercenaries from Europe—led, according to tradition, by the brothers Hengist and Horsa—who promptly turned on him in an event known as the Treachery of the Long Knives. They opened the door for a huge immigration of Angles, Saxons, and Jutes from the European continent, who brought their lifestyles, culture, and language to Britain. The Groans of the Britons were the dying gasps of one period of English history and the birth cries of the modern English language and modern England.

OPPOSITE: An illustration of King Vortigern meeting the mercenaries Hengist and Horsa on the Isle of Thanet, Kent. The two brothers led a wave of immigration to southeast England.

English barons try to flex their legal muscle after Magna Carta

(June 19, 1215)

The Magna Carta, the Great Charter, marked a turning point in English democracy. Under pressure from his nobles, King John relinquished the absolute power that monarchs assumed. A recently discovered letter shows just what a revolutionary moment the king's signature at Runnymede had been.

Politics and power were ruthless games in the Middle Ages. As young men, King John's elder brothers had rebelled against their father, Henry II, and John himself had tried to overthrow the rule of his brother Richard Lionheart, while Richard was fighting the Third Crusade in the Middle East. Despite losing that family squabble, John became king upon the death of Richard in 1199.

As king he earned the nickname "John Lackland" by losing large parts of England's Angevin territories through war in France. He offended his French barons, who deserted him, and without consultation imposed new taxes on the English barons to fund another French campaign.

The barons objected, and what began as a chaotic chorus of disaffected baronial voices became a more organized campaign of military rebellion that captured the cathedral cities of Lincoln, Exeter, and London itself. King John was forced to negotiate a peace for his kingdom through the Archbishop of Canterbury.

A peace treaty, the Magna Carta, was the result. It outlined limits to the king's abuse of traditional feudal practice; in other words, how he conducted business with the barons. It offered written guarantees of access to judicial procedure regardless of wealth, not only for the nobility but for all freemen. And it established a sort of League of Justice, a council of twenty-five barons to oversee and enforce these devolved privileges—by force if necessary. This was a new kind of government, and England's baffled enemies could only joke that England now had twenty-six kings.

It is a document still revered by legal systems around the world for enshrining basic human rights. But at the time, in 1215, it seemed not to be taken very seriously by either party to its signing. The rebels reneged on a promise to give back London; and far from accepting a peace, John renewed his attacks on them. The civil war that ensued only ended with John's death the following year.

A newly discovered letter, however, proves that, at least at first, some of the barons were trying to exercise their new powers. Only four days after the signing of the Magna Carta, five of the new council members wrote to the authorities in the county of Kent. It advised them that the barons were to be present at the swearing in of twelve knights, to be appointed in Kent as in each county "to enquire into evil customs committed by sheriffs and their ministers, in regard to forests and foresters, warrens and warreners, riverbanks and their keepers, and to ensure the suppression of such evil customs."

This was one of the terms of the Magna Carta, and the letter was making clear that there was a new rule of law: whatever evil customs the sheriffs and their ministers, foresters, warreners, and riverbank keepers had been getting away with until then, was going to stop. Here was a new broom, intent on sweeping clean. The sheriff of Kent and all the king's bailiffs were to be in no doubt that it was to the council that their oaths should be sworn, and not to the king.

OPPOSITE TOP: *The letter was recently discovered by scholars copied into a manuscript held in Lambeth Palace Library. It is the bottom paragraph of the text. The document sheds new light on the balance of power between the King and the barons.*

Letter of five of the twenty-five barons, appointing four knights to oversee the swearing of oaths and the appointment of an inquest by twelve knights in the county of Kent.

We have sent to you the bearers of the present letters, namely William of Eynsford, William de Ros, Thomas de Canville and Richard of Graveney, whom we attorn in our place to receive on our behalf the oaths of all you as in the letters of the lord King which he sent to the sheriff and the others aforesaid, ordering you that you swear oaths to the aforesaid four knights as in the form set out in the lord King's letters, and that you have oaths made at a certain time and place to be determined by the aforesaid four knights. We wish moreover that the aforesaid four knights be present when the twelve knights are elected in your county who will swear oaths to enquire into evil customs committed by sheriffs and their ministers, in regard to forests and foresters, warrens and warreners, river banks and their keepers, and to ensure the suppression of such evil customs as is set out in the lord King's charter.

Letter from Joan of Arc to the besieging Henry VI

King of England, and you duke of Bedford, who call yourself regent of the kingdom of France; you, William Pole, count of Suffolk; John Talbot, and you Thomas Lord Scales, who call yourselves lieutenants of the said duke of Bedford, make satisfaction to the King of Heaven; surrender to the Maid who is sent here by God, the King of Heaven, the keys of all the good towns which you have taken and violated in France. She is come here by God's will to reclaim the blood royal. She is very ready to make peace, if you are willing to grant her satisfaction by abandoning France and paying for what you have held. And you, archers, men-at-war, gentlemen and others, who are before the town of Orléans, go away into your own country, in God's name. And if you do not do so, expect tidings from the maid, who will come to see you shortly, to your very great harm. King of England, if you do not do so, I am a chieftain of war, whatever place I meet your people in France, I shall make them leave, whether they will it or not. And if they will not obey, I will have them all put to death. I am sent here by God, the King of Heaven, body for body, to drive you out of all France. And if they wish to obey, I will show them mercy. And be not of another opinion, for you will not hold the kingdom of France from God, the King of Heaven, son of Saint Mary; for the king Charles, the true heir, will hold it, as is revealed to him by the Maid, he will enter Paris with a good company. If you do not believe these tidings from God and the Maid, in whatever place we find you, we shall strike therein and make so great a tumult that none so great has been in France for a thousand years, if you do not yield to right. Know well that the King of Heaven will send greater strength to the Maid and her good men-at-arms than you in all your assaults can overwhelm; and by the blows it will be seen who has greater favor with the God of Heaven. You, duke of Bedford, the maid prays and requests that you do not bring destruction upon yourself. If you will grant her right, you may still join her company, where the French will do the fairest deed ever done for Christianity. Answer if you wish to make peace in the town of Orléans; and if you do not, you will be reminded shortly to your very great harm.

LEFT: The Maid of Orléans as painted in 1865 by John Everett Millais, a founding member of the Pre-Raphaelite Brotherhood.

Joan of Arc tells Henry VI she has God on her side

(March 22, 1429)

After receiving a vision of three saints, Jeanne d'Arc set about turning the tide of English rule in northern France. The illiterate daughter of a sheep farmer dictated a letter to be sent to Henry VI and the Duke of Bedford, who were besieging Orléans.

The Hundred Years' War raged across France from 1337 to 1453. It was fought between the English under Henry V, who believed England had a right to rule France, and the French, who backed their own king, Charles VI.

The war was complicated by the mental illness of Charles VI. His brother Louis of Orléans, and his cousin John of Burgundy could not agree about how to run the country on his behalf. Civil war erupted: John had Louis assassinated and Louis's supporters assassinated John, whose Burgundian supporters then sided with England. It's no wonder that by the early fifteenth century, England had the upper hand.

In 1422, Henry V and Charles VI both died. In 1425, Joan of Arc was tending her father's sheep when she had a vision of Saints Michael, Catherine, and Margaret, who told her to drive out the English and convey the French claimant, Charles VI's son Charles VII, to his coronation. Her little village, in a corner of France still loyal to the French king, had itself been raided and burned down by supporters of the English claim to the French throne.

Charles VII was planning an expedition to relieve the siege of Orléans when, in 1429, Joan of Arc arrived. Charles, either impressed with Joan or desperate because all else had failed, agreed that she could travel with his army. As they approached Orléans, Joan dictated a letter to Henry VI and his cousin the Duke of Bedford, who commanded the English army.

She was illiterate, although she could sign her name; but there was no lack of confidence in the demands from the sheep farmer's daughter to the English ruling classes. "Surrender to the Maid who is sent here by God, the King of Heaven, the keys of all the good towns which you have taken and violated in France.

"King of England," she continued, "if you do not do so, I am a chieftain of war, and in whatever place I meet your people in France, I shall make them leave, whether they will it or not. And if they will not obey, I will have them all put to death."

Joan's presence galvanized the French forces. They began to take the fight to the English, and only a month after their arrival at Orléans, forced the English to withdraw. By contrasting the king of England with the king of Heaven, she transformed the Hundred Years' War into a holy war. "I am sent here by God, the king of Heaven, body for body, to drive you out of all France."

The tide turned and the French won a string of victories. Joan was ever-present, and insisted on carrying a banner rather than a sword. She was wounded on several occasions but succeeded in her holy mission when, only four months after her letter to the English, Charles VII of France was crowned king at Reims.

In 1430, Joan was captured by Burgundian forces and put on trial by the pro-English Bishop of Beauvais, Pierre Cauchon. After Cauchon declared her guilty of heresy, she was burned at the stake on May 30, 1431, at around nineteen years old. But it was too late for the vengeful English. France was ruled by a French king, and in time Saint Joan joined the company of the saints who had visited her.

Leonardo da Vinci sets out his skills to the Duke of Milan

(c. 1480s)

Leonardo da Vinci's letter setting out his skills to his prospective employer was no run-of-the-mill résumé. It showed the great artist's stunning ingenuity and mechanical insight, hardly touching on his ability to draw and paint.

In 1482, Leonardo da Vinci was living in Florence and working for the ruling Medici family in an intellectual and creative hothouse called the Garden of the Piazza San Marco. He had begun a commission to paint *The Adoration of the Magi* for the Church of San Donato in Scopeto, just outside Florence's city walls, when his services were offered to another noble Italian family. The Medicis had loaned him to Ludovico Sforza, the Duke of Milan, about 185 miles to the north.

It was a peace offering by the Medicis from one power center to another. Leonardo was accompanied by a magnificent lyre in the shape of a horse's head which he himself had crafted. If music has power to soothe the savage breast, the Medicis were sending not only the gift of music but the man who made it—Leonardo was reputed to be a fine musician on top of all his many other attributes.

To emphasize what a valuable gift he was, Leonardo also wrote himself a cover letter, with a summary of his skills. It was an exemplary résumé, simply presented as an itemized list with a short introductory paragraph. Among da Vinci's claims were these:

- I will make covered chariots, safe and un-attackable, which, entering among the enemy with their artillery, there is no body of men so great but they would break them
- In case of need I will make big guns, mortars, and light ordnance

It was a list of military inventions and innovations, and perhaps with Leonardo, the Medicis were offering their military secrets to the Sforzas as a show of faith in the peace process. Only at the end of the letter does Leonardo offer his artistic services:

- In times of peace I believe I can give perfect satisfaction and to the equal of any other in architecture and the composition of buildings public and private; and in guiding water from one place to another
- I can carry out sculpture in marble, bronze, or clay, and also I can do in painting whatever may be done, as well as any other, be he who he may

Whether or not Milan benefited from da Vinci's engineering ingenuity, it certainly gained from his artistry. Leonardo remained in the city until the end of the century, and Ludovico Sforza commissioned one of his most famous murals, *The Last Supper*, for the city's Church of Santa Maria delle Grazie.

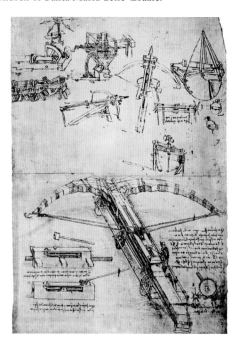

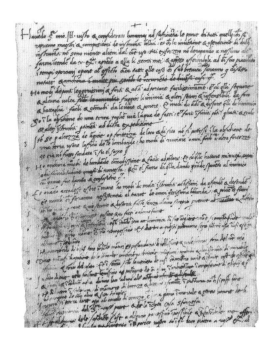

RIGHT: Da Vinci's letter.

OPPOSITE: Leonardo's drawing of a giant crossbow (a figure of a man stands by the release mechanism) is contained in the twelve-volume Codex Atlanticus, *a compilation of da Vinci drawings made from 1478 to 1519 by the sculptor Pompeo Leoni.*

Letter from Leonardo da Vinci to the Duke of Milan

My Most Illustrious Lord,

Having now sufficiently seen and considered the achievements of all those who count themselves masters and artificers of instruments of war, and having noted that the invention and performance of the said instruments is in no way different from that in common usage, I shall endeavor, while intending no discredit to anyone else, to make myself understood to Your Excellency for the purpose of unfolding to you my secrets, and thereafter offering them at your complete disposal, and when the time is right bringing into effective operation all those things which are in part briefly listed below:

1. I have plans for very light, strong and easily portable bridges with which to pursue and, on some occasions, flee the enemy, and others, sturdy and indestructible either by fire or in battle, easy and convenient to lift and place in position. Also means of burning and destroying those of the enemy.

2. I know how, in the course of the siege of a terrain, to remove water from the moats and how to make an infinite number of bridges, mantlets and scaling ladders and other instruments necessary to such an enterprise.

3. Also, if one cannot, when besieging a terrain, proceed by bombardment either because of the height of the glacis or the strength of its situation and location, I have methods for destroying every fortress or other stranglehold unless it has been founded upon a rock or so forth. …

Henry VII writes to English nobles asking for their support

(1485)

English history in the second half of the fifteenth century is a bloody saga, a tale of insatiable rivalry and treachery. Competing branches of the Plantagenet dynasty fought one another to mutual extinction. Disaffected nobility was ready to follow a new king, if one could be found.

The Wars of the Roses were so called because its two principal factions were the houses of York and Lancaster. York's coat of arms bore a white rose; Lancaster's, a red one. Yorkist Edward IV had murdered the ineffectual King Henry VI of the house of Lancaster and seized power.

Edward IV was unusual in those turbulent times in that he died of natural causes. His father and brother were killed at the Battle of Wakefield, another brother was executed for treason, and after his death, his two sons (the Princes in the Tower) were killed while "under protection" from Edward's brother, Richard. This left Richard free to be crowned in 1483 as Richard III.

Lancastrian Henry VI had been a weak ruler, losing all of England's possessions in France with the exception of Calais. In that power vacuum, the families of the English nobility fought among themselves for influence, recruiting private armies from soldiers returning from the war in France. As the conflict became national, the wealthy Neville family backed York, and under the Yorkist king Richard III, they benefited greatly from his gratitude. Others who had opposed Richard's claim found their lands forfeited.

The Yorkists' grip on power was tight and ruthless. But there was opposition to Richard III from the very start of his reign. Resistance focused on the exiled Henry Tudor, who had a tenuous claim to the English throne through illegitimate and maternal lines on the Lancastrian side. Henry was in Brittany in northwest France, where he had become a pawn in international relations between France and England.

Now, however, he sensed the possibility of a return to England at the highest level. Evading an attempt by Richard to bring him back to England to be executed, Henry fled to Paris and sent letters by trusted couriers to canvas potential supporters. Because of the secrecy necessary to plot his return, most were destroyed after being read, but one survives.

He writes that he is glad to understand that he has the recipients' backing, "to advance me to the furtherance of my rightful claim, due and lineal inheritance of that crown and for the just depriving of that homicide and unnatural tyrant which now unjustly bears dominion over you."

What will really make him happy, however, is to know "what power you will make ready and what captains and leaders you get to conduct, be prepared to pass over the sea with such force as my friends here are preparing for me." Henry was gathering an invasion force on the European mainland. And he hints at the benefits of supporting a successful rebellion: "If I have such good speed and success as I wish, according to your desire, I shall ever be most forward to remember and wholly to requite this your great and moving loving kindness in my just quarrel."

Replies to Henry's letters promised enough support for him to go ahead and land in Pembrokeshire in Wales in August 1485. As he progressed through Wales, more and more men flocked to his standard. Three weeks later at the Battle of Bosworth Field, many of Richard III's apparently loyal backers switched sides. Henry won a decisive victory, and Richard was killed during the fighting; his grave was only found in 2012, beneath a twentieth-century parking lot in Leicester.

Henry was crowned Henry VII, the first monarch of the Tudor Dynasty which included his son Henry VIII (of the six wives) and his granddaughter Queen Elizabeth. Those letters from France certainly paid off.

Letter from Henry VII to Lancastrian supporters

Right trusty, worshipful and honourable good friends, I greet you well. Being given to understand your good *devoir* and *entreaty* to advance me to the furtherance of my rightful claim, due and lineal inheritance of that crown and for the just depriving of that homicide and unnatural tyrant which now unjustly bears dominion over you, I give you to understand that no Christian heart can be more full of joy and gladness than the heart of me, your poor exiled friend, who will, upon the instant of your sure advertising what power you will make ready and what captains and leaders you get to conduct, be prepared to pass over the sea with such force as my friends here are preparing for me. And if I have such good speed and success as I wish, according to your desire, I shall ever be most forward to remember and wholly to requite this your great and moving loving kindness in my just quarrel. Given under our signet H.

I pray you to give credence to the messenger of that he shall impart to you.

ABOVE LEFT: Henry VII painted in 1505, a full twenty years after the Battle of Bosworth Field. It is the oldest painting in the National Gallery, London.

ABOVE RIGHT: Shakespeare famously depicted Richard III as a "crookback," and after the discovery of Richard's skeleton under a parking lot in Leicester, it was confirmed that he suffered from scoliosis, or curvature of the spine. This portrait is a copy of an earlier work, as it dates to the late sixteenth century, almost a hundred years after his death.

Columbus explains his discoveries to the king of Spain

(March 15, 1493)

On the return leg of his first voyage of discovery to the New World, Christopher Columbus writes a letter describing what he has found. It creates a sensation throughout Europe, and until the nineteenth century, it was the only known written first-person account of the historic events of 1492–93.

Columbus was looking for Asia. The traditional trade route to the East—over land by the Silk Route—had become dangerous since the Ottomans captured Constantinople. Doing some optimistic calculations, he reckoned that Japan was about 2,300 miles (3,700 km) west of the Canary Islands, a feasible journey for a fifteenth-century sailing ship with enough supplies of food and water.

In 1492, he finally persuaded Ferdinand, king of Castile in modern-day Spain, to sponsor a voyage. Only a year earlier, Catholic monarchs had finally defeated the Nasrid dynasty, Muslim rulers of much of the Spanish peninsula for over 250 years. Now Ferdinand wanted to give the newly unified Spain an advantage over the rest of Old Europe with a short reliable sea route to Asia.

It took Columbus and his three ships—the *Santa María*, the *Pinta* and the *Niña*—five weeks to cross the Atlantic. He named the first landfall San Salvador, the Holy Savior; it was probably the eastern Bahamian island of Plana Cays. From there he landed on neighboring Bahamas before exploring the northern coasts of Cuba (which he called Isla Juana) and Hispaniola to the east (which he called Española, today split between Haiti and the Dominican Republic).

In his letter he described Cuba as "exceedingly fertile. It has numerous harbors on all sides, very safe and wide, above comparison with any I have ever seen. Through it flow many very broad and health-giving rivers." Hispaniola, he implied, was a sort of paradise: "beautiful mountains, great farms,

groves and fields, most fertile both for cultivation and for pasturage, and well adapted for constructing buildings. The convenience of the harbors in this island, and the excellence of the rivers, in volume and salubrity, surpass human belief, unless one should see them. In it the trees, pasture-lands and fruits differ much from those of Juana.

"Besides this," he continued, "Hispana abounds in various kinds of species, gold and metals." This was the nitty-gritty—not what European civilization could do for the New World, but what the New World could do for Spain. The indigenous people, Columbus was at pains to point out, would be a pushover for conquest, being unarmed except for bows and arrows. They might, he thought, "become Christians and inclined to love our King and Queen and Princes and all the people of Spain." He captured several local inhabitants to bring back to Ferdinand as trophies, although only eight of them survived the return trip.

Ferdinand was sufficiently impressed with the West Indies' potential to send Columbus on three further voyages to Central and Southern America. Columbus's letter was quickly published in Latin and read throughout Europe, sparking the colonization of America and the eventual development of the slave trade. Columbus maintained for the rest of his life that he had discovered a sea route to Asia, despite growing evidence that he had not. It was Amerigo Vespucci, an Italian explorer, who in 1502 first refuted Columbus's claim, and whose first name was henceforth used to refer to the new continent—America.

Letter from Columbus to King Ferdinand and Queen Isabella

I have determined to write you this letter to inform you of everything that has been done and discovered in this voyage of mine.

On the thirty-third day after leaving Cadiz I came into the Indian Sea, where I discovered many islands inhabited by numerous people. I took possession of all of them for our most fortunate King by making public proclamation and unfurling his standard, no one making any resistance. The island called Juana, as well as the others in its neighborhood, is exceedingly fertile. It has numerous harbors on all sides, very safe and wide, above comparison with any I have ever seen. Through it flow many very broad and health-giving rivers; and there are in it numerous very lofty mountains. All these islands are very beautiful, and of quite different shapes; easy to be traversed, and full of the greatest variety of trees reaching to the stars. . . .

In the island, which I have said before was called Hispana, there are very lofty and beautiful mountains, great farms, groves and fields, most fertile both for cultivation and for pasturage, and well adapted for constructing buildings. The convenience of the harbors in this island, and the excellence of the rivers, in volume and salubrity, surpass human belief, unless one should see them. In it the trees, pasture-lands and fruits differ much from those of Juana. Besides, this Hispana abounds in various kinds of species, gold and metals. The inhabitants . . . are all, as I said before, unprovided with any sort of iron, and they are destitute of arms, which are entirely unknown to them, and for which they are not adapted; not on account of any bodily deformity, for they are well made, but because they are timid and full of terror. . . . But when they see that they are safe, and all fear is banished, they are very guileless and honest, and very liberal of all they have. No one refuses the asker anything that he possesses; on the contrary they themselves invite us to ask for it. They manifest the greatest affection towards all of us, exchanging valuable things for trifles, content with the very least thing or nothing at all. . . . I gave them many beautiful and pleasing things, which I had brought with me, for no return whatever, in order to win their affection, and that they might become Christians and inclined to love our King and Queen and Princes and all the people of Spain; and that they might be eager to search for and gather and give to us what they abound in and we greatly need. …

OPPOSITE: This portrait of Christopher Columbus, dating from 1519, by Sebastiano del Piombo identifies the sitter as "the Ligurian Colombo, the first to enter by ship into the world of the Antipodes, 1519." Although for many years it was viewed as the authoritative likeness, the date 1519 throws it into doubt, as Columbus died in 1506.

Martin Luther tells his friend, "Let your sins be strong"

(August 1521)

Ordained as a Roman Catholic priest in 1507, Martin Luther was excommunicated by Pope Leo X and outlawed by the Holy Roman Emperor for his alleged heresies against Catholic orthodoxy. Luther's letter to his fellow Protestant Philip Melanchthon only two months later showed him to be unrepentant.

Luther directly challenged the authority of the Church and its leader, the Pope, by attacking the practice of indulgences—the absolution of sins in return for financial donations to the Church. Salvation was only possible, he believed, by faith in God; and it was only in the gift of God, not for sale by priests.

Luther's refusal to retract his criticisms in the German town of Worms resulted in the Edict of Worms, which declared that "we forbid anyone from this time forward to dare, either by words or by deeds, to receive, defend, sustain, or favor the said Martin Luther. … Those who will help in his capture will be rewarded generously for their good work."

Luther evaded arrest thanks to Prince Frederick of Saxony, who allowed him to live in secret in his castle at Wartburg. During his time in Wartburg, Luther undertook perhaps his most revolutionary act, translating the New Testament from Latin into German so that ordinary people could read it for themselves. He also made time to write to his friend and fellow theologian Melanchthon, a key figure in the development of the Protestant Reformation.

Melanchthon and Luther were teaching colleagues at Wittenberg University, and Luther wrote in support of their fellow professor the Bishop of Kemberg, who had defied Catholic teaching as a priest by getting married. He quoted St. Paul, "the voice of the divine majesty," who wrote in his letter to Timothy that the celibacy rule had been invented by demons and therefore could be ignored. It did not come from God. Better, he argued, to be married than

to "burn with vain desire" or to act immorally outside marriage. Luther himself married a nun two years later.

Luther wrote in support of the views of Andreas Carlstadt on the subject of holy Communion. It was considered a sin not to take full Communion of both bread and wine, even if either of them was deliberately withheld. But, he writes, "scripture makes no definition by which we could declare this act a sin." What if the wine were accidentally spilled? Later that year Carlstadt would conduct the first Reformed Communion, in German instead of Latin, allowing communicants to take the bread and wine themselves instead of having them fed to them by a priest. It was another challenge to the authority of the priesthood.

This was liberation theology, and it spread rapidly through a population long oppressed by the power and corruption of the Catholic Church. Luther's impact on Christianity was far-reaching. Northern Europe is to this day a stronghold of Protestantism compared to, for example, Spain, France, and Italy.

The letter closed with another attack on priestly misinterpretations of the Bible. Just as true faith, not indulgences, produces real absolution, so there is a difference between real sins and sins invented by unfair or unbiblical laws. "You must therefore bear the true, not an imaginary sin. … Be a sinner, and let your sins be strong, but let your trust in Christ be stronger." In other words, if you're going to sin, sin properly and have faith that Christ died to absolve you. "No sin can separate us from Him, even if we were to kill or commit adultery thousands of times each day."

Letter from Martin Luther to Philip Melanchthon

… Of course, you can only know and absolve those sins which have been confessed to you; sins which have not been confessed to you, you neither need to know, nor can you absolve them. That is reaching too high, dear gentlemen.

You cannot convince me that the same is true for the vows made by priests and monks. For I am very concerned about the fact that the order of priesthood was instituted by God as a free one. Not so that of the monks who chose their position voluntarily, even though I have almost come to the conclusion that those who have entered into that state at an age prior to their manhood, or are currently at that stage, may secede with a clear conscience. I am hesitant, however, with a judgment about those who have been in this state for a long time and have grown old in it.

By the way, St. Paul very freely speaks about the priests, that devils have forbidden them to marry; and St. Paul's voice is the voice of the divine majesty. Therefore, I do not doubt that they must depend on him to such a degree that even though they agreed to this interdiction of the devil at the time, now—having realized with whom they made their contract—they can cheerfully break this contract.

This interdiction by the devil, which is clearly shown by God's Word, urges and compels me to sanction the actions of the Bishop of Kemberg. For God does not lie nor deceive when He says that this is an interdiction from the devil. If a contract has been made with the devil it must not endure since it was made in godless error against God and was damned and repudiated by God. For He says very clearly that those spirits are in error who are the originators of the interdictions.

Why do you hesitate to join this divine judgment against the gates of hell? That is not how it was with the oath of the children of Israel which they gave to the Gibeons. They had it in their laws that they must offer peace or accept peace offered to them, and accept into their midst proselytes and those who adhered to their customs. All this took place. Nothing happened there against the Lord or by the advice of spirits. For even though in the beginning they murmured, later on they approved.

In addition, consider that the state of being unmarried is only a human statute and can be readily lifted. Therefore, any Christian can do this. I would make this statement even if the interdiction had not come from a devil, but from a devout person. …

OPPOSITE: *Martin Luther believed that salvation and the gift of eternal life was not a reward for good deeds on earth, but that it was a divine gift from God through the believer's faith in Jesus Christ as the redeemer of sin.*

Letter from Henry VIII to Anne Boleyn

For a present so beautiful that nothing could be more so (considering the whole of it), I thank you most cordially, not only on account of the fine diamond and the ship in which the solitary damsel is tossed about, but chiefly for the fine interpretation and the too humble submission which your goodness hath used towards me in this case; for I think it would be very difficult for me to find an occasion to deserve it, if I were not assisted by your great humanity and favour, which I have always sought to seek, and will seek to preserve by all the kindness in my power, in which my hope has placed its unchangeable intention, which says, *Aut illic, aut nullibi**.

The demonstrations of your affection are such, the beautiful mottoes of the letter so cordially expressed, that they oblige me forever to honour, love, and serve you sincerely, beseeching you to continue in the same firm and constant purpose, assuring you that, on my part, I will surpass it rather than make it reciprocal, if loyalty of heart and a desire to please you can accomplish this.

I beg, also, if at any time before this I have in any way offended you, that you would give me the same absolution that you ask, assuring you, that henceforward my heart shall be dedicated to you alone. I wish my body was so too. God can do it, if He pleases, to whom I pray every day for that end, hoping that at length my prayers will be heard. I wish the time may be short, but I shall think it long till we see one another.

* Which means "Either there, or nowhere".

Henry VIII writes a love letter to Anne Boleyn

(1528)

Anne Boleyn was the daughter of a diplomat in the court of English King Henry VII. Henry VII's son, Henry VIII, was besotted with her, as the passionate language of seventeen surviving love letters from him to her demonstrate. It was a love affair that changed the course of British history.

Henry VIII had many reasons for wedding his six wives. In the sixteenth century, marriages were political treaties between powerful families, not love matches between two people. Henry's first arranged marriage had actually been arranged for his older brother, Arthur, heir to Henry VII's throne. It was a very desirable union: Catherine of Aragon was a daughter of the Spanish monarchs King Ferdinand and Queen Isabella. But Arthur died, aged fifteen, only six months after his wedding to Catherine.

Still, a treaty between England and Spain was too good to miss; Arthur's brother Henry was the new heir to the throne, and Catherine was married to him instead, just after his 1509 coronation. The royal couple had a daughter, Mary. But Henry desperately wanted a male heir, a future Henry IX.

And then in 1526, along came Anne Boleyn. Henry, twenty-five, still a young man and despairing of Catherine's inability to give him a son, lost his head and heart to Anne, who was ten years his junior. He pursued her and overcame her initial resistance to his charms with a series of love letters. One, written in January 1528, shows how much progress he had made in his suit and how infatuated he was with her.

Anne had sent him a present of a model ship containing a little figure of a woman, implying that Henry was her shelter from life's storms. Henry, king of England, insisted that he was not worthy of such a present. "I think it would be very difficult for me to find an occasion to deserve it," he wrote, in French, "if I were not assisted by your great humanity and favor." Anne had modestly asked him to forgive any shortcomings on her part, and he replied in kind. "I beg also, if at any time before this I have in any way offended you, that you would give me the same absolution that you ask.

"Henceforth my heart shall be dedicated to you alone," promised the husband of Catherine of Aragon. "I wish my body was so too." Henry declared his "unchangeable intention, which says, *aut illic, aut nullibi*"—"either there [in your heart] or nowhere." Her words, he wrote, "oblige me forever to honor, love and serve you." He was virtually quoting the marriage vows, and marriage is what he meant by his unchangeable intention.

There was a significant problem, though. Henry was already a married man and the Catholic Church would not countenance divorce. Henry and Anne both pleaded with Pope Clement VII but to no avail. Infuriated and frustrated, Henry appointed a new Archbishop of Canterbury in 1533 to declare his marriage to Catherine null and void—he and Anne had secretly married four months earlier. The pope in return excommunicated both Henry and the archbishop, Thomas Cranmer. Henry simply broke with Rome and placed himself at the head of the Church of England. He closed down the wealthy and powerful Catholic monasteries around which English daily life revolved, changing forever the religious, economic, and social life of the country. All this for love.

Anne, like Catherine before her, gave birth to a daughter, the future Queen Elizabeth I, but no sons. And Henry, as he had done before, began to look elsewhere—in this case, Jane Seymour. Anne was beheaded on trumped-up charges of treason, infidelity, and incest, a hateful end after such a loving beginning. Henry signed the letter in which he committed himself to marrying Anne Boleyn like a teenager carving joint initials on a tree: "H aultre AB ne cherse R"—"King Henry seeks no other but Anne Boleyn"—and the "AB" is enclosed in a heart.

Letter from Bartolomé de las Casas to King Charles V of Spain

…God has created all these numberless people to be quite the simplest, without malice or duplicity, most obedient, most faithful to their natural Lords, and to the Christians, whom they serve; the most humble, most patient, most peaceful and calm, without strife nor tumults; not wrangling, nor querulous, as free from uproar, hate and desire of revenge as any in the world . . .

Among these gentle sheep, gifted by their Maker with the above qualities, the Spaniards entered as soon as they knew them, like wolves, tiger and lions which had been starving for many days, and since forty years they have done nothing else; nor do they afflict, torment, and destroy them with strange and new, and diverse kinds of cruelty, never before seen, nor heard of, nor read of . . .

The Christians, with their horses and swords and lances, began to slaughter and practice strange cruelty among them. They penetrated into the country and spared neither children nor the aged, nor pregnant women, nor those in child labor, all of whom they ran through the body and lacerated, as though they were assaulting so many lambs herded in their sheepfold.

They made bets as to who would slit a man in two, or cut off his head at one blow: or they opened up his bowels. They tore the babes from their mothers' breast by the feet, and dashed their heads against the rocks. Others they seized by the shoulders and threw into the rivers, laughing and joking, and when they fell into the water they exclaimed: "boil body of so and so!" They spitted the bodies of other babes, together with their mothers and all who were before them, on their swords.

They made a gallows just high enough for the feet to nearly touch the ground, and by thirteens, in honor and reverence of our Redeemer and the twelve Apostles, they put wood underneath and, with fire, they burned the Indians alive. …

ABOVE: *Bartolomé de las Casas's influential letter.*

De las Casas exposes Spain's atrocities in the New World

(1542)

Spain exported many things to their colonies in the New World, including sadistic cruelties first dreamed up under the Spanish Inquisition. But in 1542, one man wrote a letter exposing the barbaric treatment of the native populations, which brought about the New Laws of the Indies for their protection.

Bartolomé de las Casas was a Spanish colonist-turned-priest working in Latin America. He had first traveled to Hispaniola (modern-day Haiti) with his father in 1502 at the age of eighteen and became a hacendado, using local people to work the land. In 1510, he became a priest in the Catholic Church and subsequently took part in the brutal colonization of Cuba, acting as chaplain to the military. Although he continued in his efforts to convert the native islanders to his European religion, he also attempted to set up a model colony for them and to improve the conditions in which they lived. He argued against enslaving them (although he suggested enslaving Africans instead) and was an early proponent of Indian rights.

Not all of his countrymen were so humanitarian, so when in 1542 the Holy Roman Emperor Charles V convened a special symposium on Spanish colonization, Bartolomé wrote a letter to the emperor. He described the atrocities that he had witnessed, committed by Spaniards against the local tribes on the islands of Hispaniola and Cuba.

The letter was read out at the conference, and it made uncomfortable listening. He related in graphic detail the cruelties inflicted for sport by Spanish settlers—the slow deaths of the local leaders by hanging and burning, the living deaths by mutilation, the mass killings by blade and spear.

"The Christians, with their horses and swords and lances … penetrated into the country and spared neither children nor the aged, nor pregnant women, nor those in child labor, all of whom they ran through the body and lacerated." It was apparently for fun. "Laughing and joking," he wrote, "they made bets as to who would slit a man in two, or cut his head off at one blow."

He had by now been arguing for the rights of the Hispaniolans for nearly thirty years, and was accustomed to being dismissed by men in power who were profiting from Spain's activities in the region. But now his shocking testimony struck home. It helped that Bartolomé had known the emperor when he was merely king of Spain. Charles V introduced what became known as the New Laws of the Indies, recalling some officials from the Spanish colonies and governing the use of local labor in the West Indies.

He introduced the gradual abolition of the practice of encomienda, whereby settlers were awarded the right to use sectors of the colonized population in perpetuity—now encomiendas would end with the death of the current encomendero or title holder. Slavery was outlawed, and in the West Indies, where harsh treatment had almost extinguished the local tribes, natives no longer had to provide any goods or services for their Spanish conquerors.

Bartolomé felt that the New Laws of the Indies did not go far enough. Encomenderos, including the Viceroy of New Spain (as the Spanish colonies throughout the Americas were known), thought they went too far. Threats were made against Bartolomé's life; there were riots; and the New Laws of the Indies were repealed after only three years. Bartolomé de las Casas left New Spain in defeat and spent the rest of his life acting as an advocate for the colonies in the Spanish imperial court.

Elizabeth I writes to Bloody Mary, begging for her life

(March 16, 1554)

Henry VIII disposed of personal relationships when they no longer suited his purpose. After his death his eldest daughter, Mary, sent her half sister, Elizabeth, to the Tower of London. Elizabeth, fearing that Mary had inherited her father's ruthlessness, wrote her a letter, begging for her life.

Mary was the daughter of Henry VIII's first wife, Catherine of Aragon. Elizabeth's mother was his second wife, Anne Boleyn. Henry annulled his marriage to Catherine and beheaded Anne before moving on to the third of his six wives, Jane Seymour. Henry's serial weddings were in pursuit of a male heir, and with Jane he finally had a son, Edward.

Edward was only nine years old when he succeeded Henry, and only fifteen when he died, without any heirs. Mary, Henry VIII's eldest child, was the obvious successor, but she was a Catholic. After Henry's excommunication by the pope, Edward had been raised as a Protestant; and his advisers now proclaimed a distant Protestant cousin, Lady Jane Grey, as the new queen. But Jane only lasted nine days in the role before Mary's supporters deposed her. Mary I, known in history as Bloody Mary, now set about undoing her father's Protestant reforms and consolidating her hold on the crown in typically brutal fashion.

On February 12, 1554, Jane was beheaded and on March 18, Elizabeth—whom Mary saw as another potential rival for the throne—was ordered to be imprisoned in the Tower of London, where Jane had been held before her execution. Elizabeth, also a Protestant, feared the worst, having been implicated in a plot to prevent Mary's marriage to the Catholic king of Spain. She wrote to Mary protesting her innocence and pleading for mercy.

"I protest before God," she insisted, "that I never practised,

counselled, nor consented to any thing that might be prejudicial to your person in any way, or dangerous to the state by any means." The evidence against her was a forged letter from the leader of the plot, Thomas Wyatt; "and as for the traitor Wyatt, he might peradventure write me a letter, but on my faith I never received any from him. And as for the copy of the letter sent to the French King, I pray God confound me eternally if I ever sent him word, message, token, or letter."

Although Elizabeth certainly knew many of the conspirators, her innocence is believed by most historians. She was at pains to persuade Mary to hear her defense for herself, and not merely take her advisers' word for it: "I humbly beseech your Majesty to let me answer afore yourself, and not suffer me to trust to your Councillors, yea, and that afore I go to the Tower (if it be possible); if not afore I be further condemned."

It took Elizabeth so long to write the letter that the tide on the River Thames had turned before she finished it and she could no longer be ferried to the Tower that day. Was that an accident? Elizabeth was a shrewd operator, and after putting her signature to the letter, she drew lines across the rest of the page to prevent anyone adding anything incriminating to it. Mary was persuaded to spare Elizabeth's life, and as she lay dying without heirs in 1558, she recognized Elizabeth as her successor to the English throne.

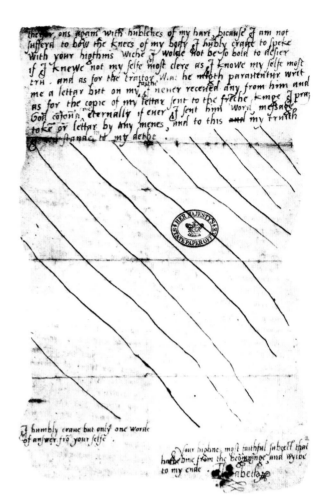

ABOVE: *Given the level of suspicion surrounding the English court, Elizabeth took no chances in leaving blank space on her letter and drew lines across it.*

OPPOSITE: *A portrait of Elizabeth, sometimes attributed to William Scrots, dated to c. 1546–47 when she was around thirteen or fourteen years old.*

Coded letter from Anthony Babington to Mary, Queen of Scots

First, assuring of invasion: Sufficient strength in the invader: Ports to arrive at appointed, with a strong party at every place to join with them and warrant their landing. The deliverance of your Majesty. The dispatch of the usurping Competitor. For the effectuating of all which it may please your Excellency to rely upon my service.... Now forasmuch as delay is extreme dangerous, it may please your most excellent Majesty by your wisdom to direct us, and by your princely authority to enable such as may advance the affair; foreseeing that, where is not any of the nobility at liberty assured to your Majesty in this desperate service (except unknown to us) and seeing it is very necessary that some there be to become heads to lead the multitude, ever disposed by nature in this land to follow nobility, considering withal it doth not only make the commons and gentry to follow without contradiction or contention (which is ever found in equality) but also doth add great courage to the leaders. For which necessary regard I recommend some unto your Majesty as fittest in my knowledge for to be your Lieutenants in the West parts, in the North parts, South Wales, North Wales and the Counties of Lancaster, Derby and Stafford: all which countries, by parties already made and fidelities taken in your Majesty's name, I hold as most assured and of most undoubted fidelity …

… Myself with ten gentlemen and a hundred of our followers will undertake the delivery of your royal person from the hands of your enemies. For the dispatch of the usurper, from the obedience of whom we are by the excommunication of her made free, there be six noble gentlemen, all my private friends, who for the zeal they bear to the Catholic cause and your Majesty's service will undertake that tragical execution. …

Babington's plot is revealed in coded letters to Mary, Queen of Scots

(1586)

When supporters of the imprisoned Mary, Queen of Scots, plotted to assassinate her captor, Queen Elizabeth I, they wisely wrote their letters in code. But the plotters had been infiltrated by government spies, and the code was cracked, with fatal consequences.

The two queens were cousins. Mary, who had her own strong claim to the English throne, had fled from Scotland after the suspicious murder of her estranged husband, Henry Stuart, Lord Darnley. At the time of the scandal, Elizabeth had written to her: "I should ill fulfil the office of a faithful cousin or an affectionate friend if I did not … tell you what all the world is thinking. Men say that, instead of seizing the murderers, you are looking through your fingers while they escape; that you will not seek revenge on those who have done you so much pleasure."

Mary married the alleged murderer, Lord Bothwell, a move that split Scottish opinion. After imprisonment and escape from Lochleven Castle, she eventually fled south to England in 1568 into the protective custody of her cousin.

At first she was kept in something approaching the royal manner. But she was a focus for Elizabeth's many enemies, and her freedoms were increasingly curtailed as she was moved from castle to castle.

As so often in British history, religion was the issue. Elizabeth and England were Protestant; Mary was a Catholic and the beacon for all who wanted a Catholic back on the English throne. These included John Ballard, a Jesuit priest, who led the plot to free Mary and kill her cousin. Ballard recruited sympathizers to the cause, among them Anthony Babington, who had been on the staff of Mary's one-time jailer, the Earl of Shrewsbury.

Babington wrote letters to Mary in early 1586, telling her of the

plot, unaware that from the outset, Elizabeth's spies had penetrated the assassins' circle. Babington's friend and colleague Robert Poley was in the pay of Elizabeth's security supremo, Sir Francis Walsingham. Walsingham had also planted Gilbert Gifford, a double agent who was allowed to smuggle letters to and from Mary in beer barrels and relay the letters' contents to Walsingham.

Mary did not instigate the plot to murder her cousin, but she certainly approved of it. She stressed in one letter to Babington the need for an invasion by Catholic Spain to put her on the throne. This, like other correspondence, was intercepted by Walsingham's code breaker Thomas Phelippes, whom Walsingham now instructed to add a postscript. When Babington received the letter, it included a forged request to send Mary the names of his fellow conspirators. One final letter, genuinely from Mary, gave Walsingham the damning evidence he needed of her treason. She wrote, "Let the great plot commence."

In September 1586, Mary's supporters were rounded up one by one, tried, and then hung, drawn, and quartered. Mary herself was given a show trial at Fotheringhay Castle, in which she was not allowed to present any defense. Her decoded letters were read out and a jury of English bishops, earls, and lords found her guilty by forty-five votes to one. Queen Elizabeth, who had for so long resisted calls to execute her troublesome cousin, could do so no longer. On February 8, 1587, Mary was beheaded.

Philip II of Spain insists the Armada press on and attack England

(July 5, 1588)

The Armada sailed from Spain in late May 1588 with 130 ships under the command of the Duke of Medina Sidonia. He was tasked with escorting an army massed in Flanders to invade England. Medina Sidonia was an aristocrat without naval command experience ... and therein lay the problem.

The aim of the Armada was to overthrow Queen Elizabeth I and her establishment of Protestantism in England and to stop English privateers who were severely disrupting trade with the lucrative colonies of New Spain.

The Duke of Medina Sidonia was a late appointment as commander of the fleet, following the death of Philip II's original choice, the Marquis of Santa Cruz. The duke's principle qualification, as far as Philip was concerned, was that he would do what he was told. He had little military and even less naval experience, being prone to seasickness.

That frailty was tested when, soon after setting off from Lisbon, the Armada was scattered by storms as it crossed the Bay of Biscay. The duke reported the setback to Philip and urged a delay, both to allow the fleet to regroup and repair back in A Coruña, and to give time for potential peace negotiations between the countries.

The king replied by letter on July 5, 1588. He was very clear in his instruction. "My intention is not to desist from the enterprise in consequence of what has happened but to carry forward the task already commenced. The expedition must not be abandoned on account of this difficulty."

The duke had complained of the mixed nature of the fleet. Of his 130 ships, only twenty-eight were purpose-built warships; the rest were converted cargo vessels and barges for carrying troops and supplies, best suited to inshore waters, not the open seas of Biscay.

Many were still missing after the storm. In his anxiety to push on with the mission, the king ordered the duke not to go looking for them and insisted the rest were perfectly seaworthy. "In order to gain time you may leave behind twelve or fifteen of the least useful of your ships, transferring their contents onto the other vessels."

The delay was putting an extra strain on the expedition's supplies. The Armada was supposed to have sailed with two months of food and drink, but some ships had soon run out of water and provisions. "Serve out fresh bread, meat and fish whilst you are in port," Philip continued, "and you may spend the reserve money in paying for this.

"Be ready to sail on your voyage as soon as you receive my further orders," the king concluded. Peace talks had already fallen through, and the following day the Duke of Medina Sidonia reluctantly but obediently set sail once more. Ill winds in the English Channel; poor communication with the Spanish reinforcements waiting in the Netherlands; an opportunistic attack by Sir Francis Drake with fireships on the anchored Spanish fleet outside Calais; and storms in the North Sea all conspired to make the ill-fated Armada an international embarrassment for the Spanish court.

Drake and Sir John Hawkins had smaller but faster warships than the ponderous Spanish galleons, and the English use of fireships caused mayhem while the fleet were waiting to take the invasion troops onboard.

Philip's stubbornness drove him to send two further, smaller armadas, in 1596 and 1597; both were defeated by storms en route. The 1588 victory confirmed the superiority of the English navy and permanently weakened the political strength of Catholicism in northern Europe. A third of the Armada was wrecked off Scotland and Ireland, and it is said that the wild horses of Connemara are descendants of Spanish cavalry mounts that swam ashore.

Letter from Philip II of Spain to the Duke of Medina Sidonia

Your letter of 28th instant arrived yesterday; and before I reply to it I may say that you will have seen by my letters of 26th ultimo and first instant, that my intention is not to desist from the enterprise in consequence of what has happened, but, in any case, to carry forward the task already commenced, overcoming the difficulties which may present themselves. I mean, however, after the Armada has been refitted, and your scattered forces have been re-united, or so much of them as may be of importance.

This intention of mine is, as I say, clearly indicated in the above-mentioned letters ; but the order given in the later of the two, for the Armada to sail by the 10th instant, is conditional upon your having been joined by the missing ships; and upon your having with the utmost speed made arrangements to refit the ships, and reinforce those which are to sail with the arms, men, and victuals of the ships which you leave behind. By ships left behind, I mean those which you find need repairs which will occupy a long time, and of these the hulls alone must remain, all the contents being put on board the other vessels.

I think well, nevertheless, to repeat clearly to you here what my meaning is. In conformity with this the Council of War will write to you saying, that, in order to gain time, you may leave behind twelve or fifteen of the least useful of your ships, transferring their contents onto the other vessels; always on the understanding that you shall have been joined by the rest of the missing ships.

I now come to your letter enclosing the report and opinion of the council you summoned. With regard to the suggestion that the Armada should leave Corunna for the purpose of seeking along the coast for the missing ships, that should not be adopted on any account. The missing ships should join you there, and when all, or a sufficient number, are united, you may proceed on your expedition, and I approve of the orders you had sent out to this effect. …

RIGHT: Philip II failed to convert England back to Catholicism by force, even though factions within the country supported the change.

Lord Monteagle gets a carefully worded warning …

(October 26, 1605)

The Gunpowder Plot of 1605 was a Catholic plan to blow up the English parliament on the first day of the new session, when the Protestant king, James I, would be present. A week before the proposed explosion a prominent Catholic noble, Lord Monteagle, received an anonymous letter.

Following the death of Queen Elizabeth without heirs, England wanted to continue her Protestant legacy and therefore invited the Scottish king to rule England too. Ironically, James was the Protestant son of ardent Catholic Mary, Queen of Scots, whom Elizabeth had put to death after uncovering a plot to seize the throne.

Lord Monteagle had himself been imprisoned for taking part in a Catholic uprising against Elizabeth. However, it was expected that King James would be more tolerant of Catholicism than his predecessor, and Monteagle wrote to James to assure him that he was "done with all formal plots."

Not all Catholics felt the same about the new king. Robert Catesby, who had taken part in the same uprising as Lord Monteagle, and like Monteagle been imprisoned, found King James less accommodating of Catholicism than anticipated after his 1603 accession. In 1604, he conceived the idea of blowing James up with gunpowder in the House of Lords, where the State Opening of Parliament would take place on November 5, 1605, and where the king was sure to be present. Catesby began to recruit other Catholics to his cause, which saw the parliamentary explosion as a prelude to a popular uprising to return a Catholic to the English throne.

He was unconcerned about the collateral deaths of hundreds of Protestant lords and commoners in the explosion. But there remained some Catholic lords such as his former fellow revolutionary Lord Monteagle who would share the king's fate. Although the letter that Monteagle received was unsigned, it seems possible that it came from Catesby or at least from one of the conspirators who knew of Monteagle's religious sympathies.

The letter was oblique in its references, but its meaning was clear. Its author spoke of Monteagle's religion only in terms of "the love I bear to some of your friends" and of Protestantism only as "the wickedness of this time" that "God and man have concurred to punish." The letter urged Monteagle "to devise some excuse to shift your attendance at this parliament" and "to retire yourself into your country [estate] where you may expect the event in safety."

It hinted strongly at the nature of that event. "They shall receive a terrible blow, this parliament, and yet they shall not see who hurts them." And Monteagle was urged not to ignore the author's advice out of fear of being implicated in the plot, "for the danger is past as soon as you have burnt the letter."

It has been suggested that Monteagle wrote the letter himself to curry favor with the new king. In any case, he was a man of his word and, having rejected "all formal plots," he took the letter to the secretary of state, who took it to the king. The rest, as they say, is history. On the eve of the State Opening of Parliament, a thorough search of the parliamentary buildings revealed one of the conspirators, Guy Fawkes, concealed in the basement with a keg of gunpowder concealed under a pile of coal.

Under torture, Fawkes revealed the names of his fellow plotters, all of whom were executed in January 1606. Monteagle received money and lands from a grateful government for his loyalty to the Protestant crown. The letter survives in Britain's National Archives.

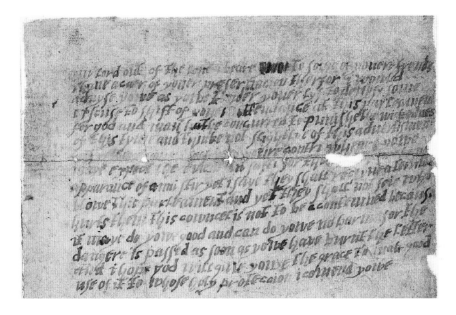

ABOVE: The warning letter that unraveled the plot.

Anonymous letter to Lord Monteagle

26 October, 1605. My lord, out of the love I bear to some of your friends, I have a care of your preservation, therefore I would advise you as you tender your life to devise some excuse to shift your attendance at this parliament, for God and man have concurred to punish the wickedness of this time, and think not slightly of this advertisement, but retire yourself into your country, where you may expect the event in safety, for though there be no appearance of any stir, yet I say they shall receive a terrible blow this parliament and yet they shall not see who hurts them, this counsel is not to be condemned because it may do you good and can do you no harm, for the danger is past as soon as you have burnt the letter and I hope God will give you the grace to make good use of it, to whose holy protection I commend you.

Letter from Galileo Galilei to Leonardo Donato, Doge of Venice

Most Serene Prince.

Galileo Galilei most humbly prostrates himself before Your Highness, watching carefully, and with all spirit of willingness, not only to satisfy what concerns the reading of mathematics in the study of Padua, but to write of having decided to present to Your Highness a telescope ("Occhiale") that will be a great help in maritime and land enterprises.

I assure you I shall keep this new invention a great secret and show it only to Your Highness.

The telescope was made for the most accurate study of distances.

This telescope has the advantage of discovering the ships of the enemy two hours before they can be seen with the natural vision and to distinguish the number and quality of the ships and to judge their strength and be ready to chase them, to fight them, or to flee from them; or, in the open country to see all details and to distinguish every movement and preparation.

Galileo explains the first sighting of the moons of Jupiter

(January 1610)

Galileo Galilei is often hailed as the father of modern science. He had the intellect and the imagination to find scientific solutions by looking at problems from new perspectives. In January 1610, he wrote a letter describing, and illustrating, his latest astronomical discoveries.

Galileo taught geometry, astronomy, and mechanics at the University of Padua in northern Italy in the first decade of the seventeenth century. In 1609, he was shown a rudimentary spyglass, the new invention from the Netherlands for seeing things that were far away. Galileo immediately understood the principle of this early telescope and set about building himself a better one.

Having done so, he wrote to Leonardo Donato, the doge (political leader) of the Republic of Venice. Venice was a powerful state that, like the Netherlands, had built its wealth on maritime trade, and Galileo felt sure the doge would be interested in his much-improved device. "This telescope," he wrote, "has the advantage of discovering the ships of the enemy two hours before they can be seen with the natural vision."

There were obvious benefits to being able to assess the enemy's strength in advance "and be ready to chase them, to fight them or to flee from them," as Galileo pointed out—and not only at sea but on land, "in open country to see all details and to distinguish every movement and preparation."

Galileo, however, saw far greater potential for the new device. When looking through a telescope, why stop at the terrestrial horizon? The astronomer had already used it to look to the heavens, and at the foot of the draft of his letter to the doge are his sketches of

four moons of Jupiter. He had discovered them in the days before he wrote the letter and drawn their relative positions to the planet on successive nights, except on January 14, which, he noted, was cloudy.

From his telescopic observations he deduced that they were not stars but moons in orbit around Jupiter. With them, Galileo was the first man to find any moons beyond our own in the solar system, and to this day they are called the Galilean moons—Io, Europa, Callisto, and the largest of them all, Ganymede.

They are the largest of some seventy-nine moons now known to circle the planet, and their discovery challenged the prevalent belief that everything in the universe rotated around Earth. Galileo famously went farther down this scientific road by suggesting that Earth revolved around the sun and not vice versa. This so shook the established worldview that in 1633, he was forced to withdraw the suggestion and spend the rest of his life under house arrest.

But he was right, and in 1989, NASA launched the Galileo space probe, named in his honor, with a mission to observe Jupiter and its moons at close quarters. In 2003, its job done, the probe crash-landed onto the surface of Jupiter, having sent back data that immeasurably increased our knowledge of the space objects first studied through that homemade telescope in 1609.

Charles II reassures Parliament that they will be in control

(April 4, 1660)

England was once a republic. The English Civil War was fought over who should govern—the king or Parliament. By the end, King Charles I had been beheaded, his son Charles II had fled to Europe, and Oliver Cromwell ruled Britain as Lord Protector. When Cromwell died, there was an opportunity …

Charles I believed that kings had an absolute right to rule, making all state decisions themselves. It was a historical irony that Cromwell ruled without Parliament for five years as a military dictator, as completely in power as Charles had wished to be.

On Cromwell's death in 1658, in a further echo of royalty, he was succeeded by his son Richard Cromwell. Richard, however, lacked his father's authority and competence, and the republic's New Model Army soon replaced him with a parliament. But when that parliament threatened to exercise its power to rule, the army removed it and splintered into factions arguing about how to govern the country. Anarchy seemed imminent.

General George Monck, Cromwell's governor in Scotland, marched south with his army to impose some stability on the situation. In a surprising move for a parliamentarian, he wrote secretly to Charles II, then in exile in the Netherlands, inviting him to return to the throne of England for the good of the country. Charles wrote a letter known to historians as the Declaration of Breda in reply.

It was essentially a job application, and in it he discussed what he would bring to the post of king. In a spirit of reconciliation he was ready to "grant a free and general pardon" to the former enemies of the Crown, provided that they "within forty days … return to the loyalty and obedience of good subjects." He made an exception here for those who had had a hand in the beheading of his father.

He promised religious freedom, having in mind the constant battle for hearts and minds between Protestant and Catholic denominations, which had marked the reigns of his predecessors. And he promised to do so by being "ready to consent to such an Act of Parliament as, upon mature consideration, shall be offered to us for the full granting that indulgence."

Here was a king ready to work with Parliament for the good of the people: "a free Parliament," he spelled it out, "by which, upon the word of a King, we will be advised." Shrewdly, he gave Parliament the task of deciding who owned what, after so much property had changed hands in the course of the civil war. And he offered financial inducement in his willingness to settle the outstanding back pay of Monck's soldiers and to take them on as his own army with no cut in wages or conditions.

The Declaration of Breda offered a way forward for all concerned. The king got his throne back, and almost no one would be penalized for taking it from him in the first place, other than those directly involved with the execution of his father. It offered the genuine possibility of a peaceful restoration of the monarchy to a country whose wounds, as Charles put it, "have so many years together been kept bleeding."

Monck convened a special parliament, which declared that Charles II had been king all along since the execution of his father. He was crowned in Westminster Abbey a year later, having ushered in a new age of British parliamentary democracy.

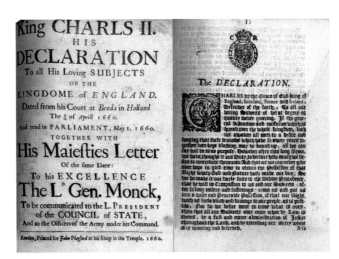

Letter from Charles II to his subjects

Charles, by the grace of God, King of England, Scotland, France and Ireland, Defender of the Faith. To all our loving subjects, of what degree or quality soever, greeting.

If the general distraction and confusion which is spread over the whole kingdom doth not awaken all men to a desire and longing that those wounds which have so many years together been kept bleeding, may be bound up, all we can say will be to no purpose; however, after this long silence, we have thought it our duty to declare how much we desire to contribute thereunto; and that as we can never give over the hope, in good time, to obtain the possession of that right which God and nature hath made our due, so we do make it our daily suit to the Divine Providence, that He will, in compassion to us and our subjects, after so long misery and sufferings, remit and put us into a quiet and peaceable possession of that our right, with as little blood and damage to our people as is possible; nor do we desire more to enjoy what is ours, than that all our subjects may enjoy what by law is theirs, by a full and entire administration of justice throughout the land, and by extending our mercy where it is wanted and deserved.

And to the end that the fear of punishment may not engage any, conscious to themselves of what is past, to a perseverance in guilt for the future, by opposing the quiet and happiness of their country, in the restoration of King, Peers and people to their just, ancient and fundamental rights, we do, by these presents, declare, that we do grant a free and general pardon, which we are ready, upon demand, to pass under our Great Seal of England, to all our subjects, of what degree or quality soever, who, within forty days after the publishing hereof, shall lay hold upon this our grace and favour, and shall, by any good subjects; excepting only such persons as shall hereafter be excepted by Parliament those only to be excepted. …

Letter from English Earls and Clergy to Prince William of Orange

We have great satisfaction to find … that your Highness is so ready and willing to give us such assistances as they have related to us. We have great reason to believe we shall be every day in a worse condition than we are, and less able to defend ourselves, and therefore we do earnestly wish we might be so happy as to find a remedy before it be too late for us to contribute to our own deliverance. But although these be our wishes, yet we will by no means put your Highness into any expectations which may misguide your own councils in this matter; so that the best advice we can give is to inform your Highness truly both of the state of things here at this time and of the difficulties which appear to us.

As to the first, the people are so generally dissatisfied with the present conduct of the government in relation to their religion, liberties and properties (all which have been greatly invaded), and they are in such expectation of their prospects being daily worse, that your Highness may be assured there are nineteen parts of twenty of the people throughout the kingdom who are desirous of a change, and who, we believe, would willingly contribute to it, if they had such a protection to countenance their rising as would secure them from being destroyed before they could get to be in a posture able to defend themselves. It is no less certain that much the greatest part of the nobility and gentry are as much dissatisfied, although it be not safe to speak to many of them beforehand; and there is no doubt but that some of the most considerable of them would venture themselves with your Highness at your first landing, whose interests would be able to draw great numbers to them whenever they could protect them and the raising and drawing men together. And if such a strength could be landed as were able to defend itself and them till they could be got together into some order, we make no question but that strength would quickly be increased to a number double to the army here, although their army should all remain firm to them; whereas we do upon very good grounds believe that their army then would be very much divided among themselves, many of the officers being so discontented that they continue in their service only for a subsistence (besides that some of their minds are known already), and very many of the common soldiers do daily shew such an aversion to the popish religion that there is the greatest probability imaginable of great numbers of deserters which would come from them should there be such an occasion; and amongst the seamen it is almost certain there is not one in ten who would do them any service in such a war. …

ABOVE: *William of Orange painted between c. 1680 and 1684. The Battle of the Boyne was the final time two crowned kings of England, Scotland, and Ireland met on the field of battle.*

The English nobility make Prince William of Orange an offer

(June 30, 1688)

History is written by winners, so the signatories of a letter inviting a foreign power to invade Britain are today known as the Immortal Seven rather than the Treacherous Seven, and the event that their letter precipitated is called the Glorious Revolution.

It was a treasonous act. In 1688, during the reign of James II, three English earls, a lord, two gentlemen, and the Bishop of London wrote a letter to a foreign prince, inviting him to bring his army across the channel and become its king. The cause of such high-ranking dissent was religion.

Although Charles II had promised religious tolerance when he regained the English throne, the Anglican Church had ensured that Catholics, Puritans, and other minority forms of Christianity were sidelined by denying them public office. Charles himself made a deathbed conversion to Catholicism and was succeeded as king by his Catholic brother, James II. James began to appoint Catholics to high rank in the army and in other public positions, and when his second wife gave birth to a son, who would be raised as a Catholic, Anglicans feared the establishment of a new Catholic dynasty.

Things came to a head when James ordered that a Declaration of Indulgence—a statement of tolerance for Catholics and non-Anglican Protestants—be read from every Anglican pulpit. Seven bishops refused to do so, and James had them arrested on a charge of sedition. On June 30, 1688, they were acquitted of the charge, a decision that undermined James's authority to impose his Catholic agenda.

That afternoon, the Immortal Seven composed their letter to William, Prince of Orange in the Netherlands. William was married to Mary, James II's daughter by his first wife, and both William and Mary were staunch Protestants. Mary had been heir to the English throne until the birth of James's new son.

The letter talked up the level of resistance to James II's new religious freedoms: "the people are so generally dissatisfied with the present conduct of the government in relation to their religion, liberties and properties … that your Highness may be assured there are nineteen parts of twenty of the people throughout the kingdom who are desirous of a change."

The authors assured William that there would be military support for him if he chose to land in Britain: "Many of the common soldiers do daily shew such an aversion to the popish religion that there is the greatest probability imaginable of great numbers of deserters."

Rumors were rife that the new male heir to the throne was not the genuine article—that the queen's baby had been stillborn and a substitute baby smuggled into the royal bedchamber in a bedpan. "Not one in a thousand believes [the baby] to be the queen's," the letter reported, suggesting that this could be the pretext for William's invasion.

William did land in Devon, and an invading Dutch army on British soil became the Glorious Revolution. The Anglican Church was established once and for all as the nation's official religion, and James II, Britain's last Catholic monarch, fled to Europe. He made one last attempt to regain the English throne by enlisting the support of Irish Catholics, but on July 1, 1690, William led an army to meet and defeat James at the Battle of the Boyne. The victory entrenched the bitter divide between Catholics and Protestants in Ireland, which is still feeling the aftereffects of that letter to William of Orange nearly 350 years later.

Letter to the printer of the *London Chronicle*, Dec. 25, 1773

Sir,

Finding that two Gentlemen have been unfortunately engaged in a Duel, about a transaction and its circumstances of which both of them are totally ignorant and innocent, I think it incumbent on me to declare (for the prevention of farther mischief, as far as such a declaration may contribute to prevent it) that I alone am the person who obtained and transmitted to Boston the letters in question. Mr. W. could not communicate them, because they were never in his possession; and, for the same reason, they could not be taken from him by Mr. T. They were not of the nature of "private letters between friends:" They were written by public officers to persons in public station, on public affairs, and intended to procure public measures; they were therefore handed to other public persons who might be influenced by them to produce those measures: Their tendency was to incense the Mother Country against her Colonies, and, by the steps recommended, to widen the breach, which they effected. The chief Caution expressed with regard to Privacy, was, to keep their contents from the Colony Agents, who the writers apprehended might return them, or copies of them, to America. That apprehension was, it seems, well founded; for the first Agent who laid his hands on them, thought it his duty to transmit them to his Constituents.

B. Franklin,
Agent for the House of Representatives of the Massachusetts-Bay.

LEFT: *Ben Franklin felt honor-bound to reveal that he was the source of the leaked letters after William Whately accused John Temple of taking the letters, which Temple vigorously denied. Temple challenged Whately to a duel and wounded him in the encounter in early December 1773. A second duel was planned, at which point Franklin wrote to the* London Chronicle.

OPPOSITE: *A portrait of Massachusetts governor Thomas Hutchinson, who spent his final years in exile in England.*

Ben Franklin's stolen mail reveals a political scandal

(1773)

Benjamin Franklin was the postmaster general for the Massachusetts Bay colony and acted as its representative in London. He was passed a bundle of correspondence from the governor of Massachusetts Thomas Hutchinson to his deputy Andrew Oliver, which had incendiary contents. …

The letters had been written a few years earlier, when discontent with rule from London was already widespread. In the 1760s, Britain imposed a series of taxes on the colonial population to help pay for the military cost of protecting its American colony. The population reasoned that if it was going to be taxed, it should have a say in how the money was spent—"No Taxation without Representation" became their slogan.

The Hutchinson-Oliver letters discussed their response to the ensuing unrest. Far from making any concessions to democracy, the letters called for an increased military presence and a curtailment of "English liberties"—so that although the settlers were British subjects, they would not have the same rights as those living in Britain.

Franklin thought these discoveries worth making known to the Massachusetts Committee of Correspondence, one of several such committees that had been formed to share information of revolutionary interest. Franklin understood the explosive implications of the letters and insisted that they were only for the eyes of the committee and not to be more widely circulated. Nevertheless, they were eventually printed in the *Boston Gazette* in June 1773, fanning the flames of colonial resentment.

At the end of the year anger boiled over in Boston. A new act that summer had given the British East India Company

a tax-free, competitive advantage over the colonies' tea importers. Boston merchants made their feelings known by boarding an East India Company vessel and throwing its cargo overboard—the famous Boston Tea Party.

In England, Benjamin Franklin was forced to admit that he had supplied the letters to the Committee of Correspondence. A parliamentary committee gave him a patronizing dressing-down during a hearing into the Tea Party and the contents of Hutchinson's letters. Franklin was accused of theft and dishonorable actions and stripped of his position as postmaster general. Hutchinson was exonerated, but soon recalled as governor and replaced by the British military commander in North America, General Thomas Gage.

Franklin remained tight-lipped throughout the hearing, but returned to America utterly convinced of the need for independence from Britain. In 1774, the British Parliament passed a series of acts designed to punish the Massachusetts colonists for their temerity in resisting its will, known as the Intolerable, or Coercive, Acts. They only served to increase outraged opposition to British rule, and within a year colonial feelings had blown up into a full-scale Revolutionary War. When it was all over, Franklin helped to draft the Declaration of Independence. Hutchinson, a Bostonian by birth, ended his life in exile in Britain, where he wrote a three-volume history of Massachusetts.

Abigail Adams tells husband John to "remember the ladies"

(March 31, 1776)

John Adams set up the committee responsible for drafting America's Declaration of Independence. It consisted of Thomas Jefferson, Benjamin Franklin, Robert Livingston, Roger Sherman, and himself. Many others had ideas of what the declaration should contain, including Adams's wife Abigail.

The archive of correspondence between John and Abigail Adams is a treasure trove of insights into the early history of the United States. Their eyewitness accounts of events before and after the Revolutionary War are invaluable. Abigail was a wholehearted supporter of independence, and the couple worked closely to develop their ideas of the political and moral shape of the new nation.

With the declaration came an opportunity for a fresh start. A nation whose pilgrim fathers sailed there on a matter of religious principle now had a clean slate on which to write the framework of laws by which they would govern and be governed. While John and his committee thrashed out the details in Philadelphia, Abigail wrote from Braintree in Massachusetts. She had been mindful of the weighty task in which he was engaged. "I long to hear that you have declared an independancy," she wrote, "and by the way, in the new Code of Laws which I suppose it will be necessary for you to make I desire you would Remember the Ladies."

Two hundred and fifty years before #MeToo, Abigail Adams called out the all-male committee: "Do not put such unlimited power into the hands of the Husbands. Remember, all Men would be tyrants if they could." One assumes that Abigail considered John an exception to the rule. "Men of Sense in all Ages abhor those customs which treat us only as the vassals of your Sex. Regard us then as Beings placed by providence under your protection and in immitation of the

Supreem Being make use of that power only for our happiness."

Perhaps only half-joking, Abigail threatened that "if perticuliar care and attention is not paid to the Laidies we are determined to foment a Rebellion, and will not hold ourselves bound by any Laws in which we have no voice, or Representation." She was making a fair comparison with the American Revolution itself, which arose from the refusal of (male) colonists to accept British laws and taxation when they had no representation in the British parliament.

Whether she was joking or not, her husband certainly took it in that spirit. "As to your extraordinary Code of Laws, I cannot but laugh." His letter in reply dismissed the idea rather patronizingly. "Depend upon it, we know better than to repeal our masculine systems. Altho they are in full force, you know they are little more than theory … and in practice you know we are the subjects. We have only the name of Masters."

When the Declaration says "all men are created equal," it means all mankind, not all males. Although the Nineteenth Amendment did not, until 1920, enshrine the right to vote regardless of gender, women had the vote in many states before then—in Massachusetts they were voting even before the Revolutionary War. But even today, not all males do as John had done for Abigail. "Such of you as wish to be happy," she observed in her letter, "willingly give up the harsh title of Master for the more tender and endearing one of Friend."

Letter from Abigail Adams to John Adams

I wish you would ever write me a Letter half as long as I write you; and tell me if you may where your Fleet are gone? What sort of Defence Virginia can make against our common Enemy? Whether it is so situated as to make an able Defence? Are not the Gentery Lords and the common people vassals, are they not like the uncivilized Natives Brittain represents us to be? I hope their Riffel Men who have shewen themselves very savage and even Blood thirsty; are not a specimen of the Generality of the people.

I am willing to allow the Colony great merrit for having produced a Washington but they have been shamefully duped by a Dunmore.

I have sometimes been ready to think that the passion for Liberty cannot be Eaquelly Strong in the Breasts of those who have been accustomed to deprive their fellow Creatures of theirs. Of this I am certain that it is not founded upon that generous and christian principal of doing to others as we would that others should do unto us. …

I long to hear that you have declared an independancy—and by the way in the new Code of Laws which I suppose it will be necessary for you to make I desire you would Remember the Ladies, and be more generous and favourable to them than your ancestors. Do not put such unlimited power into the hands of the Husbands. Remember all Men would be tyrants if they could. If perticuliar care and attention is not paid to the Ladies we are determined to foment a Rebelion, and will not hold ourselves bound by any Laws in which we have no voice, or Representation.

That your Sex are Naturally Tyrannical is a Truth so thoroughly established as to admit of no dispute, but such of you as wish to be happy willingly give up the harsh title of Master for the more tender and endearing one of Friend. Why then, not put it out of the power of the vicious and the Lawless to use us with cruelty and indignity with impunity. Men of Sense in all Ages abhor those customs which treat us only as the vassals of your Sex. Regard us then as Beings placed by providence under your protection and in immitation of the Supreem Being make use of that power only for our happiness. …

George Washington employs his first spy in the Revolutionary War

(February 4, 1777)

America as a nation dates from the 1776 Declaration of Independence. But the outcome of the Revolutionary War that followed was by no means a foregone conclusion. It took a counterespionage initiative by General George Washington to turn the tables against the superior British forces.

Britain easily held the upper hand in the early stages of the Revolutionary War. It had a trained army and a powerful navy. They also had spies. Against it were ranged a disparate group of colonies with no previous collective organization of any kind. By early 1777, the rebellious colonists seemed certain of defeat.

Although the revolutionaries understood the need for counterintelligence, their efforts in that direction were rudimentary. In that more gentlemanly age, the use of civilians as tools of war was not considered respectable, and future president George Washington at first sought volunteer spies from the army. Only when one of them, Captain Nathan Hale, was captured and executed by the British did Washington begin to consider civilians, who would be less conspicuous.

On the advice of a colleague, Washington commissioned a merchant called Nathaniel Sackett to build a network of spies. Sackett had some experience with codes and secret messages, having served on the New York Committee and Commission for Detecting and Defeating Conspiracies. Remarkably, Washington's original letter to Sackett, written over 230 years ago, still survives.

It's a short letter, but it marks the origins of modern American intelligence gathering. "The advantage of obtaining the earliest and best Intelligence of the designs of the Enemy," General Washington writes, "the good character given of you by Colonel Duer, and your capacity for an undertaking of this kind, have induced me to entrust the management of this business to your care."

Unlike the British effort, there was no Revolutionary budget for this sort of thing, but Washington, as a wealthy plantation owner, had the financial muscle to get his spy ring off the ground. "I agree, on behalf of the Public, to allow you Fifty Dollars per Kallendar Month, and … the sum of Five hundred Dollars to pay those whom you may find necessary to Imploy in the transaction of this business."

Sackett delivered his first report a month later. He had already recruited several agents and sworn them to secrecy. Unfortunately, Sackett was not the greatest of spymasters. The information that he and his network gathered came in too slowly and too inaccurately. After a few months Washington was forced to replace him with another army officer, Major Benjamin Tallmadge.

Tallmadge was altogether better at the work. He established a spy network known as the Culper Ring, which was so effective that even George Washington did not know who its members were. Its existence was only revealed to the public in the 1930s. It gave America's revolutionaries the advantage they needed to anticipate British plans, and the tide of the conflict turned. After the war, Washington presented Congress with an expenses claim of $17,000 for the operation. It was money well spent, and Congress repaid him in full.

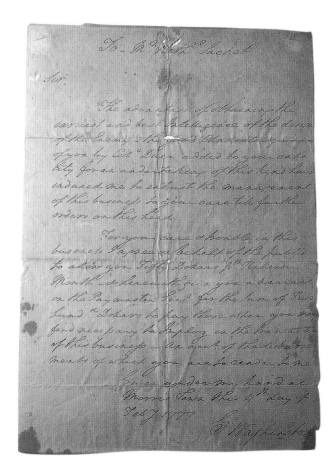

Letter from George Washington to Nathaniel Sackett

The advantage of obtaining the earliest and best Intelligence of the designs of the Enemy, the good character given of you by Colonel Duer, and your capacity for an undertaking of this kind, have induced me to entrust the management of this business to your care till further orders on this head.

For your own trouble in this business I agree, on behalf of the Public, to allow you Fifty Dollars per Kallendar Month, and herewith give you a warrant upon the Paymaster General for the sum of Five hundred Dollars to pay those whom you may find necessary to Imploy in the transaction of this business, an acct of the disbursements of which you are to render to me.

Given at Head Quarters at
Morristown this 4th day of Feby, 1777
G. Washington

Letter from Thomas Jefferson to Peter Carr

Dear Peter

I have received your two letters of Decemb. 30 and April 18, and am very happy to find by them, as well as by letters from Mr. Wythe, that you have been so fortunate as to attract his notice & good will; I am sure you will find this to have been one of the most fortunate events of your life, as I have ever been sensible it was of mine. I inclose you a sketch of the sciences to which I would wish you to apply in such order as Mr. Wythe shall advise; I mention also the books in them worth your reading, which submit to his correction. …

Italian. I fear the learning this language will confound your French and Spanish. Being all of them degenerated dialects of the Latin, they are apt to mix in conversation. I have never seen a person speaking the three languages who did not mix them. It is a delightful language, but late events having rendered the Spanish more useful, lay it aside to prosecute that.

Spanish. Bestow great attention on this, & endeavor to acquire an accurate knowlege of it. Our future connections with Spain & Spanish America will render that language a valuable acquisition. The antient history of a great part of America, too, is written in that language. I send you a dictionary. …

Religion. Your reason is now mature enough to examine this object. In the first place divest yourself of all bias in favour of novelty & singularity of opinion. Indulge them in any other subject rather than that of religion. It is too important, & the consequences of error may be too serious. On the other hand shake off all the fears & servile prejudices under which weak minds are servilely crouched. Fix reason firmly in her seat, and call to her tribunal every fact, every opinion. Question with boldness even the existence of a god; because, if there be one, he must more approve of the homage of reason, than that of blindfolded fear. You will naturally examine first the religion of your own country. Read the bible then, as you would read Livy or Tacitus. The facts which are within the ordinary course of nature you will believe on the authority of the writer, as you do those of the same kind in Livy & Tacitus. …

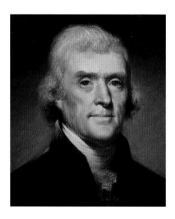

LEFT: *The classic 1800 portrait of Thomas Jefferson by Rembrandt Peale.*

Jefferson advises his nephew to question the existence of God

(August 10, 1787)

In 1787, a letter from an uncle to his seventeen-year-old nephew contained advice about how to get the best out of his education. Thomas Jefferson was serving as the Minister to France in Paris. Had it been published at the time, he might never have become president of such a God-fearing nation.

Thomas Jefferson wrote to his nephew Peter Carr because the latter was about to begin his studies with Mr. George Wythe, Jefferson's former teacher. Wythe had been one of the signatories of the Declaration of Independence and now taught at William and Mary College in Williamsburg, Virginia.

Jefferson was a learned man who prized education highly and wanted to pass his love of learning to Peter. Attached to his letter was a comprehensive reading list for each subject that Carr was likely to study, including advice on what *not* to read—in modern history for example, "omit Clarendon [a history of the English Civil War] as too seducing for a young Republican."

Other subjects on the list included ancient, foreign, and American history, and poetry recommendations from Homer to Shakespeare. Beside a thorough classical education Jefferson placed an emphasis on the sciences. There were books on agriculture, anatomy, astronomy, botany, chemistry, mathematics, and physics. In politics and the law he deferred to George Wythe's choices; but he suggested some weighty tomes in the fields of philosophy (which he called morality) and religion.

In the body of the letter, Jefferson expanded on the list with his general thoughts on several subjects. With admirable foresight he recommended that Peter study Spanish rather than Italian: "our future connections with Spain and Spanish America will render that language a valuable acquisition. I send you a dictionary."

He advised seventeen-year-old Peter Carr to resist any urge to travel. "This makes men wiser, but less happy. Travel broadens the mind but makes men less satisfied with their home country. This observation," he added ruefully—writing to Peter from Paris—was "founded in experience."

Half the letter was devoted to Jefferson's views on philosophy and religion. On morality, "I think it lost time to attend lectures on this." Jefferson argued that morality was innate and therefore did not need to be refined except by practice and by reading the books on his list. On religion, he was startlingly challenging. "Question even the existence of a God; because, if there is one, he must approve of the homage of reason [rather] than that of blindfolded fear."

Peter should apply reason to the Bible just as he would to classical authors like Tacitus: "Those facts in the Bible which contradict the laws of nature must be examined with more care." Jesus was either (implausibly) "begotten of God, born of a virgin … and ascended into heaven" or (more rationally) "of illegitimate birth, of benevolent heart … punished capitally for sedition by being gibbeted according to Roman law." An inquiring mind was more useful than blind belief.

Jefferson concluded with sound advice. "Be good, be learned, be industrious … to render you precious to your country, dear to your friends, happy within yourself." Peter Carr took his advice, serving four terms in the Virginia House of Delegates. Jefferson would have been even prouder that his nephew helped to found Albemarle Academy, which evolved into the University of Virginia.

Mozart's final letter to his wife, Constanze

Dearest, most beloved little Wife

Hofer drove out with me yesterday, Thursday the 13th, to see our Karl. We lunched there and then we all drove back to Vienna. At six o'clock I called in the carriage for Salieri and Madame Cavalieri—and drove them to my box. Then I drove back quickly to fetch Mamma and Karl, whom I had left at Hofer's. You can hardly imagine how charming they were and how they liked, not only my music, but the libretto and everything. They both said that it was an *operone*, worthy to be performed for the grandest festival and before the greatest monarch, and that they would often go to see it, as they had never seen a more beautiful or delightful show. Salieri listened and watched most attentively and from the overture to the last chorus there was not a single number that did not call forth from him a *bravo!* or *bello!* It seemed as though they could not thank me enough for my kindness. They had intended in any case to go to the opera yesterday. But they would have to be in their places by four o'clock. As it was, they saw and heard everything in comfort in my box. When it was over, I drove them home and then had supper at Hofer's with Karl. Then I drove him home and we both slept soundly. Karl was absolutely delighted at being taken to the opera. He is looking splendid. As far as health is concerned, he could not be in a better place, but everything else there is wretched, alas! All they can do is turn out a good peasant into the world. But enough of this. As his serious studies (God help them!) do not begin until Monday, I have arranged to keep him until after lunch on Sunday. I told them that you would like to see him. So tomorrow, Saturday, I shall drive out with Karl to see you. You can then keep him, or I shall take him back to Heeger's after lunch. Think it over. A month can hardly do him much harm. In the meantime the arrangement with the Piarists, which is now under discussion, may come to something. On the whole, Karl is no worse; but at the same time he is not one wit better than he was. He still has his old bad manners; he never stops chattering just as he used to do in the past; and he is, if anything, less inclined to learn than before, as out at Perchtoldsdorf all he does is run about in the garden for five hours in the morning and five hours in the afternoon, as he has himself confessed. In short, the children do nothing but eat, drink, sleep and run wild. Leutgeb and Hofer are with me at the moment. The former is staying to supper with me. I have sent out my faithful comrade Primus to fetch some food from the Burgerspital. I am quite satisfied with the fellow. He has only let me down once, when I was obliged to sleep at Hofer's, which annoyed me intensely, as they sleep far too long there. I am happiest at home, for I am accustomed to my own hours. This one occasion put me in a very bad humour. Yesterday the whole day was taken up with the trip to Perchtoldsdorf, so I could not write to you. But that you have not written to me for two days is really unforgivable. I hope that I shall certainly have a letter from you today, and that tomorrow I shall talk to you and embrace you with all my heart. Farewell. Ever your Mozart.

I kiss Sophie a thousand times. Do what you like with N. N. Adieu

OPPOSITE: Constanze Mozart

Mozart writes to his wife as he struggles to finish *Requiem*

(October 14, 1791)

It is thanks to his prolific correspondence that we know so much of the life—and death—of Wolfgang Amadeus Mozart. The earliest surviving letter was written to a girlfriend when he was thirteen. One of the last was to his wife, Constanze, as his health declined and he raced to complete his *Requiem*.

The mysterious stranger who commissioned Mozart to write a requiem has been the subject of conspiracy theories almost from the day he arrived at Mozart's house in July 1791 and offered a fee for the work and for all the rights to it. Was it Mozart's rival Antonio Salieri?

Mozart never knew what we know now—that it was a servant of Count Franz von Walsegg, an Austrian noble with a great love of music. Von Walsegg maintained an ensemble at his castle in Lower Austria. He was a competent musician but not a great composer; and so he would commission others to write music for him, which he would then pass off as his own.

When the count's wife died, he commissioned the *Requiem*—a choral mass for the dead—which he intended to have performed on the anniversary of her death each year. He paid well; and Mozart, constantly beset by money woes and expecting another child with his beloved wife, Constanze, willingly accepted the work.

His new son, Franz, was born at the end of July, when Mozart's workload was already heavy. Several of his works were to be played at the coronation of the emperor Leopold II in September, including a new and as yet unfinished opera, *La Clemenza di Tito*. Mozart was still working on it in the coach from Salzburg on the way to the coronation in Prague. At the same time he was putting the finishing touches to a clarinet concerto and composing another new opera, *The Magic Flute*.

The workload began to take its toll. He became depressed and interpreted the onset of kidney failure as an attempt

by someone to poison him. Constanze was not around to comfort him, having traveled to the health spa at Baden. He wrote letters to her almost every day that she was there, including his last on October 14.

It's a chatty, upbeat report of recent events, of which the highlight was a night out in Vienna at a performance of *The Magic Flute*. He was accompanied by his mother, his son Karl, the opera singer Caterina Cavalieri and the composer Salieri. Never self-effacing, Mozart wrote that everyone loved it and that in particular, "Salieri listened and watched most attentively and from the overture to the last chorus there was not a single number that did not call forth from him a *bravo!* or *bello!*"

In his last letter Mozart was critical of the school in Perchtoldsdorf, a village southeast of Vienna, which Karl was attending—the country air was good for the boy's health but "all they can do is turn out a good peasant into the world." He proposed to take Karl out of it for a month and travel to be with Constanze. "Tomorrow I shall talk to you and embrace you with all my heart."

Mozart never finished his *Requiem*, and as his health deteriorated he declared, "I am writing this *Requiem* for myself." Confined to bed, he was entertained by friends who sang parts of the *Requiem* with him. As he sank into unconsciousness on the evening of December 4, he could be heard dictating a percussion part for the *Requiem* to his student Franz Xaver Süssmayr. He died in the early hours of the following morning, and Constanze commissioned Süssmayr to complete Mozart's *Requiem* so that she might collect the rest of the fee.

Maria Reynolds tells Alexander Hamilton her husband has found out

(December 15, 1791)

Alexander Hamilton was a Founding Father of the United States. Under the patronage of George Washington he shaped the nation's economy, establishing its financial systems and terms of international trade. He might have become president himself, but blackmail and a sex scandal brought his downfall.

The affair between Alexander Hamilton and his married lover, Maria Reynolds, had been going on for six months. In the summer of 1791, Mrs. Reynolds approached Hamilton for financial help, claiming that her husband, Mr. James Reynolds was cruel and had abandoned her. But when Hamilton visited her to give her some money, he was very easily seduced. As he later recalled, "some conversation ensued from which it was quickly apparent that other than pecuniary consolation would be acceptable."

By the end of the year Hamilton wanted to end the affair, and although James and Maria Reynolds had recently become reconciled, Maria had no desire to end things with Alexander. It has been suggested that Mr. Reynolds knew of the affair all along, and that he and his wife may even have planned it together, in the light of what then followed.

Matters came to a head in December 1791, when Hamilton received a letter from Maria Reynolds. All was discovered, she wrote, in a mixture of great distress and poor spelling: "Mr. [Reynolds] has rote to you this morning and I know not wether you have got the letter or not and he has swore that If you do not answer It or If he dose not se or hear from you to day he will write Mrs. Hamilton."

After a series of angry letters between Mr. Reynolds and Hamilton, Reynolds did not—as was the common practice of the time—challenge Hamilton to a pistol duel. Instead, he blackmailed Hamilton, the serving secretary of the treasury, to the tune of $1,000. Nor was that the end of the business, because in January 1792, Reynolds wrote to Hamilton encouraging him to return to the house "as a friend," to resume the affair.

Whether or not Maria Reynolds was coerced by her husband, she did indeed seduce Hamilton again

on several occasions. And each time, Hamilton was persuaded by Mr. Reynolds to pay him more blackmail money, between $30 and $50 a visit until James Reynolds changed his mind again and, in June 1792, demanded an end to Hamilton's visits.

Hamilton had so far managed to keep the affair secret. But toward the end of the year Reynolds was imprisoned for another money-making scheme in which he had forged the claims of Revolutionary War veterans for back pay. Both James and Maria wrote to Hamilton, asking for his help in the case, and when he refused they tried to implicate him in the forgery.

As treasury secretary he faced ruin if he was implicated in a financial scandal. Alexander Hamilton had no choice but to reveal the true nature of his connection to the Reynoldses, backing up his version of events by surrendering all the correspondence as proof. Unfortunately for him, the letters were then leaked to his political enemy, Thomas Jefferson, who used them to destroy his rival's reputation. Although Washington remained loyal to his colleague, America's first sex scandal brought an end to Hamilton's ambitions for higher office.

Letter from Maria Reynolds to Alexander Hamilton

Dear Sir

I have not tim to tell you the cause of my present troubles only that Mr. has rote to you this morning and I know not wether you have got the letter or not and he has swore that If you do not answer It or If he dose not se or hear from you to day he will write Mrs. Hamilton he has just Gone oute and I am a Lone I think you had better come here one moment that you May know the Cause then you will the better know how to act Oh my God I feel more for you than myself and wish I had never been born to give you so mutch unhappisness do not rite to him no not a Line but come here soon do not send or leave any thing in his power

Maria

OPPOSITE: A typically effusive letter written by Alexander Hamilton to his long-suffering wife, Elizabeth Schuyler Hamilton. After his death in a duel with Aaron Burr, she would spend the rest of her life burnishing his reputation.

RIGHT: Alexander Hamilton painted in 1792 by artist and friend John Trumbull.

Thomas Jefferson wants a French botanist to explore the northwest

(January 23, 1793)

Thomas Jefferson's vision of the United States did not stop with the thirteen colonies. In the early years of the new nation, he was keen to support an expedition westward, in the hope of finding a route to the Pacific coast. In French botanist André Michaux he thought he'd found the man to accomplish it.

André Michaux was a man caught between two worlds. He had been appointed by the French king, Louis XVI, to study American plants that might have been useful to the French agricultural economy. But while he was in the New World, France had a revolution in the Old World, and Louis was sent to the guillotine. Would Michaux still have a job, or his head, if he returned to France?

Michaux was impressed with the biodiversity of the North American continent. He is reputed to have dispatched some 60,000 trees back to France as well as other plants and animals. He also introduced new species from Europe to America. But when the payment of his salary was interrupted by the shocking events of the French Revolution, he had to look elsewhere for gainful employment.

He turned to the American Philosophical Society, an organization founded in Philadelphia in 1743, still in existence today, and devoted to expanding human scientific knowledge. Jefferson was a member of the society, and Michaux knew that another of Jefferson's proposed expeditions had fallen through. He offered to undertake a similar journey in return for an advance equal to the debts he had now run up.

The letter in which Jefferson set out the terms of such an undertaking had been thought lost for nearly two hundred years until it was rediscovered in 1979 in the society's archives. It reveals his vision not only for the expedition but for the nation whose Declaration of Independence he had helped to draft.

Michaux was to follow the Mississippi and Missouri rivers and find a low-altitude connection between those navigable waterways and another that led to the Pacific. There he would meet up with other Europeans, send a report, then return to Philadelphia "to give into [the members of the Society] a full narrative of your journey and observations, and to answer the enquiries they shall make of you." Michaux would, however, retain the right to publish his own findings.

His scientific brief from Jefferson was very broad—he was to record the location of any useful animal, vegetable, and mineral resources, and prepare anthropological notes on local populations. Although Jefferson was careful not to be too specific in his instructions, he did ask Michaux to keep an eye out for any mammoths and llamas "to learn … how far north they come."

At the last minute Michaux got word that the new French regime was going to employ him in the same capacity as the late king had. Eager to prove his Franco-republican credentials, he became involved in an unsanctioned scheme by the new French ambassador to the US to recapture Louisiana from the Spanish. The ambassador was recalled, the liberation of Louisiana was abandoned, and the perfidious Michaux himself returned to France without having explored west of the Mississippi.

France regained Louisiana in 1800 and sold it to the US in the Jefferson-negotiated purchase of 1803. In 1804, Jefferson, then president, formed an elite army unit called the Corps of Discovery and at last commissioned Meriwether Lewis and William Clark to lead the expedition of which he had always dreamed.

Letter from Jefferson to André Michaux

ABOVE: In the uncertain post-revolutionary world of French politics, the former royal botanist appears to have changed his name to Andrew Michaud.

Sundry persons having subscribed certain sums of money for your encouragement to explore the country above the Missouri, & thence Westwardly to the Pacific ocean, having submitted the plan of the enterprise to the direction of the American Philosophical society, & the Society having accepted of the trust, they proceed to give you the following instructions.

They observe to you that the chief objects of your journey are to find the shortest & most convenient route of communication between the US. & the Pacific ocean, within the temperate latitudes, & to learn such particulars as can be obtained of the country, through which it passes, its productions, inhabitants & other interesting circumstances. As a channel of communication between these states & the Pacific ocean; the Missouri, so far as it extends, presents itself under circumstances of unquestioned preference. It has therefore been declared as a fundamental object of the subscription (not be dispensed with) that this river shall be considered & explored as a part of the communication sought for. To the neighborhood of this river therefore, that is to say to the town of Kaskaskia, the society will procure you a conveyance in company with the Indians of that town now in Philadelphia.

From thence you will cross the Missisipi and pass by land to the nearest part of the Missouri above the Spanish settlements, that you may avoid the risk of being stopped. You will then pursue such of the largest streams of that river, as shall lead by the shortest way, & the lowest latitudes to the Pacific ocean.

When, pursuing these streams, you shall find yourself at the point from whence you may get by the shortest & most convenient route to some principal river of the Pacific ocean, you are to proceed to such river, & pursue its course to the ocean. It would seem by the latest maps as if a river called Oregon interlocked with the Missouri for a considerable distance, & entered the Pacific ocean, not far Southward of Notka sound. But the Society are aware that these maps are not be trusted so far as to be the ground of any positive instruction to you. …

Letter from Charlotte Corday to Charles Barbaroux

We are such good Republicans in Paris that we cannot conceive how a useless woman, whose life at its best could be of no great value, can sacrifice herself in cold blood to save her country.

I quite expected instant death, but some courageous men, who were really above all praise, saved me from the very excusable fury of those whom I had bereaved. As I was really calm, I suffered much from the lamentations of some women; but whoso saves his country does not count the cost.

I hope that peace may be established soon. This is a great preliminary, without which we should never have had it. I have enjoyed a delicious peace of mind for two days; the happiness of my country constitutes mine, and there is no act of self-sacrifice that does not confer more pleasure than pain.

I have no doubt they will torment my father somewhat although he has already enough to afflict him in my loss. If I indulged in my last letter I made him think that, fearing the horrors of civil war, I was going to England; at that time my plan was to remain incognita, kill Marat publicly, and, dying myself immediately afterwards, let the Parisians seek my name in vain.

I beg you, citizen—you and your colleagues—to undertake the defense of my relatives and friends if they are troubled. I say nothing to my dear aristocrat friends, but I preserve their memory in my heart.

I have never hated but one human being, and I have already shown with how great a hatred, but there are thousands for whom my love is stronger even than was my hate. The possession of a lively imagination and a sensitive heart give promise of a stormy life, and I beg those who might mourn for me to consider that fact; they will then be glad to think of me as being at peace in the Elysian fields with Brutus and the ancients. As for the moderns, there are but few true patriots among them who could die for their country; almost all are selfish. Alas, what a poor people this is to found a Republic. ...

LEFT: The Assassination of Marat, *painted in 1860 by Paul-Jacques-Alimé Baudry.*

OPPOSITE: *At her request, Charlotte Corday was painted a few hours before her execution by a National Guard officer she had seen sketching her in court. She made a few suggestions on his work before mounting the tumbrel.*

After murdering Marat in his bath, Charlotte Corday writes in despair

(July 16, 1793)

The high optimism of the French Revolution gave way to the horrors of *La Terreur*—The Terror—all too soon. One woman, Charlotte Corday, made it her mission to stand up for the principles of *liberté*, *égalité*, and *fraternité* on which the original revolution was founded.

Broadly speaking, the French Revolution of 1789 was driven by two factions: the Montagnards, and the Jacobins. The Montagnards, led by Maximilien Robespierre, held the most powerful positions in the new government, but when they steered the country toward more extreme forms of revolution, some more moderate Jacobins resisted.

This group of objectors known as the Girondists were most popular in regional France, away from the political hotbed of Paris. Charlotte Corday, from a village in Normandy, northwest of the capital, sympathized with the Girondist cause. She was incensed when, in September 1792, the radical Jacobin Jean-Paul Marat ordered the execution of around 1,500 prisoners in Paris, mostly nonpolitical ones, merely so that any counterrevolutionary movement at home or abroad could not draw on them for support.

The killing was repeated in around seventy other cities and towns throughout France; and then in June 1793 twenty-one Girondist members of the government were purged and beheaded. Corday decided that, as she later claimed during her trial, "Marat was perverting France … One man must die to save a hundred thousand." On July 13, 1793, she visited Marat at his home on the pretense of giving him the names of leading Girondists. Finding him in a medicinal bath, she stabbed him with a six-inch kitchen knife, which she had bought for that purpose. The scene was

immortalized in a painting by Jacques-Louis David later the same year.

Corday was captured on the spot. While in prison awaiting trial, she wrote two famous letters. The first was to her father, apologizing "for having ended my existence without your permission. I avenged many innocent victims, I prevented many other disasters. The people, when they become disillusioned some day, will rejoice to be rid of a tyrant." This letter was produced at the trial as evidence that her crime was premeditated.

The second was to Charles Barbaroux, a Girondist leader whom she had met in Normandy. She complained to him of her lack of privacy under arrest, and wrote that "there are but few true patriots among them who could die for their country; almost all are selfish. Alas, what a poor people this is to found a Republic." Her remark at the trial that "it's only in Paris that people have eyes for Marat. In the other departments, he is regarded as a monster" sums up the centralized nature of French political life even today.

Her act did not immediately have the desired effect. Some 17,000 Girondists were murdered in the following months throughout France. This marked the start of the *Terreur*, a proto-Stalinist period in which almost any act or belief could be interpreted as a crime against the new revolutionary government, punishable by dispossession or death. Corday was guillotined. Barbaroux fled and tried to shoot himself, but he was captured and guillotined before he could die of his gunshot wound.

On the eve of battle, Nelson sends a message to his fleet

(October 21, 1805)

In the nineteenth century, pen and paper were not always the best way to get a message across, especially on the eve of battle. In 1805, Vice Admiral Horatio Nelson sent a memorable message by the naval equivalent of texting—flags.

Trafalgar is a name left by Spain's one-time Arabic rulers, and Cape Trafalgar lies south of Cádiz on the Spanish Atlantic. About five miles west of there, in 1805, the British fleet under Nelson met a Franco-Spanish fleet in the largest naval engagement of the Napoleonic Wars.

Britain's tactic of blockading French ports to prevent any attempt to invade England was proving successful. But French Vice Admiral Villeneuve managed to break out of Toulon on the French Mediterranean coast and join forces with other French ships in the Caribbean. When Villeneuve returned with these reinforcements, he sailed to Cádiz.

At Cádiz there was now a large fleet of French and Spanish ships. As supplies ran low in port, Villeneuve was ordered to sail for Naples. Nelson, confident of the British navy's superior fighting abilities, saw his chance to draw the enemy into a decisive battle. For his part Villeneuve was certain that in a straight fight his fleet would overwhelm the British strength: the French fleet, now augmented with Spanish vessels, included some of the largest then navigating the world's oceans.

A naval battle of the period was by convention a straight fight—that is to say, two fleets filed past each other in single lines, shooting at each other's broadsides. This facilitated signalling, and meant that the losing side could disengage relatively easily. Nelson, however, had a radical battle plan. He intended to approach the enemy not side-on but at ninety degrees, with not one but two columns of British ships, breaking the Franco-Spanish fleet into three smaller sections, which could be more easily dealt with.

Nelson circulated his orders as his two columns approached the French line, using a coded system of signal flags. All that remained was for Nelson to send the final signal: "Engage the enemy more closely." But first he wanted to encourage the men under his command with a more personal message.

He trusted them to do their best and asked the signal officer to send "England confides that every man will do his duty." Confides, meaning "has confidence in." The officer, Lieutenant John Pasco, pointed out that there was no codeflag for "confide" and so it would take longer to compose the signal. "If your Lordship will permit me to substitute the 'confides' for 'expects' the signal will soon be completed, because the word 'expects' is in the vocabulary, and 'confides' must be spelt." Nelson agreed, although the resulting message—more of a postscript than a full letter—was less trusting and more commanding.

Out went the message: "England expects that every man will do his duty." The last three letters of it and the "end of message" flag are clearly visible in J. M. W. Turner's evocative painting of Nelson's ship HMS *Victory* in the midst of battle. The rest, really, is history. Trafalgar was a momentous victory for the British navy. Of the Franco-Spanish fleet of thirty-three ships, twenty-two—fully two-thirds—were sunk. Not one of Britain's twenty-nine went down. In the closing stages of the battle, however, Nelson was struck by a musketball from a French sniper. He died knowing that his unconventional attack plan and inspiring signal had won the day.

OPPOSITE TOP: Turner's painting of HMS Victory *at Trafalgar hangs in the National Maritime Museum in Greenwich.*

OPPOSITE: After his victory at the Battle of the Nile, the sultan of Turkey sent Nelson a plume of feathers made of thirteen diamond sprigs, representing the number of French ships sunk or captured.

Napoleon informs Alexander I that France and Russia are at war

(July 1, 1812)

In 1807, souvenir medallions were produced depicting the French and Russian emperors in a brotherly embrace. Five years later they were at each other's throats. Napoleon had crossed into Russian territory, threatening invasion, and he wrote a letter to the Russian tsar explaining why it was the tsar's fault.

Following Napoleon's victory at the Battle of Friedland in 1807, he signed two treaties at Tilsit, which ended his wars with Prussia and Russia, disposing of half of all Prussian lands to French satellite states (including the newly created Duchy of Warsaw) and to Russia. Everyone except the Prussians was happy with the new arrangements, which consolidated Napoleon's grip on central Europe and made Russia and France allies in Napoleon's ongoing war with Britain.

In 1809, Napoleon, who was continually testing the boundaries of the French Empire, made peace with Austria in the Treaty of Schönbrunn, as a result of which part of Austria was transferred to the Duchy of Warsaw. This enlarged duchy now had a greater border with Russia and appeared to the tsar to make a French invasion of Russia more likely. Alexander began to push back against the Tilsit allocations of land. Napoleon had already made some concessions in 1808, but now Russia began to prepare militarily for counterattacks on cities under French control, such as Warsaw and Danzig.

As border tensions increased, Napoleon sent an offer of peace to St. Petersburg. But before he received a reply, he crossed the Neman River into Russia on June 24, 1812, with an army of nearly half a million men, about three times the size of the Russian forces in the area. He entered Vilna—modern-day Vilnius—four days later. There he received a communication, delivered by the tsar's general Alexander Balashov, who refused to negotiate so long as French troops were on Russian soil.

In reply to this message, Napoleon wrote a long letter to his fellow emperor Alexander. It was a letter of self-justification, giving the French perspective of events and painting Napoleon as the injured party who had "marched on the Neman profoundly convinced that I had done all I could to spare mankind these fresh misfortunes." He listed all his efforts to make peace and all Alexander's moves toward war. "You armed on a large scale … I also armed but six months after Your Majesty … I have missed no opportunity of explaining my intentions … for eighteen months you refused to give any explanation of your proceedings …" and so on.

Napoleon rather too easily concluded in his letter that "We are at war then. God himself cannot undo what has been done." But of course, "if Your Majesty wishes to end hostilities, you will find me ready to do so."

Alexander, fighting with patriotic ferocity on home ground, was not inclined to do so. Napoleon's vast army was ill-equipped for the Russian terrain and too large to feed either from the land through which it passed or from the inadequate French supply lines. Even during the push to Vilna, Napoleon lost some 10,000 horses; starvation and illness decimated the troops; and deserters from his Grande Armée, adrift in a foreign land, ran amok in lawless bands.

Although Napoleon did reach Moscow, it was at enormous cost in lives and equipment, and his disastrous retreat from the capital during a harsh Russian winter was a humiliating blow to his pride and power and a debilitating blow to the French army.

OPPOSITE TOP LEFT: A letter from Alexander to Napoleon dating to mid-June 1812. In reality, the huge logistical investment of supporting the 680,000 soldiers of the Grand Armée meant that whatever the Tsar wrote, Napoleon was not turning back.

OPPOSITE TOP RIGHT: Napoleon's disingenuous letter to the Tsar. Having arrived at the gates of Moscow, instead of entering the city as a grand conqueror, he found that Count Rostopchin had set his great prize on fire.

Letter from Alexander I to Napoleon

My brother, yesterday I learned that, in spite of the conscientiousness with which I fulfilled my obligations to your Majesty, your troops crossed the borders of Russia, and just now I received a note from St. Petersburg, in which Count Lauriston, speaking of the cause of this attack, declares that your Majesty considered themselves at war with me from the very moment Prince Kurakin requested passports. The motives that the Duke of Bassano had given in support of his refusal to issue him passports, by no means serves as a pretext for an attack. In fact, Ambassador Prince Kurakin, as he himself said, never received orders to act in this way … I completely disapprove of his actions and ordered him to remain at his post. If it is not the intention of your Majesty to shed the blood of our peoples because of a misunderstanding of this kind and if you agree to withdraw your troops from the Russian territory, that everything that happened was not the case and agreement between us is still possible. Otherwise your majesty compels me to see you as an enemy, whose actions are not caused by my actions. It is up to your Majesty to save mankind from the scourge of a new war. …

Letter from Napoleon to Alexander I about the fires in Moscow

Dear sir, my brother! … There is no more beautiful, proud city of Moscow: Rostopchin set fire to it … I started a war against your Majesty without anger: one note from you before or after the last battles would stop my procession, and I really would like to sacrifice you the advantage of being the first to enter Moscow. If your Majesty keeps some more of those past feelings, you will favorably receive this letter. Nevertheless, you can only be grateful to me for being aware of what is happening in Moscow. By this, my dear sir, my brother, I pray to God that he will guard your Majesty and shore under his holy and dignified protection. …

As machines replace farm labor, Captain Swing issues a threat

(1830)

In 1830, farmers all over the south of England began to receive handwritten letters from a mysterious Captain Swing, threatening to burn their crops or property. Who was this man who menaced the livelihoods of so many over such a great distance?

One of the oldest arguments against technical progress is that it puts people out of jobs. As the Industrial Revolution transformed economies and labor practices around the world, opposition to new factory technology increased. A well-known early example was the action of the Luddites, who protested not only at the loss of employment but at the de-skilling of the labor force. Their destruction of new textile machinery in the English Midlands was only halted in 1816 by political and military forces.

In Kent, in 1830, another movement emerged that protested the introduction of the threshing machine on the county's farms. It was a time of high unemployment, and the arrival of these machines threatened to make things worse for the poorest in rural society who worked on the land. Threshing is the process of separating the grains from the stalks of a cereal crop, traditionally done by workers with flails. This provided valuable work in the autumn and winter months, and in the late eighteenth century it employed a quarter of all agricultural workers. The wheat lay stacked in ricks around the farmyard waiting to be threshed, but could easily be set alight.

Farmers had already been lowering their workers' wages, safe in the knowledge that should they become destitute, the local parish would have to support them under the country's Poor Law. Added to this strife were the rising tithes, or levies demanded by the church, who were traditionally due 10 percent of the harvest. At this sensitive time, the introduction of a device that made laborers redundant was inflammatory.

Protests spread across southern England. Landowners began to receive letters from a certain Captain Swing, who threatened to smash up machinery and burn down haystacks if they did not themselves destroy their hated threshing machines. For example:

"Sir, This is to acquaint you that if your threshing machines are not destroyed by you directly we shall commence our labours. Signed on behalf of the whole … Swing."

This one-man arson campaign was harder to police than demonstrations that, by their nature, were designed to be visible. Arson was a criminal, covert action often conducted at night. Historians continue to argue about the connection between Captain Swing and protesters arguing against church tithes and the burden of the Poor Law. They shared an enemy—the threshing machine—but their methods were very different.

One thing is clear: "Captain Swing" was a nom de plume used by many who favored more violent means to their end. The handwriting and the degree of literacy vary too much between letters.

Some have suggested that the Captains Swing were agent provocateurs, trying to accelerate a confrontation between workers and employers. Others have suggested a collusion between farm laborers and those who would benefit by having to repair the broken machines—wheelwrights, blacksmiths, and carpenters. The protests died out during 1831, but not before over 500 protesters had been transported to Australia and nineteen of them executed for their actions.

Res Sir
I am afraid you have
not had one of the inclosed
Bills You See what your
Damnable Dean has done
if thare Should Be a Row
hear he is marked he
will have the old
Dance of

Swing

Dr Agnus

The college that thou holdest
Shalt be fired very Shortly,
Thou shalt here further from one
when it is in flames.

Swing

Head Quarters

SWING!
taken from the Life.
Dedicated to Mess.ʳˢ Cobbett. Carlisle. & Cᵒ

ABOVE: A rare watercolor portrait of Darwin painted in the 1830s after his return from the five-year voyage of the HMS Beagle.

Darwin gets an offer to become the naturalist on a surveying ship

(August 24, 1831)

John Stevens Henslow wrote to the twenty-two-year-old Charles Darwin, advising him of a place on the admiralty surveying vessel HMS *Beagle*, which was traveling to South America. But the trip needed to be sanctioned by Darwin's father, who wanted his son to become an Anglican priest.

Darwin's observations during the voyage of the *Beagle* to the Galápagos Islands and elsewhere, formed the basis for his groundbreaking theory of evolution, a cornerstone of modern science. It was a two-year trip that stretched to five and informed Darwin's theory of natural selection. But it was an offer that was almost not taken up.

Charles Darwin had followed in his father's footsteps to study medicine in Edinburgh; but the young man spent more time studying geology and marine life than medical matters. His father was displeased and moved his son to Cambridge to study for the Anglican priesthood instead. Here, Charles applied himself rather more earnestly to the subject at hand, but continued to be fascinated by natural history, which he studied under pioneering geologist Adam Sedgwick and the Cambridge professor of botany, John Stevens Henslow.

In the summer of 1831, having graduated from the university, he received a letter from Henslow, who recognized Darwin's remarkable instinct and enthusiasm for the study of plants and animals. He had heard of a position that might suit Darwin and had recommended him for the job. "I have been asked by Peacock [a tutor at Cambridge] … to recommend him a naturalist as companion to Captain Fitzroy employed by Government to survey the S. extremity of America—I have stated that I consider you to be the best qualified person I know of who is likely to undertake such a situation."

Although it was a golden opportunity to observe unfamiliar habitats, Henslow added that "Captain F. wants a man (I understand) more as a companion than a mere collector and would not take any one however good a Naturalist who was not recommended to him likewise as a gentleman." Darwin would have a free hand to follow his interests. "If you take plenty of books with you, anything you please may be done."

Darwin was keen to go, but his father disapproved, and so Darwin wrote to Peacock declining the offer. However, while discussing the madcap idea of a two-year ocean voyage with his father, he had told Charles: "If you can find any man of common sense who advises you to go I will give my consent." The following day Charles was out shooting with his uncle Josiah Wedgwood (the famous pottery manufacturer), whom his father had always maintained was one of the most sensible men in the world. Charles mentioned the *Beagle's* expedition, and Wedgwood thought it a terrific idea. With Wedgwood on Charles's side, Darwin senior "at once consented," as Charles recalled in later life, "in the kindest manner."

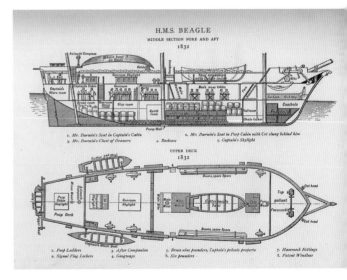

ABOVE: *HMS* Beagle, *launched in 1820, was one of a hundred Cherokee-class brig sloops built for the Royal Navy.*

The first postage stamp transforms the sending of letters

(May 1, 1840)

In the 2,500-year history of the letter, the postage stamp has been around for less than 200 of them. Rowland Hill's invention of the postage stamp revolutionized communication, not only in Great Britain, but around the world.

Great Britain's General Post Office (GPO) was established in 1660 during the reign of Charles II, although the Royal Mail traces its history back to 1516, when Henry VIII created a position called Master of the Posts (later known as postmaster general).

The Royal Mail was, as its name suggests, only for use by the monarchy, and after the union of the English and Scottish crowns, King James VI set up a Royal Mail service between the two countries to keep in touch with his Scottish government.

Charles I allowed the public to use the Royal Mail network for the first time; and his son Charles II's GPO built a network of post offices around the country. Mail coaches began delivering long-distance mail in 1784, and the first mail train service ran in 1830.

As letter writing became more popular, *sending* a letter remained, for the large part, free. The GPO charged a fee to the *recipient*, based on the size of the letter and the distance it had been carried. Every item of post therefore had to be priced individually, and postal rates were generally high. As a result, penny-pinching correspondents worked out codes, which could be seen and read on the outside of any postal packet. By this means the recipient could receive a message without accepting the item and without paying for the postage.

In 1839, a short-lived remedy was introduced, the Uniform Fourpenny Post. This was a flat prepaid rate of four pence per half-ounce letter, regardless of distance carried. Letters that were not prepaid were charged double. The immediate result was a sharp increase in the volume of post

carried by the Royal Mail, which doubled between November 1839 and February 1840.

Prepaid letters were marked with a "4," either by hand or with a rubber stamp—in either case the mark was open to abuse and forgery. The rate was lowered to only one penny in January 1840, and to combat forgery and evasion, a label printed in black—the Penny Black—was introduced in May, the world's first adhesive stamp for a public postal service.

Accompanying the Penny Black was the Twopenny Blue. Because they were designed for inland use, there was no need to print "Great Britain" on them, and Great Britain remains the only nation in the world to issue stamps without the name of the country. All British stamps, however, carry a portrait of the reigning monarch.

The stamps were cancelled in red ink after posting, but it proved difficult to see the cancellation against the black of the stamp, and the red ink was quite easily removed by those wishing to cheat and reuse the Penny Black. So in February 1841, the Penny Black was replaced with the Penny Red, which was cancelled in much more visible and permanent black. Despite their short life, nearly 69 million Penny Blacks were printed—in sheets of 240, which had to be cut with scissors. Perforations between stamps were introduced in 1850.

LEFT: The portrait of Victoria on the Penny Black dated to 1834, when she was Princess Victoria, and remained on stamps until her death in 1901. The letters in each bottom corner refer to their position on the printed sheet of 240.

ABOVE: *Three examples of Penny Black letters with red cancellation marks—which proved too easy to remove.*

Friedrich "Fred" Engels begins a lifelong correspondence with Karl "Moor" Marx

(October 1844)

When Friedrich Engels met Karl Marx in Paris he was impressed with the radical socialist's vision for the working classes. But Marx had been banished from Germany, and Engels was keen to continue their collaboration, even though it demanded a stealthy correspondence. ...

Friedrich Engels and Karl Marx wrote *The Communist Manifesto*, published in 1848. Although the philosophy behind it is nowadays called Marxist, it is built at least in part on Engels's experiences of the English working classes, gained while he worked in his father's textile mill in Salford, northwest England.

On Engels's return home to the Wupper valley in Germany in August 1844, after his two-year sojourn in England, he stopped off in Paris to meet Karl Marx, who already had a certain left-wing notoriety. Marx, unwelcome in Germany following the banning of his newspaper *Rhineland News,* had moved to Paris in 1843, to edit a new internationalist socialist newspaper, *The German-French Yearbook.* It had folded after only one issue.

Engels and Marx hit it off at once. They met in the Café de la Régence, a venue popular with chess players and other strategists. Their socialist visions coincided, and Engels, with his English experiences, talked excitedly about the power of the working classes to bring about the political and economic changes they both wanted. They made plans for the dissemination of their ideas in a series of proposed articles, pamphlets, and books, before Engels continued on his way to his hometown of Barmen.

From there he wrote a long letter to Marx, determined to cement their friendship. "I have not been able to recapture the mood of cheerfulness and goodwill I experienced during the ten days I spent with you." He reported in detail on the rise of communism in Germany: In Cologne, "our people are very active"; in Düsseldorf, "we also have some able fellows." He admired the inhabitants of Elberfeld, "in whom a humane way of thinking has truly become second nature," and "in Barmen the police inspector is a communist."

The only remaining German-language left-wing organ *Vorwärts* had to be published in Paris and smuggled into German bookshops in plain wrappers. "We writers," Engels wrote, "have to keep quiet if we're not to be nabbed." Throughout the letter Engels uses "we" to emphasize his friendship with Marx.

Even private correspondence had to be disguised. "If this letter reaches you unopened," Engels advised, "send your reply under sealed cover to F. W. Strücker & Co, Elberfeld, with the address written in as commercial a hand as possible (so as not to appear to be personal). ... I shall be curious to know whether the postal sleuth-hounds are deceived by the ladylike appearance of this letter."

The pair collaborated on communist publications throughout Marx's life, and with his father's wealth behind him, Engels was able to subsidize Marx while he wrote his masterpiece *Das Kapital.* It is one of the ironies of communism that one of its greatest architects was the privileged son of a rich German industrialist.

Letter from Friedrich Engels to Karl Marx

Dear Marx,

No doubt you are surprised, and justifiably so, not to have heard from me sooner; however I still cannot tell you even now anything about my return. I've been stuck here in Barmen for the past three weeks, amusing myself as best I can with few friends and many relations amongst whom, fortunately, there are half a dozen amiable women. Work is out of the question here, more especially since my sister [Marie] has become engaged to the London communist, Emil Blank, an acquaintance of Ewerbeck's and, of course, the house is now in a hellish state of turmoil. Moreover, it's clear to me that considerable obstacles will continue to be placed in the way of my return to Paris, and that I may well have to spend six months or a whole year hanging about in Germany; I shall, of course, do everything I can to avoid this, but you have no idea what petty considerations and superstitious fears I have to contend with.

I spent three days in Cologne and marvelled at the tremendous propaganda we had put out there. Our people are very active, but the lack of adequate backing is greatly felt. Failing a few publications in which the principles are logically and historically developed out of past ways of thinking and past history, and as their necessary continuation, the whole thing will remain rather hazy and most people will be groping in the dark. Later I was in Duesseldorf, where we also have some able fellows. The ones I like best, by the way, are my Elberfelders, in whom a humane way of thinking has truly become second nature; these fellows have really begun to revolutionise their family lives and lecture their elders whenever these try to come the aristocrat over the servants or workmen -- and that's saying a great deal in patriarchal Elberfeld. But besides this particular group there's another in Elberfeld which is also very good, though somewhat more muddled. In Barmen the police inspector is a communist. The day before yesterday I was called on by a former schoolfellow, a grammar school teacher, who's been thoroughly bitten although he's had no contact whatever with communists. If we could bring direct influence to bear on the people, we'd soon get the upper hand, but such a thing is virtually impossible, especially since we writers have to keep quiet if we're not to be nabbed. Otherwise it's safe enough here, no one bothers much about us so long as we keep quiet, and it seems to me that Hess' fears are little more than phantoms. I've not been molested at all here so far, although the public prosecutor once insistently questioned one of our people about me, but up till now I haven't had wind of anything else.

OPPOSITE LEFT: Karl Marx.

OPPOSITE RIGHT: Friedrich Engels.

Baudelaire writes a suicide letter to his mistress … and lives

(June 30, 1845)

A letter written by French poet Charles Baudelaire sold at auction in 2018 for nearly a quarter of a million euros. This item attracted a bid three times higher than the others, because of its unusual opening. "By the time you receive this letter," it began, "I will be dead."

Charles Pierre Baudelaire was the very archetype of a struggling, suffering poet—a tortured soul—though often the torture was self-inflicted. He was a spendthrift and consumed alcohol and opium to considerable excess.

In 1845, he wrote the letter announcing his death. It was addressed to his lover, Jeanne Duvall, an actress of mixed French and Haitian descent whom Caroline Baudelaire, the poet's mother, described as a Black Venus. The two women did not get along—Caroline thought Jeanne spent all of Charles's money and made him miserable. Whatever the truth, the couple remained part-time lovers for twenty years until Jeanne's death in the 1860s.

Baudelaire's own death might have come a lot sooner. His excessive expenditure on clothes, prostitutes, drink, and drugs were all classic signs of a young man unhappy with himself. He could not bear his mother's disapproval of his lover and the rest of his lifestyle.

Mounting debts and doubts about his ability as a writer compounded his depression. In his 1845 letter to Jeanne, he explained why he was about to commit suicide. "I am killing myself because I can no longer live, because the exhaustion of going to sleep and the exhaustion of waking up are unbearable to me. I am killing myself because I believe myself to be immortal, and I hope for it."

Fortunately for the literary world, Baudelaire was as bad at suicide as he was at financial management. He stabbed himself in the chest, yet managed to miss all his vital organs and survived the attempt. Ironically, in so doing, he ensured the immortality that he believed he possessed. With this new lease of life he went on to write poetry that reflected the new aesthetic values of the industrial age and influenced a whole generation of poets.

His first published work was a review of the Paris Salon of 1845, and he went on to build a reputation as an insightful critic of both literature and fine art. In 1847, he published *La Fanfarlo*, a fictionalized version of his affair with Jeanne, and ten years later he published the poetry collection that cemented his reputation, *Les Fleurs du Mal (The Flowers of Evil)*.

Some of its contents were banned for offending public decency. "I don't care a rap about all these imbeciles," he wrote to his mother, "and I know that this book, with its virtues and its faults, will make its way in the memory of the lettered public, beside the best poems of Hugo, Gautier and even Byron."

In later life he adoringly told his mother, "believe that I belong to you absolutely, and that I belong only to you." After his eventual death she wished he had followed his stepfather in a diplomatic career: "He would not have left a name in literature, it is true, but we should have been happier."

Following a massive stroke he spent the last two years of his life paralyzed. He died a cruel death for a wordsmith, unable to speak or understand words, in 1867 in a Paris sanatorium.

OPPOSITE TOP: Baudelaire was influenced by the works of Edgar Allan Poe. Apart from translating many of his novels, he set about becoming the French Poe.

OPPOSITE: In 1845, Baudelaire's poetry career was as successful as his suicide bid. But all that would change with Les Fleurs du Mal.

Major Robert Anderson reports he has surrendered Fort Sumter

(April 18, 1861)

The commander of a Federal army fort in Charleston Harbor sends a hurried message to the secretary of war in Washington, informing him of his garrison's surrender. It means that the Confederacy has staged its first attack against the Union. The War Between the States has begun.

Following South Carolina's secession from the United States, and Abraham Lincoln's inauguration as president, on April 10, 1861, Brigadier General Pierre G. T. Beauregard of the provisional Confederate forces demanded the surrender of the besieged US garrison of Fort Sumter in Charleston Harbor.

The rebel forces numbered 10,000 well-equipped men while the defenders had only sixty-eight soldiers with inferior armaments and scant food and supplies. But the fort's commander, US Army Major Robert Anderson, refused to concede.

On Friday, April 12 at 4:30 a.m., Confederate Lieutenant Henry S. Farley, commanding a battery of two 10-inch siege mortars on James Island, fired the first shot at the US fort, beginning a long cannonade. At about 7:00 a.m., Captain Abner Doubleday, Sumter's second-in-command, fired the first salvo in response, aware that his guns weren't capable of reaching their target. The Confederates' bombardment continued for thirty-four hours.

Realizing that resistance was futile and lacking hope of immediate reinforcements, Anderson raised a white flag of surrender on April 13 at 2:30 p.m. He was allowed to evacuate the following day and escaped to the North.

As soon as he was able to do so, on April 18 at 10:30 a.m., Anderson telegraphed from the steamship SS *Baltic* off Sandy Hook to US Secretary of War Simon Cameron in Washington, informing him of what had transpired.

"Having defended Fort Sumter for thirty four hours," he reported, "until the quarters were entirely burned the main gates destroyed by fire. The gorge walls seriously injured. The magazine surrounded by flames and its door closed from the effects of heat."

The document's significance was immediately clear. Robert Toombs, the Confederate secretary of state, said at the time, "The firing upon that fort will inaugurate a civil war greater than any the world has yet seen …" Upon receiving the telegram, President Lincoln ordered 75,000 volunteers and called Congress into session. The assault became a rallying cry for the Union cause.

Although the attack resulted in just two Union soldiers killed and two wounded, with no casualties on the other side, the incident marked the opening engagement of the exceptionally bloody Civil War.

Four years later, after the fort had been pounded into rubble by shore batteries on nearby Morris and Sullivan islands, Beauregard ordered the evacuation of Charleston. The fort was abandoned on February 22, 1865. Major Robert Anderson and Captain Abner Doubleday returned on April 14 to raise the same flag that they had lowered in 1861.

The original Fort Sumter telegram is kept in the National Archives in Washington, D.C.

S.S.BALTIC.OFF SANDY HOOK APR.EIGHTEENTH.TEN THIRTY A.M. .VIA

NEW YORK. . HON.S.CAMERON. SECY.WAR. WASHN. HAVING DEFENDED

FORT SUMTER FOR THIRTY FOUR HOURS UNTIL THE QUARTERS WERE EN

TIRELY BURNED THE MAIN GATES DESTROYED BY FIRE.THE GORGE WALLS

SERIOUSLY INJURED.THE MAGAZINE SURROUNDED BY FLAMES AND ITS

DOOR CLOSED FROM THE EFFECTS OF HEAT .FOUR BARRELLS AND THREE

CARTRIDGES OF POWDER ONLY BEING AVAILABLE AND NO PROVISIONS

REMAINING BUT PORK.I ACCEPTED TERMS OF EVACUATION OFFERED BY

GENERAL BEAUREGARD BEING ON SAME OFFERED BY HIM ON THE ELEV

ENTH INST.PRIOR TO THE COMMENCEMENT OF HOSTILITIES AND MARCHED

OUT OF THE FORT SUNDAY AFTERNOON THE FOURTEENTH INST.WITH

COLORS FLYING AND DRUMS BEATING.BRINGING AWAY COMPANY AND

PRIVATE PROPERTY AND SALUTING MY FLAG WITH FIFTY GUNS. ROBERT

ANDERSON.MAJOR FIRST ARTILLERY.COMMANDING.

ABOVE: The fateful dispatch from Major Anderson. The War Between the States had begun.

OPPOSITE: Damage to Fort Sumter after the Confederate assault.

Letter from Sullivan Ballou to his wife, Sarah

My very dear Sarah:

The indications are very strong that we shall move in a few days—perhaps tomorrow. Lest I should not be able to write you again, I feel impelled to write lines that may fall under your eye when I shall be no more.

Our movement may be one of a few days duration and full of pleasure—and it may be one of severe conflict and death to me. Not my will, but thine O God, be done. If it is necessary that I should fall on the battlefield for my country, I am ready. I have no misgivings about, or lack of confidence in, the cause in which I am engaged, and my courage does not halt or falter. I know how strongly American Civilization now leans upon the triumph of the Government, and how great a debt we owe to those who went before us through the blood and suffering of the Revolution. And I am willing—perfectly willing—to lay down all my joys in this life, to help maintain this Government, and to pay that debt.

But, my dear wife, when I know that with my own joys I lay down nearly all of yours, and replace them in this life with cares and sorrows—when, after having eaten for long years the bitter fruit of orphanage myself, I must offer it as their only sustenance to my dear little children—is it weak or dishonorable, while the banner of my purpose floats calmly and proudly in the breeze, that my unbounded love for you, my darling wife and children, should struggle in fierce, though useless, contest with my love of country.

Sarah, my love for you is deathless, it seems to bind me to you with mighty cables that nothing but Omnipotence could break; and yet my love of Country comes over me like a strong wind and bears me irresistibly on with all these chains to the battlefield. The memories of the blissful moments I have spent with you come creeping over me, and I feel most gratified to God and to you that I have enjoyed them so long. And hard it is for me to give them up and burn to ashes the hopes of future years, when God willing, we might still have lived and loved together and seen our sons grow up to honorable manhood around us. …

On the eve of battle, Sullivan Ballou writes to his wife, Sarah

(July 14, 1861)

Sullivan Ballou was an ordinary man. An East Coast lawyer, married father of two sons, he was active in local politics and Speaker of the Rhode Island House of Representatives. Then in 1861, he answered Lincoln's appeal for volunteers for the Federal army.

The first shots of the American Civil War were fired on April 12, 1861, when Confederate forces captured Fort Sumter in Charleston Harbor. President Lincoln responded with a call to arms to defeat the rebels. Ballou, a fellow Republican, was among the first to volunteer.

As a respectable member of Rhode Island society, he was officer material, and Ballou was given the rank of major in the 2nd Rhode Island Infantry regiment. In July 1861, the regiment was on the move, first to Washington, D.C. and then to join up with other troops in northeastern Virginia. He was now part of a massive force, some 35,000 men under the command of newly appointed General Irvin McDowell. Until only a few days earlier, McDowell had held the same rank as Ballou, although he had been a serving soldier before the outbreak of war.

Ahead of the move to Virginia, Ballou, like many of the men under his command, sensed that they were about to see action, and wrote a letter to his wife, Sarah, "lest I should not be able to write you again." He was afraid, and although he was fighting out of conviction— "I know how strongly American Civilization now leans upon the triumph of the Government"—he was acutely aware of what he was leaving behind. "Is it weak or dishonorable, while the banner of my purpose floats calmly and proudly in the breeze, that my unbounded love for you, my darling wife and children, should struggle in fierce though useless contest with my love of country?"

What follows is a moving declaration of love. Faced with the possibility of death, Ballou begins: "Sarah, my love for you is deathless. … If I do not (return), my dear Sarah, never forget how much I love you, and when my last breath escapes me on the battlefield it will whisper your name."

An orphan himself after the early death of his father, Ballou could not bear the thought of leaving his children to the same fate, and his wife a widow. "I must watch you from the spirit land and hover near you, while you buffet the storms with your precious little freight." In a paragraph of pure poetry, he cannot contain his love. "But, O Sarah! If the dead can come back to this earth and flit unseen around those they loved, I shall always be near you; in the brightest day and in the darkest night— amidst your happiest scenes and gloomiest hours— always, always; and if there be a soft breeze upon your cheek, it shall be my breath; or the cool air fans your throbbing temple, it shall be my spirit passing by."

As a major in his regiment, he rode ahead of his infantry troops when he led them into battle a week later near Manassas. Confederate spies knew McDowell's strategy, and his army was outmaneuvered in this, the first pitched battle of the Civil War. The Union side, perhaps overconfident at this early stage of the war, underestimated the determination of the rebels. This was the battle, after all, where Confederate General Thomas "Stonewall" Jackson earned his nickname.

The First Battle of Bull Run, as it is also known, was a resounding victory for the South. Ballou was hit by a cannonball in the first moments of the charge, losing his horse and his right leg. He died of his wounds a week later in a field hospital.

His letter to Sarah was found among his effects. Ballou's final letter to his wife was published and has become the most celebrated of farewell letters written by a soldier from the frontline. Sarah Ballou never remarried, and died fifty-six years later.

Abraham Lincoln sends General McClellan an ultimatum

(1862)

Union General George McClellan was often insubordinate and disobeyed orders, trusting his own judgment over others'. A telegram to him from President Lincoln during the Civil War reveals tensions between the two at a point where the tide of the conflict was finely balanced.

General McClellan was a career soldier with an attitude. One episode illustrates his tendency not to respect his superiors. Asked to survey a railroad route across the Cascade mountains he was not thorough and picked the worst of four passes, having refused to inspect them in winter conditions. He also refused to hand over his survey journals because—it's believed—they were full of disparaging remarks about the Washington Territory governor who had commissioned the survey.

At the outbreak of war he reentered military service with the Ohio militia on the Union side, although his views on slavery might have led him to the secessionists. A couple of early victories under his command went to his head, especially after he was summoned to advise the president and lead a new force, the Army of the Potomac. "I almost think," he wrote in a letter to his wife, "that were I to win some small success now I could become Dictator or anything else that might please me."

He was not as good as he thought. He constantly overestimated the enemy's strength and was therefore timid in attack; and he showed no respect or obedience for his commander in chief Lincoln's overview and strategy. He once described Lincoln as "nothing more than a well-meaning baboon."

Things came to a head over the battle for Richmond, Virginia, which was held by Confederate troops. Lincoln telegraphed McClellan on May 25, 1862, to say "the enemy is moving north in sufficient force to drive [Union] General Banks before him. I think the movement is a general and concerted one, such as would not be if he was acting upon the purpose of a very desperate defense of Richmond."

In other words, the defense of Richmond was not a priority for the enemy, and now would be a good time to capture the town. But if the enemy was moving north, Washington, D.C. was threatened. Time was of the essence. "I think," Lincoln concluded, "the time is near when you must either attack Richmond or give up the job and come to the defense of Washington."

McClellan disagreed. He moved only slowly toward Richmond, and when he repelled an unexpected Confederate attack, he missed an opportunity to counterattack and take the town. By the end of June, Confederate General Robert E. Lee had had time to greatly strengthen Richmond's defenses. McClellan withdrew and blamed Lincoln for the setback. "If I save this army now," he telegraphed the war office, "I tell you plainly I owe no thanks to you or to any other persons in Washington. You have done your best to sacrifice this army."

Despite this, and despite the pleas of most of the war cabinet, McClellan was eventually put in charge of the defense of Washington. But his failure once again to pursue the enemy after the bloody but decisive Union victory at Antietam on September 17 gave Lincoln the opportunity he was looking for to sack McClellan. For his part, McClellan continued to live in his bubble, reporting to his wife that "those in whose judgment I rely tell me that I fought the battle splendidly and that it was a masterpiece of art." He ran against Lincoln in the 1864 presidential election, and lost.

McClellan did, however, make a lasting contribution to the US Army. His equestrian design, the McClellan saddle, remained in use until the army stopped using horses in the twentieth century.

Time Received 9 P.m

United States Military Telegraph,

War Department,

Head Quarters A.P.P. 6. P. m.
October 25th. 1862.

His Excellency
The President.

In reply to your telegram
of this date I have the honor to
state, from the time this army left
Washington on the 17th of September
my Cavalry has been constantly
Employed in making reconnoisances,
scouting & picketing. Since the battle
of Antietam six (6) Regiments have
made a trip of two hundred (200)
miles marching fifty five (55) miles
in one day while Endeavoring to
reach Stuarts Cavalry.

Genl Pleasanton in his
official report states that he

19190

ABOVE: *Lyndon Johnson famously said of troublesome FBI director Edgar Hoover that he would sooner have him inside the tent than out. President Abraham Lincoln talks to his insubordinate general in September 1862, at Antietam—after which McClellan was thrown out.*

LEFT: *On October 25, McClellan responded to a barbed enquiry from Lincoln, with an indignant three-page response. This is the first page. Lincoln had written to McClellan: "I have just received your dispatch about sore-tongued and fatigued horses. Will you pardon me for asking what the horses of your army have done since the battle of Antietam that fatigue anything?"*

WASHINGTON.

"LIBERTY AND UNION, NOW AND FOREVER, ONE AND INSEPARABLE."

SATURDAY, AUGUST 23, 1862.

A LETTER FROM THE PRESIDENT.

EXECUTIVE MANSION,
Washington, August 22, 1862.

Hon. HORACE GREELEY:

DEAR SIR: I have just read yours of the 19th, addressed to myself through the New York Tribune. If there be in it any statements, or assumptions of fact, which I may know to be erroneous, I do not now and here controvert them. If there be in it any inferences which I may believe to be falsely drawn, I do not now and here argue against them. If there be perceptible in it an impatient and dictatorial tone, I waive it in deference to an old friend whose heart I have always supposed to be right.

As to the policy I "seem to be pursuing," as you say, I have not meant to leave any one in doubt.

I would save the Union. I would save it the shortest way under the Constitution. The sooner the national authority can be restored the nearer the Union will be "the Union as it was." If there be those who would not save the Union unless they could at the same time *save* slavery, I do not agree with them. If there be those who would not save the Union unless they could at the same time *destroy* slavery, I do not agree with them. My paramount object in this struggle *is* to save the Union, and is *not* either to save or to destroy slavery. If I could save the Union without freeing *any* slave I would do it, and if I could save it by freeing *all* the slaves I would do it; and if I could save it by freeing some and leaving others alone, I would also do that. What I do about slavery and the colored race, I do because I believe it helps to save the Union; and what I forbear, I forbear because I do *not* believe it would help to save the Union. I shall do *less* whenever I shall believe what I am doing hurts the cause, and I shall do *more* whenever I shall believe doing more will help the cause. I shall try to correct errors when shown to be errors; and I shall adopt new views so fast as they shall appear to be true views.

I have here stated my purpose according to my view of *official* duty; and I intend no modification of my oft-expressed *personal* wish that all men everywhere could be free.   Yours,

A. LINCOLN.

ABOVE: Horace Greeley was the founder of the New-York Tribune *in 1841. He was a fervent social campaigner and abolitionist.*

LEFT: How Lincoln's reply to Greeley appeared in the press.

Abraham Lincoln spells out his Civil War priorities to Horace Greeley

(August 22, 1862)

When abolitionist Horace Greeley, the combative founder and editor of the *New-York Tribune*, wrote and published a highly critical open letter to Abraham Lincoln during the Civil War, the president felt obliged to reply.

Perhaps it was the changing tide of the Civil War in 1862 that emboldened Greeley to print his letter in the *Tribune*'s pages on August 19 that year. After initial defeats, the Federal army was winning battles, and its supporters could begin to think about the future of the nation after victory. Greeley was a longtime advocate of the abolition of slavery. As far as he was concerned, that was what the Civil War was being fought over, and he did not believe that Lincoln was focused enough on that goal.

Beneath a headline that read "The Prayers of Twenty Million," Greeley wrote, "Dear Sir: I do not intrude to tell you that a great proportion of those who triumphed in your election are sorely and deeply pained by the policy with regard to the slaves of the Rebels." The very opening of the letter—"Dear Sir" instead of "Dear Mr. President"—was a calculated snub.

As the letter continued it became more blunt and aggressive in its tone. A new law passed in 1862 legitimized the confiscation of lands held by rebels and the emancipation of their slaves. Greeley demanded, "We require of you to EXECUTE THE LAWS. We think you are remiss in the discharge of your official duty with regard to the emancipating provisions of the new Confiscation Act. Those provisions were designed to fight Slavery with Liberty."

Lincoln's reply was published in the *Tribune* on August 22 and repeated in other newspapers the following day. He did not directly argue with Greeley, a valuable supporter of the Republican and Union causes. "If there be perceptible in [your open letter] an impatient and dictatorial tone," Lincoln gently chided

Greeley, "I waive it in deference to an old friend, whose heart I have always supposed to be right." But the president was at pains to set out, directly and clearly, his overriding motivation.

Slavery may have been the reason for the Southern states to secede, but it was their secession that offended the president of the United States, not their slavery. "My paramount object in this struggle is to save the Union, and is not either to save or to destroy slavery. If I could save the Union without freeing any slave I would do it, and if I could save it by freeing all the slaves I would do it; and if I could save it by freeing some and leaving others alone I would also do that."

Lincoln's letter continues in this vein, leaving absolutely no doubt about his mission as president. Only in the last paragraph does he state a personal position. "I have here stated my purpose according to my view of official duty; and I intend no modification of my oft-expressed personal wish that all men everywhere could be free."

What Lincoln did not admit in his letter to Horace Greeley was that he had already drafted his Emancipation Proclamation, which declared all slaves in the rebel states to be free men. He waited until the Union victory at Antietam in September 1862 to announce it so that he could not be accused of making it out of desperation. Although as a war measure it only applied to the enemy states and not to those remaining in the Union, it effectively liberated three and half million slaves; and it led directly to the passage of the Thirteenth Amendment after the war.

William Banting wants the world to know how he lost weight

(1863)

Royal funeral director William Banting had the profile of a Charles Dickens character, the portly Mr. Pickwick. In earlier Victorian times, it was a sign of wealth to be fat. But Banting was struggling to do up his own boot laces and felt he should do something about it.

The family firm of William Banting conducted royal funerals from George III in 1820 to Edward VII in 1910. They organized proceedings after the death in 1861 of Queen Victoria's husband, Prince Albert, when perhaps William's rotundity as he walked slowly before the coffin helped to convey a certain respectful dignity.

Nevertheless he wanted to lose weight. Banting sought help from several eminent doctors of the day, without success. In August 1862, he visited William Harvey, a doctor with consulting rooms in London's Soho Square. Harvey's interest in diets was not for weight loss but for any benefit they brought to other medical conditions. In any case, his advice brought results for Banting. In gratitude, Banting wrote a glowing testimonial, which, at the end of 1863, he circulated among friends and other interested parties.

This was his lengthy *Letter on Corpulence*, a tract that was so popular with the public that it was revised and reprinted three times within a year, and remains in print today. He was sixty-nine when he wrote it and died at the age of eighty-one, a walking advertisement for the regime that he promoted. He is remembered today because his was the first popular diet craze, and also the first to recommend a low-carbohydrate approach.

Today's low-carbohydrate adherents are stricter than Banting was: in the diet that his letter describes, he allowed himself "two or three glasses of good claret, sherry, or Madeira" at lunch, "a glass or two of claret or sherry" at dinner, and "for nightcap, if required, a tumbler of grog—gin, whisky, or brandy, without sugar—or a glass or two of claret or sherry."

He also admits that he could not entirely give up a little toast. But twenty-first century followers of the Atkins diet will recognize his denial of champagne, port, and beer; potato, parsnip, beetroot, turnip, and carrot; and, of course, sugar. "My former dietary table," he writes, "was bread and milk for breakfast, or a pint of tea with plenty of milk, sugar, and buttered toast; meat, beer, much bread (of which I was always very fond) and pastry for lunch, the meal of dinner similar to that of breakfast, and generally a fruit tart or bread and milk for supper. I had little comfort and far less sound sleep."

Some of the letter is taken up with descriptions of his earlier, unsuccessful attempts to lose weight. For example, he took up rowing after being advised to take vigorous exercise, only to find that it increased his appetite and made him put on more weight. Harvey's regime lost him forty-six pounds in the first year and thirteen inches in girth, and its health benefits included improved eyesight and the ability to "perform every necessary office for myself." He had been unable even to lace up his boots.

Dietary science has progressed since Banting, but William Banting's letter is still a very personable read, admitting of both failures and successes, and evocative of a successful man's private life and battles. Banting's diet was so popular around the world that in some countries, including Sweden, his name is still in use for the act of dieting—*banta*.

LETTER

ON CORPULENCE,

Addressed to the Public

By WILLIAM BANTING.

THIRD EDITION.

LONDON:
PUBLISHED BY HARRISON, 59, PALL MALL,
Bookseller to the Queen and H.R.H. the Prince of Wales.

1864.

It is truly gratifying to me to be able now to add that many other of the most exalted members of the Faculty have honoured my movement in the question with their approbation.

I consider it a public duty further to state, that Mr. Harvey, whom I have named in the 43rd page as my kind medical adviser in the cure of Corpulence, is not Dr. John Harvey, who has published a Pamphlet on Corpulence assimilating with some of the features and the general aspect of mine, and which has been considered (as I learn from correspondents who have obtained it) the work of my medical friend. It is not.

I am glad, therefore, to repeat that my medical adviser was, and is still, Mr WILLIAM HARVEY, F.R.C.S., No. 2, Soho Square, London, W.

WILLIAM BANTING.

April, 1864.

PRINTED BY HARRISON AND SONS, ST. MARTIN'S LANE, LONDON.

ABOVE: By 1862, the sixty-five-year-old Banting was tipping the scales at 202 lbs (92 kg), a lot for a man of 5'5" (165 cm) height who didn't like exercise. He managed to reduce it to 156 lbs (70 kg) by diligent "banting."

General Sherman reminds the citizens of Atlanta that war is hell

(September 12, 1864)

After his capture of Atlanta, General Sherman corresponded with the city's military and civilian leaders. He wrote with great honesty about the hell of war and his determination to pursue it ruthlessly for the sake of his cause.

The battle for Atlanta, Georgia, in the summer of 1864 was one of the fiercest of the American Civil War. It was a central hub of the South's war effort, and its population swelled from under 10,000 before the conflict to over 20,000, with workers manufacturing everything from buttons for uniforms to armor-plating for Confederate battleships.

Despite being deep inside Confederate territory, it became an obvious target for advancing Union forces led by General William T. Sherman, who targeted the railroads. When Union troops took control of all four rail supply lines into the city, General Hood recognized his position as hopeless and led the Confederate forces quietly out of the city under cover of darkness on the night of September 1. The following morning, the city's mayor James Calhoun formally surrendered to an advance party of Sherman's army.

Hood had destroyed some vital industrial plants and blown up eighty-one rail wagons full of Confederate ordnance before quitting Atlanta. Sherman was determined to finish the job and render Atlanta useless as a Confederate manufacturing center before he moved on to his next target, Savannah. He was going to blow it up. Before doing so he called a two-day truce to allow the evacuation from the city of all civilians, to the north or to the south according to their preferences.

Sherman's reply to letters of protest from both Hood and Calhoun was a wise and sorrowful reflection on the reality of warfare. "War is cruelty," he wrote, "and you cannot refine it." He bluntly refuted the mayor's accusation of cruelty to the families of Atlanta. "Now that war comes home to you, you feel different. You deprecate its horrors, but did not feel them when you sent car-loads of soldiers … to desolate the homes of hundreds and thousands of good people who only asked to live in peace … under the Government of their inheritance."

Without admitting his intention to destroy Atlanta's industrial assets, he insisted, "my military plans make it necessary for the inhabitants to go away. … You might as well appeal against the thunderstorm as against these terrible hardships of war."

Sherman was unbending in his opposition to the rebels. "The only way the people of Atlanta can hope once more to live in peace and quiet at home is … by admitting that the war began in error and is perpetuated by pride." He declared the defense of the Union to be his priority. "Once more acknowledge the authority of the National Government … and this army becomes at once your protectors and supporters.

"I want peace, and believe it can now only be reached through union and war. But, my dear sirs," he concluded, "when that peace does come, you may call on me for anything. Then I will share with you the last cracker and watch with you to shield your homes and families against danger from every quarter."

And then Atlanta burned.

Letter from Major-General William T. Sherman to Mayor James M. Calhoun and representatives of the City Council of Atlanta

GENTLEMEN: I have your letter of the 11th, in the nature of a petition to revoke my orders removing all the inhabitants from Atlanta. I have read it carefully, and give full credit to your statements of the distress that will be occasioned by it, and yet shall not revoke my orders, simply because my orders are not designed to meet the humanities of the case, but to prepare for the future struggles in which millions of good people outside of Atlanta have a deep interest.

We must have peace, not only at Atlanta but in all America. To secure this we must stop the war that now desolates our once happy and favored country. To stop war we must defeat the rebel armies that are arrayed against the laws and Constitution, which all must respect and obey. To defeat these armies we must prepare the way to reach them in their recesses provided with the arms and instruments which enable us to accomplish our purpose. Now, I know the vindictive nature of our enemy, and that we may have many years of military operations from this quarter, and therefore deem it wise and prudent to prepare in time. The use of Atlanta for warlike purposes is inconsistent with its character as a home for families.

There will be no manufactures, commerce, or agriculture here for the maintenance of families, and sooner or later want will compel the inhabitants to go. Why not go now, when all the arrangements are completed for the transfer, instead of waiting till the plunging shot of contending armies will renew the scenes of the past month? Of course, I do not apprehend any such thing at this moment, but you do not suppose this army will be here until the war is over. I cannot discuss this subject with you fairly, because I cannot impart to you what I propose to do, but I assert that my military plans make it necessary for the inhabitants to go away, and I can only renew my offer of services to make their exodus in any direction as easy and comfortable as possible.

You cannot qualify war in harsher terms than I will. War is cruelty and you cannot refine it, and those who brought war into our country deserve all the curses and maledictions a people can pour out. I know I had no hand in making this war, and I know I will make more sacrifices to-day than any of you to secure peace. But you cannot have peace and a division of our country. If the United States submits to a division now it will not stop, but will go on until we reap the fate of Mexico, which is eternal war. …

The United States does and must assert its authority wherever it once had power. If it relaxes one bit to pressure it is gone, and I know that such is the national feeling. This feeling assumes various shapes, but always comes back to that of Union. Once admit the Union, once more acknowledge the authority of the National Government, and instead of devoting your houses and streets and roads to the dread uses of war, and this army become at once your protectors and supporters, shielding you from danger, let it come from what quarter it may. …

OPPOSITE: The elegance of Sherman's handwriting belies its steely message.

Letter from Vincent van Gogh to Theo van Gogh

It's with some reluctance that I write to you, not having done so for so long, and that for many a reason. Up to a certain point you've become a stranger to me, and I too am one to you, perhaps more than you think; perhaps it would be better for us not to go on this way. …

As you may perhaps know, I'm back in the Borinage; my father spoke to me of staying in the vicinity of Etten instead; I said no, and I believe I acted thus for the best. Without wishing to, I've more or less become some sort of impossible and suspect character in the family, in any event, somebody who isn't trusted, so how, then, could I be useful to anybody in any way? …

I, for one, am a man of passions, capable of and liable to do rather foolish things for which I sometimes feel rather sorry. I do often find myself speaking or acting somewhat too quickly when it would be better to wait more patiently. I think that other people may also sometimes do similar foolish things. Now that being so, what's to be done, must one consider oneself a dangerous man, incapable of anything at all? I don't think so. But it's a matter of trying by every means to turn even these passions to good account. …

I must now bore you with certain abstract things; however, I'd like you to listen to them patiently. For example, to name one passion among others, I have a more or less irresistible passion for books, and I have a need continually to educate myself, to study, if you like, precisely as I need to eat my bread. You'll be able to understand that yourself. When I was in different surroundings, in surroundings of paintings and works of art, you well know that I then took a violent passion for those surroundings that went as far as enthusiasm. And I don't repent it, and now, far from the country again, I often feel homesick for the country of paintings. …

And now for as much as five years, perhaps, I don't know exactly, I've been more or less without a position, wandering hither and thither. Now you say, from such and such a time you've been going downhill, you've faded away, you've done nothing. Is that entirely true? Perhaps you'll say, "but why didn't you continue as people would have wished you to continue, along the university road?" To that I'd say only this, it costs too much and then, that future was no better than the present one, on the road that I'm on.

It's true that sometimes I've earned my crust of bread, sometimes some friend has given me it as a favour; I've lived as best I could, better or worse, as things went; it's true that I've lost several people's trust, it's true that my financial affairs are in a sorry state, it's true that the future's not a little dark, it's true that I could have done better, it's true that just in terms of earning my living I've lost time, it's true that my studies themselves are in a rather sorry and disheartening state, and that I lack more, infinitely more than I have. But is that called going downhill, and is that called doing nothing? …

Vincent van Gogh writes an emotional letter to his brother, Theo

(June 23, 1880)

Vincent van Gogh was a troubled, restless soul, searching around for the meaning of life and the role he should play in it. After a long stream-of-consciousness letter to his brother, Theo suggested that Vincent should channel his energies into his art. …

After a happy few years working for an art dealer in The Hague and in London, Vincent van Gogh drifted through life in a variety of roles, including schoolteacher in southern England and missionary to a Belgian coal-mining community. He became almost monastic in his habits, sleeping on straw, eating little and losing himself in religious and secular introspection.

His family was very concerned for his state of mind, and in early 1880, his father thought he should be committed to a lunatic asylum. After a brief spell at his parents' home, Vincent returned to live among his Belgian miners and it was from there that he at last wrote to Theo—ostensibly to thank him for sending some much-needed money and to hope for some reconciliation with their despairing father.

But once Vincent's pen was flowing, he started to expound on his retreat from conventional life and a profoundly philosophical analysis of the nature of art as he saw it. "I must bore you now with certain abstract things," he begins. What emerges is a mind in overload, overwhelmed by complex thoughts and trying to find some release.

He reflects on having lost his way, "for as much as five years" and admits that "the future's not a little dark. … But on the road that I'm on I must continue. If I do nothing, if I don't study, if I don't keep on trying, then I'm lost." He had been reading voraciously and had begun to make connections across the arts and to see glimpses of some universal idea, God, which all of them are trying to express.

"There's something of Rembrandt in Shakespeare," he says, "something of Delacroix in Victor Hugo, something in Bunyan of Millet, something of Rembrandt in the Gospels. Everything in men and in their works that is truly good comes from God. Someone will love Rembrandt: that man will know there is a God."

Of his own apparent inactivity and detachment from the world, he argues, "Does what goes on inside show on the outside? Someone has a great fire in his soul and nobody ever comes to warm themselves at it, and passers-by see nothing but a little smoke at the top of the chimney and then go on their way." He knows the family perceives him as an idler, but he feels instinctively that "I'm good for something, even so! I have a *raison d'être*. If it became possible for you to see in me something other than an idler of the bad kind, I would be very pleased about that."

It is in many ways a sad letter, from a man wrestling with demons of depression and unrealized creativity. It is a cry for help. But having read it, Theo had the insight to advise his brother to pursue a course as an artist.

Vincent began sketching the people and places of his mining village, and that autumn he studied art in Brussels. Although his chronic depression haunted him for the rest of his life, from then on he was released to make his life's work with purpose and passion. As he wrote in hope to Theo in the same letter, "One who has been rolling along for ages as if tossed on a stormy sea arrives at his destination at last. One who has seemed good for nothing finds a role in the end and, active and capable of action, shows himself entirely different."

LEFT: Theo van Gogh.

A Chicago Methodist training school launches a moneymaker

(1888)

Chain letters in the twentieth century were at best a fad and at worst a pyramid scheme. But the first moneymaking chain letter was started by a supremely respectable Methodist training school for female missionaries in Chicago.

Some chain letters come with threats of bad luck, or worse should you break the chain. The recipient of the letter must make six copies and send them on within a week or fate will have something unkindly in store. Before the rise of the Internet and the decline of letter writing, many countries had outlawed them as nuisance mail.

In 1888, the first chain letter was an honest attempt by an institution above reproach, the Chicago Training School—a women's college for Methodist missionaries. The college was deep in debt and not raising enough in collections at its religious services to get it out of financial trouble.

The college's founders, Lucy and Josiah Meyer, wished that they could pass the collection plate farther afield than the confines of the school. They discussed the idea of leaving contribution boxes in the community, and of mailshots to potential donors, but all that would cost precious funds in construction, collection, stationery and postage. Then they hit on the idea of a chain letter: Why send hundreds of letters when you could send one?

The Meyers sent the letter, asking for a donation of a dime, and requesting that the recipient send a similar letter to three sympathetic friends. At the time it was lawful to send money through the US mail. It was a brilliant idea. It relieved the school not only of the cost in letterheads, stamps, and time, but of the need to draw up a list of possible donors: the recipients would do it all themselves.

Meyer produced 1,500 initial copies of the letter and waited for the response. It was immediate. The school raised around $6,000, with many people sending more than a dime and others encouraged to find out more about the college's work. The missionaries dubbed their chain letter a "peripatetic contribution box." Not only

was it an early form of the chain letter, it was a new way to solicit public subscription, or crowdfunding.

In 1898, a seventeen-year-old Red Cross volunteer devised a chain letter that solicited money for ice to send to troops stationed in Cuba during the Spanish-American War. So many thousands of letters arrived at her local post office in Babylon, New York, that her mother was forced to issue an open letter to stop people from sending more.

The Chicago Training School survived and thrived, weathering not only this financial crisis but also attacks on it for daring to educate young women in the service of God. Lucy Meyer went further and promoted the idea of the female deacon, an early Christian tradition that had died out before being revived in the nineteenth century, first in Germany, then in England, and eventually, thanks to Lucy, in the US.

Lucy died in 1922, and in 1935, the college merged with another in Evanston, 12 miles north of Chicago. Today, it continues her work as the Garrett–Evangelical Theological Seminary. It's perhaps the only story of a chain letter in which all those involved got what they wanted out of it.

OPPOSITE TOP: Lucy Meyer opened the Chicago Training School for Home and Foreign Missions with her husband Josiah (right) in 1885 and acted as principal from 1885 to 1917.

OPPOSITE: Following the success of early chain letters with charitable aims, the chain letter as a pyramid scheme soon appeared.

PROSPERITY CLUB—"IN GOD WE TRUST"

1. Ed. Judd   703 N. Flores San Antonio Tex

2. Harry Crapt   114 School St San Antonio Tex

3. Mrs. J. M Crapt   114 School St San Antonio Tex

4. James Craig   3811-S. Presa San Antonio Tex

5. P. M. Percy   3811-S. Presa San Antonio Tex

6. B. R. Brent   891 Liberty Beaumont Tex   Beaumont

FAITH! HOPE! CHARITY!

This chain was started in the hope of bringing prosperity to you. Within three (3) days make five (5) copies of this letter leaving off the top name and address and adding your own name and address to the bottom of the list, and give or mail a copy to five (5) of your friends to whom you wish prosperity to come.

In omitting the top name send that person ten (10c) cents wrapped in a paper as a charity donation. In turn as your name leaves the top of the list (if the chain has not been broken) you should receive 15,625 letters with donations amounting to $1,536.50.

NOW IS THIS WORTH A DIME TO YOU?

HAVE THE FAITH YOUR FRIENDS HAD AND THIS CHAIN WILL NOT BE BROKEN

TALLEY PRINTING CO

Williams sends a furious open letter to King Leopold II of Belgium

(July 18, 1890)

George Washington Williams was an African American who fought for the Union in the Civil War; he fought to be elected the first African American delegate in the Ohio state legislature; and as a lawyer he fought for clients in court. His biggest battle, however, was with the king of Belgium.

Williams would be worthy of attention if he had done nothing else than write the first definitive history of the African American, *History of the Negro Race in America 1619–1880*, published in 1882. Williams traveled to Europe in 1889 to write articles for his publisher, the Associated Literary Press. In the course of his trip he met Leopold II, king of Belgium, and was impressed.

The king spoke enthusiastically about one of his personal possessions, the Congo, and his plans to develop it. Leopold described his intentions as a benevolent enterprise for the local population, with every "honest and practical effort made to increase their knowledge and secure their welfare." Williams visited the Congo the following year to see this "benevolent enterprise" for himself.

He was horrified by what he found. Leopold was carving out a private kingdom for himself, exploiting its resources and enslaving its populations. His nominal government was little more than an abusive committee of management for rubber plantations and their unfortunate workforces, who were subjected to appalling cruelty by a private army of European and African mercenaries.

Williams wrote an open letter to the king, bluntly detailing acts of inhumanity being conducted in his name. "How thoroughly I have been disenchanted, disappointed and disheartened, it is now my painful duty to make known to your Majesty in plain but respectful language." Leopold had engaged the services of the celebrity explorer Henry Morton Stanley to open up the country along the Congo. Stanley's name, Williams told the king, "produces a shudder among this simple folk when mentioned; they remember his broken promises, his copious profanity, his hot temper, his heavy blows."

Stanley had a well-rehearsed routine for gaining the cooperation of local leaders. He would dazzle them with tricks such as lighting a cigar with the sun and a lens, or electrifying a handshake with a battery. "By such means as these … and a few boxes of gin, whole villages have been signed away to your Majesty."

A list of twelve specific allegations in the letter included the import of women "for immoral purposes"; the excessive cruelty shown to natives, fitted with ox chains around their necks and beaten with abrasive strips of hippopotamus hide until they bled; engagement in the slave trade, "wholesale and retail"; and a complete lack of medical facilities—"only three sheds for sick Africans," he wrote, which were "not fit to be occupied by a horse."

Williams circulated the letter and sent more detailed allegations to the British foreign secretary. Although Leopold II tried to suppress it, it aroused a national outcry in Belgium, which resulted in the king being forced to cede control and management of the Congo to the Belgian government. It was a crowning achievement for an African American with firsthand knowledge of slavery and cruelty.

Leopold never visited the Congo. George Washington Williams died of tuberculosis and pleurisy on his way back from Africa to the US in 1891. By this twist of fate he is buried not in America but in the British seaside resort of Blackpool, where in 1975, a new gravestone was erected in his honor.

Open Letter to King Leopold II

... It afforded me great pleasure to avail myself of the opportunity afforded me last year, of visiting your State in Africa; and how thoroughly I have been disenchanted, disappointed and disheartened, it is now my painful duty to make known to your Majesty in plain but respectful language. Every charge which I am about to bring against your Majesty's personal Government in the Congo has been carefully investigated; a list of competent and veracious witnesses, documents, letters, official records and data has been faithfully prepared, which will be deposited with Her Britannic Majesty's Secretary of State for Foreign Affairs, until such time as an International Commission can be created with power to send for persons and papers, to administer oaths, and attest the truth or falsity of these charges.

There were instances in which Mr. HENRY M. STANLEY sent one white man, with four or five Zanzibar soldiers, to make treaties with native chiefs. The staple argument was that the white man's heart had grown sick of the wars and rumours of war between one chief and another, between one village and another; that the white man was at peace with his black brother, and desired to "confederate all African tribes" for the general defense and public welfare. All the sleight-of-hand tricks had been carefully rehearsed, and he was now ready for his work. A number of electric batteries had been purchased in London, and when attached to the arm under the coat, communicated with a band of ribbon which passed over the palm of the white brother's hand, and when he gave the black brother a cordial grasp of the hand the black brother was greatly surprised to find his white brother so strong, that he nearly knocked him off his feet in giving him the hand of fellowship. When the native inquired about the disparity of strength between himself and his white brother, he was told that the white man could pull up trees and perform the most prodigious feats of strength. Next came the lens act. ...

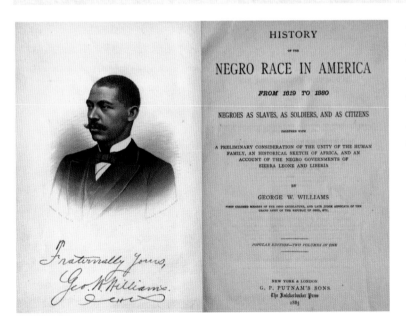

ABOVE: An extract from the "Open Letter to His Serene Majesty Leopold II, King of the Belgians." Before setting out his most serious grievances about how the country was being run, Williams painted an unflattering picture of the king's agent, the celebrated Henry Morton Stanley, who was using cheap Victorian magic tricks to impress the natives.

LEFT: George Washington Williams was a Civil War hero, a clergyman, and an accomplished writer.

WASHINGTON, D.C., January 21, 1892.

MISS A. M. SULLIVAN, TEACHER OF HELEN KELLER.

Perkins Institution for the Blind, South Boston, Mass.

DEAR MISS SULLIVAN:—Allow me to thank you for the privilege of reading your account of how you taught Helen Keller, which you have prepared for the second edition of the Souvenir issued by the Volta Bureau. Your paper is full of interest to teachers of the deaf, and it contains many valuable and important suggestions.

I am particularly struck by your statement that you gave Helen books printed in raised letters *"long before she could read them,"* and that *"she would amuse herself for hours each day in carefully passing her fingers over the words, searching for such words as she knew,"* etc.

I consider that statement as of very great significance and importance when I try to account for her wonderful familiarity with idiomatic English. She is such an exceptional child that we are apt to attribute every thing to her marvellous mind, and forget that language comes from without, and not from within. She could not intuitively arrive at a knowledge of idiomatic English expressions. It is absolutely certain that such expressions must have been *taught to her* before she could use them; and if you can show us how it was done, teachers of the deaf all over the world will owe you a debt of gratitude.

The great problem in the education of the deaf is the teaching of idiomatic language.

I am sure that instructors of the deaf will support me in urging you to tell us all you can as to the part played by books in the instruction of Helen Keller. We should like to form an idea of the quantity and quality of the reading-matter presented for her examination "long before she could read the books."

How much time did she devote to the examination of language which she could not understand, in her search for the words that she knew? I would suggest that you give us a list of the books she has read, arranging them, as well as you can, in the order of presentation. Teachers of the deaf find great difficulty in selecting suitable books for their pupils; and I am sure they would thank you especially for the names of those books that have given Helen pleasure, and have proved most profitable in her instruction.

You say, *"I have always talked to Helen as I would to a seeing and hearing child, and have insisted that others should do the same,"* etc. I presume you mean by this that you talked *with your fingers* instead of your mouth; that you spelled into her hand what you would have spoken to a seeing and hearing child. You say that you have "always' done this. Are we to understand that you pursued this method from the very beginning of her education, and that you spelled complete sentences and idiomatic expressions into her hand *before she was capable of understanding the language employed ?* If this is so, I consider the point to be of so much importance that I would urge you to elaborate the statement, and make your meaning perfectly clear and unmistakable.

Yours very Sincerely

Alexander Graham Bell

LEFT: Alexander Graham Bell was fascinated with the methods that Anne Sullivan used to communicate with Helen. With his help and support from the likes of industrialist H. H. Rogers, Keller was able to become the first deaf-blind person to earn a Bachelor of Arts degree.

Alexander Graham Bell writes to Helen Keller's teacher Anne Sullivan

(January 21, 1892)

Helen Keller was born healthy, but at the age of nineteen months contracted a disease (now believed to be scarlet fever) that left her both blind and deaf. She owed her subsequent long and rich life as an author and political activist to two people who corresponded often about her education.

Helen Keller's only experience of the sights and sounds of the world was a baby's first year and a half before being robbed of those senses. By 1887, at the age of seven, Helen's only way of communicating was with a vocabulary of sixty hand signals that she had worked out with the daughter of the family cook in Alabama. Then a doctor advised her parents to contact Alexander Graham Bell. Bell is best known today as the inventor of the telephone, but he put considerable energy into research about elocution and the instruction of the deaf—both his wife and his mother were profoundly deaf.

Bell in turn referred the Kellers to the Perkins Institution for the Blind in Boston, which allocated one of its former students, twenty-year-old Anne Sullivan, as an instructor for Helen. In 1892, Anne wrote an early account of her success in teaching Helen, which brought Helen's case back to the attention of Bell. He wrote to Anne to congratulate her on her remarkable success with Helen.

"Your paper is full of interest to teachers of the deaf," he wrote to Anne, herself partially sighted. It was already becoming clear that, thanks to Anne's work, Helen was being released from her sensory prison to express herself with exceptional maturity and depth. "She is such an exceptional child," Bell considered, "that we are apt to attribute everything to her marvellous mind and forget that language comes from without, and not from within."

What particularly intrigued Bell was the richness of Helen's language after only three years with Anne. It went far beyond merely functional statements or requests—say, of tiredness, or hunger, or pleasure—to idiomatic expressions. This was language not only for facts but for rhetoric and literature. How did she acquire it? "If you can show us how it was done," Bell asked Sullivan, "teachers of the deaf all over the world will owe you a debt of gratitude."

Anne Sullivan had already hinted at how it was done. She described giving Helen books printed in raised letters "long before she could read them" and how "she would amuse herself for hours each day in carefully passing her fingers over the words, searching for such words as she knew." As such, it was a departure from the usual practice of limiting communication with deaf people to the most basic of expressions. "I have always talked to Helen as I would to a seeing or hearing child," Anne explained, "and have insisted that others should do the same."

Helen Keller was writing poetry within a year, which Bell thought "surpasses most of [our great poets] in maturity of thought and beauty of expression." Thanks to Bell's encouragement of Sullivan, Keller would become a national and international figure. Mark Twain, who was introduced to her when she was thirteen, was astonished by her prowess, an intellect that blossomed under Anne Sullivan's tutelage.

(For an additional exchange of letters between the adult Helen Keller and the elderly Alexander Graham Bell, see page 214.)

OPPOSITE FAR LEFT: *Helen Keller with her teacher and lifelong companion, Anne Sullivan. The photograph was taken in July 1888, when Helen was just eight years old.*

OPPOSITE: *Alexander Graham Bell.*

Beatrix Potter illustrates a letter to cheer up five-year-old Noel Moore

(September 4, 1893)

Beatrix Potter and her brother, Bertram, had an isolated childhood, educated at home in southwest London by a succession of governesses. It was thanks to the last of them, Anne Moore, that she became a successful children's author. And it all began with a letter to Anne's son, Noel.

Beatrix met few other children and spent most of her childhood family holidays in the beautiful countryside of the English Lake District or Perthshire in Scotland. She became a keen observer of nature and the countryside and, like her parents, showed a talent for painting. In time, Anne Moore became less of a governess and more of a lady's companion to Beatrix, who as a young adult wrote often to Anne's young children.

Anne's eldest son Noel fell ill in the summer of 1893, and Beatrix often wrote letters to him to cheer him up. Beatrix, on holiday in the village of Dunkeld on the banks of the River Tay in Scotland, had little in the way of news, or indeed new ways to say "get well soon." As she said in a letter on September 4 that year, "I don't know what to write to you, so I shall tell you a story about four little rabbits, whose names were Flopsy, Mopsy, Cottontail, and Peter."

As all Beatrix Potter fans will know, this was the start of *The Tale of Peter Rabbit*. Peter was a real rabbit, Beatrix's pet, which she often sketched or painted. Peter was her second rabbit after Benjamin, who also achieved fame later in *The Tale of Benjamin Bunny*. Beatrix was in the habit of illustrating her letters with little cameos in ink of what she was writing about, and that September letter to Noel contains not only the story of Peter Rabbit but the first versions of Potter's distinctive illustrations.

Noel was no doubt delighted to receive it, and Anne was sufficiently impressed by her former pupil to suggest that the tale would make a good children's book. Beatrix and Bertram were not strangers to publication, having previously had designs for Christmas cards produced.

She tried without success to interest a publisher, and in 1901, printed 250 black-and-white copies at her own expense. In one of the copies she recorded the following sad news:

> "In affectionate remembrance of poor old Peter Rabbit, who died on the 26th of January 1901 at the end of his 9th year … whatever the limitations of his intellect or outward shortcomings of his fur, and his ears and toes, his disposition was uniformly amiable and his temper unfailingly sweet. An affectionate companion and a quiet friend."

A further run of 200 copies soon followed, and their successful sales attracted the attention of Frederick Warne, who had previously turned down the book. Warne was a publisher of similar illustrated children's books by artists such as Edward Lear, Kate Greenaway, and Walter Crane. Published by Warne in a new color edition, *The Tale of Peter Rabbit* sold 20,000 copies in its first year, and twenty-two more tales came from Potter's pen over the next twenty-seven years. They included some characters—Squirrel Nutkin and Jeremy Fisher the frog—who had also made their debut in letters to Noel Moore.

Beatrix Potter retired to the Lake District, where she preserved the countryside through the purchase of several farms in the area, all funded by the success of her tales. Today, there are museums of her work in both the Lake District and Dunkeld, where a small public garden is inhabited by sculptures of the creatures who she first imagined in a letter.

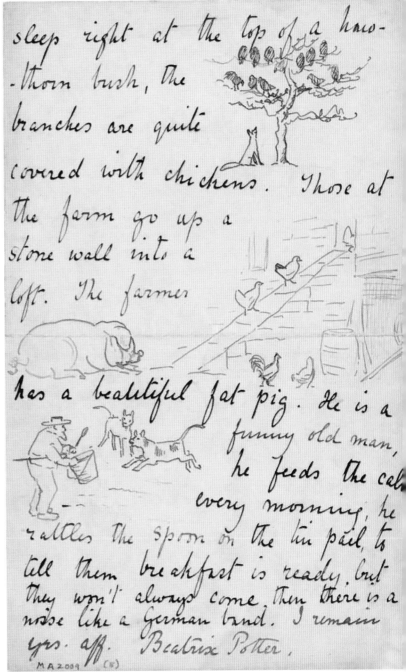

sleep right at the top of a haw-thorn bush, the branches are quite covered with chickens. Those at the farm go up a stone wall into a loft. The farmer has a beautiful fat pig. He is a funny old man, he feeds the calves every morning, he rattles the spoon on the tin pail, to tell them breakfast is ready, but they won't always come, then there is a noise like a German band. I remain yrs. aff. Beatrix Potter.

MA2009 (8)

Pierre Curie sends Maria a letter begging her to come back and study

(August 10, 1894)

After a brief spell as Pierre Curie's student in Paris, Maria Skłodowska returned to Poland, intent on continuing her work there. Pierre Curie had fallen in love and set about charming the woman many people would call "Pierre's greatest discovery," the only woman to win two Nobel prizes for science.

Maria Skłodowska was born in Warsaw. Poland at the time was part of the Russian Empire, and she studied science in secret at the underground Flying University, where nationalist Poles resisted the Russianization of Polish culture and education. In 1891, she moved to Paris to continue her studies more freely, and it was there that she found a position as a student in the laboratory of Pierre Curie.

Pierre was conducting groundbreaking research into piezoelectricity, the technology behind most digital circuitry today. He was introduced to Maria in 1894 by another Polish physicist, Józef Wierusz-Kowalski. Maria proved to be the ideal student; not only did she not hinder his work, she understood it and enhanced it. Pierre at first admired her scientific mind, then found himself relying on her insights. She became his inspiration, and finally his love.

He proposed to her. She turned him down. In the summer of 1894, she left Paris for two months to go to Freiburg, where Kowalski was now teaching, and from where she sent Pierre a note to say she was enjoying the fresh air. Pierre's heart skipped a beat. "Nothing could have given me greater pleasure than to get news of you," he wrote to her on August 10. "I hope you are laying up a good stock of air and that you will come back to us in October."

It's a tender, gentle letter. Having been rebuffed once, Pierre was anxious not to push too hard for fear of losing Maria altogether. "We have promised each other—haven't we?—to be at least great friends," he hoped. "It would be a fine thing, just the same, in which I hardly dare believe, to pass our lives near each other, hypnotized by our dreams: your patriotic dream, our humanitarian dream, and our scientific dream."

It was the latter that he most wanted to pursue, arguing that they were powerless to realize their other dreams. "From the scientific point of view, on the contrary, we may hope to do something." Little did he know how much they would do together. "See how it works out." He sounded casual, almost offhanded, but then continued, "If you leave France in a year it would be an altogether too Platonic friendship … Wouldn't it be better for you to stay with me?" Then he backed off again. "I know that this question angers you, and that you don't want to speak of it again."

Maria did not leave France a year later, and they did speak of it again. She finally agreed to marry Pierre on July 25, 1895. They were a devoted couple for the rest of their life together. As a sort of belated wedding present to each other, Pierre and Marie Curie, as Maria became known, shared the 1903 Nobel Prize for Physics. Marie won a second, for chemistry, in 1911, the only woman to win two and the only person to win two in different disciplines. Love, and Nobel prizes, are worth waiting for.

Letter from Pierre Curie to Maria Skłodowska

Nothing could have given me greater pleasure than to get news of you. The prospect of remaining two months without hearing about you had been extremely disagreeable to me: that is to say, your little note was more than welcome.

I hope you are laying up a stock of good air and that you will come back to us in October. As for me, I think I shall not go anywhere; I shall stay in the country, where I spend the whole day in front of my open window or in the garden.

We have promised each other—haven't we?—to be at least great friends. If you will only not change your mind! For there are no promises that are binding; such things cannot be ordered at will. It would be a fine thing, just the same, in which I hardly dare believe, to pass our lives near each other, hypnotized by our dreams: your patriotic dream, our humanitarian dream, and our scientific dream.

Of all those dreams the last is, I believe, the only legitimate one. I mean by that that we are powerless to change the social order and, even if we were not, we should not know what to do; in taking action, no matter in what direction, we should never be sure of not doing more harm than good, by retarding some inevitable evolution. From the scientific point of view, on the contrary, we may hope to do something; the ground is solider here, and any discovery that we may make, however small, will remain acquired knowledge.

See how it works out: it is agreed that we shall be great friends, but if you leave France in a year it would be an altogether too Platonic friendship, that of two creatures who would never see each other again. Wouldn't it be better for you to stay with me? I know that this question angers you, and that you don't want to speak of it again—and then, too, I feel so thoroughly unworthy of you from every point of view.

I thought of asking your permission to meet you by chance in Fribourg. But you are staying there, unless I am mistaken, only one day, and on that day you will of course belong to our friends the Kovalskis.

Believe me your very devoted

Pierre Curie

LEFT: *Maria's work overturned established ideas in physics and chemistry, and as feminist precursor, the role of women in science.*

OPPOSITE: *Maria turned down Pierre Curie's first proposal of marriage as she wanted to return and pursue a scientific career in Poland.*

Oscar Wilde writes a letter to Lord Alfred Douglas from Reading Gaol

(January to March 1897)

Oscar Wilde was not suited to prison life. He suffered both physically and emotionally after being sentenced in 1895 to two years' hard labor for "gross indecency"—his homosexual relationship with Lord Alfred Douglas. A new governor at Reading Gaol encouraged him to write a letter as therapy.

Wilde was deprived of intellectual stimulation in the form of conversation and books for most of his time behind bars. But a change of governor at the beginning of 1897 improved his circumstances. One of the first acts of Major James Nelson, the new man in office, was to lend Wilde a book from his own library, a move so compassionate that it brought Wilde to tears.

Nelson made another generous concession to Oscar Wilde. For the first time during his incarceration, the celebrated author and razor-sharp wit was allowed to write. Nelson provided Wilde with pen and paper with which to exercise his brilliant gifts as a wordsmith. Wilde was not allowed to keep his writings overnight or to send them to anyone. The governor regarded them as purely therapeutic, or as he put it, "for medicinal purposes."

Wilde began to write a letter to his former lover Lord Alfred, for whom his pet name was Bosie. Bosie, whose affair with Wilde had cost the latter his reputation and his freedom, had merely been using Wilde as a way of outraging his father and never wrote to Wilde in prison. "Dear Bosie," he began, "After long and fruitless waiting I have determined to write to you myself, as much for your sake as for mine, as I would not like to think that I had passed through two long years of imprisonment without ever having received a single line from you."

The notoriously flippant playwright of comedies like *Lady Windermere's Fan* and *The Importance of Being Earnest* was in no mood to joke. After two years of solitary reflection with no opportunity to express

himself and his thoughts, Wilde's letter became a twenty-page meditation on Bosie and on Wilde's own spirituality.

No longer blinded by his love for Lord Alfred (although still in love with him), Wilde used the first part of his letter to consider the effect of the hedonistic, self-centered Bosie on Oscar's work and life. Three years of conspicuous wild living had drained him financially and intellectually while he pursued an "imperfect world of coarse uncompleted passions, of appetite without distinction, desire without limit, and formless greed." While criticizing Alfred's selfish vanity, Wilde blamed himself for neglecting his genius in favor of his lusts. "Most people live *for* love and admiration," he observed. "But it is *by* love and admiration that we should live."

Moving in the letter from his secular relationship with Bosie to a consideration of Christianity, he quoted from the Book of Isaiah: "He is despised and rejected of men, a man of sorrows and acquainted with grief." He now believed that suffering, not pleasure and success, was the key to inner peace. This was demonstrated by his own experience in jail, those of his fellow inmates and of Jesus Christ. "There is not a single wretched man in this

wretched place along with me who does not stand in symbolic relation to the very secret of life. For the secret of life is suffering."

The letter shows a new sense of balance in Wilde's life, no longer simply the pursuit of pleasure. "He who can look at the loveliness of the world and share its sorrow," he reflected, "and realise something of the wonder of both … has got as near to God's secret as anyone can get."

Letter from Oscar Wilde to Lord Alfred Douglas

… Suffering is one very long moment. We cannot divide it by seasons. We can only record its moods, and chronicle their return. With us time itself does not progress. It revolves. It seems to circle round one centre of pain. The paralysing immobility of a life every circumstance of which is regulated after an unchangeable pattern, so that we eat and drink and lie down and pray, or kneel at least for prayer, according to the inflexible laws of an iron formula: this immobile quality, that makes each dreadful day in the very minutest detail like its brother, seems to communicate itself to those external forces the very essence of whose existence is ceaseless change. Of seed-time or harvest, of the reapers bending over the corn, or the grape gatherers threading through the vines, of the grass in the orchard made white with broken blossoms or strewn with fallen fruit: of these we know nothing and can know nothing.

For us there is only one season, the season of sorrow. The very sun and moon seem taken from us. Outside, the day may be blue and gold, but the light that creeps down through the thickly-muffled glass of the small iron-barred window beneath which one sits is grey and niggard. It is always twilight in one's cell, as it is always twilight in one's heart. And in the sphere of thought, no less than in the sphere of time, motion is no more. The thing that you personally have long ago forgotten, or can easily forget, is happening to me now, and will happen to me again to-morrow. Remember this, and you will be able to understand a little of why I am writing, and in this manner writing. …

A week later, I am transferred here. Three more months go over and my mother dies. No one knew how deeply I loved and honoured her. Her death was terrible to me; but I, once a lord of language, have no words in which to express my anguish and my shame. She and my father had bequeathed me a name they had made noble and honoured, not merely in literature, art, archaeology, and science, but in the public history of my own country, in its evolution as a nation. I had disgraced that name eternally. I had made it a low by-word among low people. I had dragged it through the very mire. I had given it to brutes that they might make it brutal, and to fools that they might turn it into a synonym for folly.

What I suffered then, and still suffer, is not for pen to write or paper to record. My wife, always kind and gentle to me, rather than that I should hear the news from indifferent lips, travelled, ill as she was, all the way from Genoa to England to break to me herself the tidings of so irreparable, so irremediable, a loss. Messages of sympathy reached me from all who had still affection for me. Even people who had not known me personally, hearing that a new sorrow had broken into my life, wrote to ask that some expression of their condolence should be conveyed to me. …

OPPOSITE: Wilde's therapeutic letter was partially published as
De Profundis *in 1905 and in its entirety in* The Letters of
Oscar Wilde *in 1962.*

Conclusion of Émile Zola's open letter

…But this letter is long, Sir, and it is time to conclude it.

I accuse Lt. Col. du Paty de Clam of being the diabolical creator of this miscarriage of justice—unwittingly, I would like to believe—and of defending this sorry deed, over the last three years, by all manner of ludicrous and evil machinations.

I accuse General Mercier of complicity, at least by mental weakness, in one of the greatest inequities of the century.

I accuse General Billot of having held in his hands absolute proof of Dreyfus's innocence and covering it up, and making himself guilty of this crime against mankind and justice, as a political expedient and a way for the compromised General Staff to save face.

I accuse General de Boisdeffre and General Gonse of complicity in the same crime, the former, no doubt, out of religious prejudice, the latter perhaps out of that *esprit de corps* that has transformed the War Office into an unassailable holy ark.

I accuse General de Pellieux and Major Ravary of conducting a villainous enquiry, by which I mean a monstrously biased one, as attested by the latter in a report that is an imperishable monument to naïve impudence.

I accuse the three handwriting experts, Messrs. Belhomme, Varinard and Couard, of submitting reports that were deceitful and fraudulent, unless a medical examination finds them to be suffering from a condition that impairs their eyesight and judgement. …

Writer Émile Zola accuses the French army of an anti-Semitic conspiracy

(January 13, 1898)

It was an affair that split French society. French army captain Alfred Dreyfus was convicted in 1894 of espionage on the basis that the handwriting on a document supposedly written by him was so unlike his that he must have written it. Literary giant Émile Zola came to his defense.

Émile Zola was a playwright and novelist, a pioneer of the naturalist school of writing that favored realism and social commentary over romanticism. His grim portrait of capitalism at work in a mining community, *Germinal*, brought him mass popularity, and by 1898, he was a literary celebrity.

When a telegram was discovered that cleared Alfred Dreyfus of spying and implicated another officer, Major Ferdinand Esterhazy, the army moved to cover up the story and protect Esterhazy. It forged documents to further implicate Dreyfus and posted the soldier who had found the new evidence to Tunisia. Nevertheless, when news of the discovery leaked out, belief in Dreyfus's innocence began to spread.

Zola wrote an open letter to the French president, which filled the front page of the *L'Aurore* newspaper on the morning of January 13, 1898, under the banner headline "J'Accuse … !" The letter directly named ten people, including the handwriting experts ("unless a medical examination finds them to be suffering from a condition that impairs their eyesight and judgement") who had decided that Dreyfus must be a spy because the handwriting looked so unlike his own handwriting.

The author opened with a lengthy diatribe against the processes that had convicted Dreyfus and allowed Esterhazy to walk free, "an outrageous inquiry from which criminals emerge glorified and honest people sullied." Zola was certain that anti-Semitism had played a part in "this human sacrifice of an unfortunate man, a 'dirty Jew.'" He mocked Dreyfus's accusers: "he knew several languages: a crime! He carried no compromising

papers: a crime! He was hard-working, and strove to be well informed: a crime! He did not become confused: a crime! He became confused: a crime!"

Zola's greatest opprobrium was reserved for Major Armand du Paty de Clam, the officer who pursued the conviction of Dreyfus with such zeal. "He was the one," wrote Zola, "who 'invented' the Dreyfus affair, who orchestrated the whole affair and made it his own."

Naming Du Paty de Clam exposed Zola to a charge of libel under French law. Six weeks after the publication of his letter, Zola was convicted of the offense and fled to England temporarily to escape imprisonment. Esterhazy, the real spy in the affair, whose acquittal at a show trial had prompted Zola to write his letter, was quietly pensioned off; but by the end of the year he too had fled to Britain where he spent the rest of his life under an assumed name.

The officer who had forged the papers that damned Dreyfus was arrested and committed suicide while awaiting trial. Major Du Paty de Clam was sidelined because of his role in the Dreyfus affair and, in 1901, resigned from the army. He reenlisted as World War I loomed, and died from wounds sustained in the First Battle of the Marne in 1916.

Dreyfus, who had been publicly stripped of his rank and had his sword snapped in two in front of fellow soldiers, was exiled to France's notorious Devil's Island. In 1899, thanks to Émile Zola's letter, he was offered a pardon, which, to win his liberty and despite his innocence, he accepted. In 1906, he was finally exonerated of any wrongdoing.

RECEIVED at

176 C KA 63 63 Paid.   Via Norfolk Va

Kitty Hawk N C Dec 17

Bishop M Wright

            7 Hawthorne St

Success four flights thursday morning all against twenty one mile

wind started from Level with engine power alone average speed

through air thirty one miles longest 57 seconds inform Press

home phong Christmas .   Orevelle Wright   525P

ABOVE: The telegram that announced aviation history.

TOP: The first powered, controlled, sustained flight—120 feet in 12 seconds. Orville Wright is at the
controls of the machine, lying prone on the lower wing. Wilbur Wright, running alongside to balance the
machine, has just released his hold on the forward upright of the right wing.

Orville and Wilbur Wright send news to their father, Bishop Milton Wright

(December 17, 1903)

On December 17, 1903, two brothers had some very big news indeed for their father, Milton Wright, a bishop of the Church of the United Brethren in Christ. They couldn't wait to tell him; what they had just achieved made the world a lot smaller and humanity's dreams a lot bigger.

If the news was urgent, the road to it was anything but. Since 1896, the brothers had been experimenting with airplane designs. Their father, Milton, deserves credit for igniting the initial spark of enthusiasm in the boys, with a childhood gift of a flying toy based on the spinning sycamore seed.

Wilbur and Orville began with kites and progressed to gliders. They were innovative not only in aircraft design but in control systems, breaking with the received wisdom that an ideal flight should be level, even when changing direction. They introduced the idea of banking into a turn and of changing the shape of the wings to enable steering. The latter is the basis for today's fixed wings and flaps.

They only turned their attention to powered flight in early 1903. They used an engine the mechanic in their bicycle shop built to their specifications, and propellers they modeled themselves in the absence of existing design theories. Tests conducted in wind tunnels on reproductions of their original propellers showed them to be 75 percent efficient— quite an achievement for a first attempt.

With less imagination for names than for aeronautics, they called their first powered flying machine "The Flyer." The first test flight was on Monday, December 14, a three-second journey ending in a stall, which was encouraging if unsuccessful. It was, by coincidence, the same day that 121 years earlier had witnessed the first test flight by two other brothers, the ballooning Montgolfiers of France.

Three days later, near Kitty Hawk, North Carolina, four successful flights were witnessed by five people: a local businessman; three members of the local lifeguard team; and a teenage boy, Johnny Moore, who was walking in the area. After the fourth, a gust of wind flipped The Flyer over, causing irreparable damage. It never flew again, but its work was done.

On December 17, 1903, they had at last achieved the world's first powered flights. Punctuation cost extra when you were sending a telegram, so here's how they announced the milestone in human endeavor to their father:

> "success four flights thursday morning all against twenty one mile wind started from Level with engine power alone average speed through air thirty one miles longest 57 seconds inform Press home Christmas."

ABOVE: Wilbur and Orville Wright in 1904, with their second powered machine at Huffman Prairie, Dayton, Ohio.

John Muir lobbies Teddy Roosevelt about incursions into Yosemite

(September 9, 1907)

The naturalist John Muir and President Teddy Roosevelt became friends in 1903, during a private camping trip through Yosemite Valley. When part of the Yosemite National Park came under threat from developers in 1907, Muir wrote an impassioned letter to Roosevelt to seek his support in defending it.

Their camping trip was an attempt to convince the president that Muir's beloved Yosemite Valley should be part of Yosemite National Park, and therefore under national rather than state protection. Roosevelt was indeed enchanted by the place, especially after waking up one morning under canvas to find that a blanket of snow covered their surroundings. In 1906, he signed a bill incorporating the valley into the park.

That was also the year of a devastating earthquake in nearby San Francisco. In its wake, fires raged throughout the city, destroying much that had survived the quake. There simply wasn't enough water to put them out. Plans were proposed in 1907 to solve that by damming the Hetch Hetchy Valley, in the northwest of Yosemite National Park.

Muir was horrified. The park had been established in 1890, largely along the lines and terms recommended by Muir. It was something of a holy place for the naturalist, an immigrant from Scotland who had eventually settled in San Francisco and studied the geology and botany of the region for decades. He built, and for two years inhabited, a cabin that overhung Yosemite Creek, so that he could live with the sound of running water. Although he never lost his Scottish accent, Yosemite became his spiritual home.

His letter to Roosevelt was a cry from the heart. "I am anxious," he began without preamble, "that the Yosemite National Park may be saved from all sorts of commercialism and marks of man's work other than the roads, hotels etc required to make its wonders and blessings available … For its falls and groves and delightful camp-grounds are surpassed or equalled only in Yosemite [Valley]."

Damming it, he said, would be second only to damming the Yosemite river itself as an act of vandalism against nature. "All the water required can be obtained from sources outside the Park," insisted Muir, and the arguments that Hetch Hetchy was expendable all showed "the proud sort of confidence that comes from a good sound substantial irrefragable ignorance."

In a way the letter springs no surprises. It's a well-argued two-page defense of the valley. But it was accompanied by Muir's own description of the place, a four-page summary of its unique geological and botanical value. It is Muir's hymn to Hetch Hetchy.

In one sense it is a straightforward enumeration of Hetch Hetchy's rocks, mountains, waters, plants, and climate. But it is couched in a language of such poetry and love that it's impossible at this distance not to regret what happened next. "Air, water, sunlight, woven into stuff that spirits might wear … not only in its crystal river and sublime rocks and waterfalls but in the gardens, groves and meadows of its flowery park-like floor. … Into this glorious mountain temple Nature has gathered her choicest treasures to draw her lovers into close confiding communion with her."

After a seven-year battle by environmentalists to save the valley, work began in early 1914 on building the O'Shaughnessy Dam (named after its chief engineer) at Hetch Hetchy's narrowest point. John Muir died at the end of the year, having lost his last battle for nature after so many victories. The dam was completed, and in May 1923, the valley flooded.

The most abundant and influential are the great Yellow pines, the tallest over 200 feet in height, and the oaks with massive rugged trunks four to six or seven feet in diameter, and broad heads, assembled in magnificent groves. The shrubs forming conspicuous flowery clumps and tangles are Manzanita, Azalea, Spiraea, Brier-rose, Ceanothus, Calycanthus, Philadelphus, Wild cherry, etc; with abundance of showy and fragrant herbaceous plants growing about them or out in the open in beds by themselves – Lilies, Mariposa tulips, Erodiaeas, Orchids – several species of each, Iris, Spragues, Draperia, Collomia, Collinsia, Castilleia, Nemophilia, Larkspur, Columbine, Goldenrods, Sunflowers and Mints of many species, Honeysuckle etc etc. Many fine ferns dwell here also, especially the beautiful and interesting rock-ferns, – Pellaea, and Cheilanthes of several species, – fringing and rosetting dry rock piles and ledges; Woodwardia and Asplenium on damp spots with fronds six or seven feet high, the delicate Maidenhair in mossy nooks by the falls, and the sturdy broad-shouldered Pteris beneath the oaks and pines.

It appears therefore that Hetch Hetchy Valley far from being a plain common rock-bound meadow, as many who have not seen it seem to suppose, is a grand landscape garden, one of Nature's rarest and most precious mountain mansions. As in Yosemite the sublime rocks of its walls seem to the Nature lover to glow with life whether leaning back in repose or standing erect in thoughtful attitudes giving welcome to storms and calms alike. And how softly these mountain rocks are adorned, and how fine and reassuring the company they keep – their brows in the sky, their feet set in groves and gay emerald meadows, a thousand flowers leaning confidingly against their adamantine bosses, while birds bees butterflies help the river and waterfalls to stir all the air into music – things frail and fleeting and types of permanence meeting here and blending as if into this glorious mountain temple Nature had gathered her choicest treasures, whether great or small to draw her lovers into close confiding communion with her.

John Muir

LEFT: *John Muir's lyrical entreaties fell on deaf ears.*

BELOW: *President Theodore Roosevelt with John Muir at Glacier Point in 1903. Yosemite was preserved in 1906, something Muir had lobbied for since 1890. Today, Muir Woods National Monument, north of San Francisco, is named for the Scottish-born preservationist.*

canneries, to have the children get their jobs first and then have them apply for permits. (The weakness of this system is obvious) A working woman told Miss Rife that one cannery requires no permits and that there are lots of children there.

There are several dangers connected with this work when x children do it. On every hand, one can see little tots toting boxes or pans full of beans, berries or tomatoes, and it is self-evident that the work is too hard. Then there are mach-ines which no young persons should be working around. Unguarded belts, wheels, cogs and the like are a xxx menace to careless children. See photos 858 to 860.

In the fields convenient to Baltimore in Anne Arundel County, and on Rock Creek and Stony Creek, children are employed as a matter of course. I investigated a number of farms on Rock Creek (and am convinced that we have been too lenient with the "agricultural pursuits.") (In the first place,) the long hours mf these children work ixx in the hot sun and in company, too often, with foul-mouthed negroes and whites more than compensates many times over for the boasted advantages of fresh air and country life. The living conditions in the shacks they occupy are not only harm-ful in physical ways, but the total lack of privacy where several families live in one room is extremely bad. One mother told me "it is bad for the children. They get to know too much." There is little rest for the children in these crowded shacks. (See photos 846 to 852) I admit that it is a big problem for these parents to handle, but with the right kind of help, it can be done. There were, on these farms on Rock

Lewis Wickes Hine reports to the National Child Labor Committee

(July 1909)

The US economy boomed before World War I. Employment levels were high and factories, determined to keep wage bills down, turned not only to poor immigrant labor but to young children. One man's photographs and persistent lobbying exposed these practices to the American public.

The National Child Labor Committee (NCLC) was formed in 1904. Its aim was to combat an alarming rise over the preceding twenty years in the number of preteen children being employed in harsh adult work. By 1900 one in six American children was earning meagre wages to supplement the family's income, and missing out on childhood and education as a result.

Lewis Hine taught sociology in New York at the time. He believed that photography could not only record events and conditions but open the eyes of others to them, in a way that mere words could not. He cut his documentary teeth photographing the immigrants arriving on Ellis Island, and in 1908 he was hired by the NCLC to expose the poverty traps which forced parents to rely on their infants' paychecks.

A letter which Hines wrote to the NCLC in July 1909 accompanied some of his photos. He had been observing child labor in the food canning industry in Maryland, and his letter contained distressing reports of the very young at work. "Incredibly small are the fingers that work along with those of the rest of the family, and if the child is too small to sit up it is held on the lap of the worker, or stowed away in boxes near at hand." Parents, living in crowded company shacks, were not allowed to leave children at home. "On every hand, one can see little tots toting boxes or pans full of beans, berries or tomatoes, and it is self-evident that the work is too hard."

The children grew up fast—"they get to know too much"—working in the hot sun "with foul-mouthed negroes and whites." When the canning season was over, families migrated south to the Carolinas to pack oysters there. Everywhere, abuse was rife—workers' fares and rent were deducted from their wages, which they had to spend in overpriced company stores. Factory scales were tampered with so that their efforts were under-weighed, under-recorded, and underpaid.

Testimonies from those Hine interviewed despaired of the conditions. One woman had children aged one, three, six, eight and nine; even the three-year old was put to work, and the whole family was roused by the overseer at 3 a.m., working from then until 4 p.m. "You can talk about the days of slavery being over," another told him, "but this is worse."

Factory owners were naturally keen to conceal the conditions of their workers, old and young. Hine often faced threats and intimidation, and sometimes used subterfuge to gain access, posing as a Bible salesman or a photographer of factory machinery. His images captured the story however, and in 1912 the NCLC had its first major success when President Taft signed an Act which created the United States Children's Bureau.

Its role was to "investigate the questions of infant mortality, the birth-rate, orphanage, juvenile courts, desertion, dangerous occupations, accidents and diseases of children, employment, legislation affecting children in the several states and territories." It still exists today, and tackles the modern forms of child abuse so sadly prevalent in society. The work of people like Lewis Hine is never finished.

OPPOSITE: *Hine captioned this photo: "A little spinner in Globe Cotton Mill, Augusta, Georgia. The overseer admitted she was regularly employed."*

OPPOSITE TOP: *Part of Lewis Wickes Hine's submission to the committee.*

ABOVE: One of the final photos taken of the Antarctic expedition team. Robert Falcon Scott is standing in the center (front).

RIGHT: Scott realized he could not be rescued and wrote eight last letters as he faced death. To Admiral Sir Francis Bridgeman he wrote: "Excuse writing, it is minus 40, and has been for nigh a month." This is his final diary entry.

We shall stick it out to the end but we are getting weaker of course and the end cannot be far.

It seems a pity but I do not think I can write more —

R Scott

Last Entry

For Gods Sake look after our people

Captain Scott: "We have been to the Pole and we shall die like gentlemen"

(March 16, 1912)

As he confronted the prospect of death during his return across the vast Ross Ice Shelf, Scott of the Antarctic wrote several letters, which he hoped would be found along with his body. One was to Sir Edgar Speyer, the treasurer of his ill-fated expedition to the South Pole.

Sir Edgar Speyer was an American of Jewish German roots who became a British subject. Besides his financial interests, he was a great patron of the arts, a friend of the composers Elgar and Debussy, and sponsor of London's famous Promenade concerts, for which he received his knighthood.

Explorer Robert Falcon Scott's expedition team was undertaking an 800-mile homeward trek from the South Pole in treacherous weather, without even the boost of having succeeded in its goal: the explorers had discovered on their arrival at the pole on January 17 that the Norwegian explorer Roald Amundsen had beaten them to it.

On foot and still 150 miles short of their base, they missed a vital rendezvous with a team of dogs and supplies in poor visibility. As their existing resources dwindled, they could wait for its arrival no longer.

"I write to many friends hoping the letter will reach them sometime after we are found next year," wrote Captain Robert Scott to Sir Edgar, who had coordinated the funding of this, Scott's last polar adventure. Scott knew that there was now no hope of survival. "I fear we must go," he told Sir Edgar, "and that it leaves the expedition in a bad muddle—But we have been to the Pole and we shall die like gentlemen."

Scott, already a national hero following an earlier expedition, represented the finest qualities of a British officer and gentleman. Writing to Speyer in a spidery hand on pages from his journal, he commented, "If this diary is found it will show how we stuck by dying companions and fought this thing out well to the end—I think this will show that the spirit of pluck and the power to endure has not passed out of the race." This was the very epitome of the British stiff upper lip. Later, the ailing Captain Oates, realizing he was hampering his colleagues chances of survival, walked out into the snow saying, "I am just going outside. I may be some time."

Scott noted with typical understatement that "we very nearly came through and it's a pity to have missed it [the rendezvous]." And in a very British way he took full responsibility for the outcome of the expedition. "No one else is to blame and I hope no attempt will be made to suggest that we lacked support."

In this letter and others, he expressed his great concern: the fate of the team's families. "I have my wife and child to think of—the wife is a very independent person but the country ought not to let my boy want an education and a future." In the days that followed, the survivors of the expedition struggled another 20 miles before becoming trapped in their tent by a blizzard. From there, in Scott's final letter to his wife, he asked her to "make the boy interested in natural history if you can; it is better than games." Scott's son, Peter, only two years old when his father died, became a world-renowned naturalist and founder of the World Wildlife Fund.

On March 29, 1912, Robert Scott was the last of his men to die. Edgar Speyer withdrew from British public life when he became the target of anti-German sentiment at the start of World War I. He returned to America in 1915. His letter from Scott was sold at auction on March 30, 2012, the day after the centenary.

The very final letter from the *Titanic* that was never sent

(April 13, 1912)

The world's fascination with memorabilia from White Star Line's RMS *Titanic* shows no sign of fading. Among those who perished in freezing waters was one Alexander Oskar Holverson; a letter found in his pocket book after his body was recovered sold at auction in 2017 for £120,000 ($166,000).

Holverson was the son of a first-generation Norwegian immigrant to Minnesota. He was a successful traveling salesman for the firm of Cluett, Peabody & Company. They made shirts, including the famous Arrow brand; and Sanford L. Cluett invented the process of sanforization—the preshrinking of textiles before cutting—which is still used today.

Oskar married a Pennsylvania girl, Mary Alice Towner, seven years his junior. They had no children, and his success paid for an extended holiday in 1911 and 1912. They traveled first to Buenos Aires and then on to London. On April 10, 1912, they boarded the *Titanic* to return to New York. The following day he wrote a letter, the last by any of the *Titanic*'s passengers so far discovered. "My dear Mother," it began, "we had good weather while we were in London. It is quite green and nice in England now."

Oskar was excited about the ship: "This boat is a giant in size and fitted up like a palatial hotel," he said. "The food and music is excellent." And he was thrilled to be rubbing shoulders with the rich and famous, including one of the world's wealthiest men at the time, John Jacob Astor. "He looks like any other human being," Oskar wrote in awe, "even though he has millions of money. They sit out on the deck with the rest of us."

The letter is in remarkable condition. The ink is faded but has not run; and the embossed letterhead of the White Star Line still reads, in bright blue, "On board R.M.S. 'Titanic.'" The image of a fluttering red pennant with a white star in its center still fills the top left corner of each page.

The purpose of the letter was to give notice of Alice and Oskar's expected timetable. "If all goes well we'll arrive in New York on Wednesday," he told her. But in the early hours of Monday, April 15, 1912, the Titanic struck an iceberg and sank with the loss of 1,522 lives, including Oskar's and Astor's. Thanks to the principle of "women and children first," Alice survived.

The letter also survived, unposted, in Oskar's pocket book, stained by seawater but still legible. It was passed down through the family until they sold it in 2017, along with a poignant note from Oskar's mother to Oskar's brother Walter. "I see that you have seen in the papers what has happened to my dear son Oskar," she wrote. "It was a dreadful shock to us all. To think that he is gone and that we never see him any more in this world.

"But," she consoled herself, "the best is that I know he is somewhere there is no more parting. That is my wish and prayer."

OPPOSITE TOP: *The heavily discolored letter from Holverson survived immersion in water.*

OPPOSITE: *First-class accommodation on board the* Titanic. *The Holversons were thrilled to be moving in the same social sphere as millionaire John Jacob Astor, who, like Oskar, perished in the North Atlantic.*

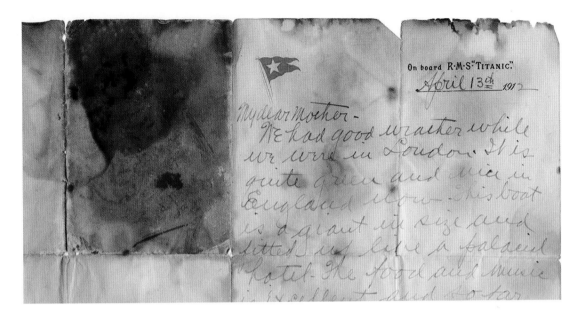

On board R·M·S "TITANIC".

April 13th 1912

My dear Mother –

We had good weather while we were in London. It is quite green and nice in England now. This boat is a giant in size and fitted up like a palatial hotel. The food and music is excellent and so far

Zimmermann offers Mexico the return of Texas, Arizona, and New Mexico

(January 19, 1917)

When British Intelligence intercepted and decoded a secret telegram from German Foreign Secretary Arthur Zimmermann, it not only thwarted German plans to enlarge the sphere of conflict, but drew America into the fighting and helped shorten World War I.

The United States remained resolutely neutral at the outbreak of World War I. Although the country's sympathies might have lain with the Allied powers, many Americans were not of British or French origin; and those of German ancestry were strongly opposed to supporting the British war effort. President Woodrow Wilson hoped to find a negotiated end to the fighting.

For Britain's part, the primary aim of its new War Propaganda Bureau was to persuade the US to join the Allies by stressing the shared values and cultures of the two countries. What really changed American hearts and minds, however, were German atrocities, such as the sinking in 1915 of the RMS *Lusitania*, the world's largest oceangoing liner, off the coast of Ireland, with the loss of nearly 1,200 civilian lives, many American.

The *Lusitania* was sunk by a German torpedo, amid claims that the British liner was carrying a cargo of ammunition. The outcry about its loss, both from Wilson and from within Germany, persuaded Germany to restrict submarine warfare to the North Sea. There, in the waters between Germany and Britain, there could be no doubt about the purpose and allegiance of any shipping.

However, in 1917, Germany decided once again to engage in unrestricted submarine attacks on any vessels anywhere it considered to be engaged in enemy activity—including those flying the US flag. In doing so it knew that it would probably provoke America into joining the war. On January 19, the German Foreign Secretary Arthur Zimmermann sent a telegram to the German ambassador to Mexico, ordering him to "make Mexico a proposal of alliance on the following basis: make war together, make peace together." This the

ambassador could accompany with an offer of "generous financial support and an understanding on our part that Mexico is to reconquer the lost territory in Texas, New Mexico, and Arizona."

Germany had been trying to foment war between Mexico and the US throughout World War I, in the hope of tying up American forces and distracting them from the European conflict. Now Zimmermann went even further, suggesting that the Mexican president "should, on his own initiative, invite Japan to immediate adherence and at the same time mediate between Japan and ourselves." Japan was at the time supporting the Allied powers in the war.

This was a calculated effort to escalate the war, to bring about a quick, decisive victory. "Please call the President's attention," Zimmermann concluded, "to the fact that the ruthless employment of our submarines now offers the prospect of compelling England in a few months to make peace."

The decoded message was shown to the US ambassador to Britain and then passed to President Wilson, who released it to the press on February 28. A few days later, when challenged by an American correspondent, Zimmermann admitted that the telegram was genuine. US shipping began to fall prey to German submarines, and on April 6, Congress declared war on Germany.

Zimmermann's telegram thus escalated and shortened the war in a way that he had not anticipated. Far from being distracted by Mexico, America withdrew forces that had been hunting for the Mexican revolutionary Pancho Villa. And Japan declared that it had no intention of switching sides.

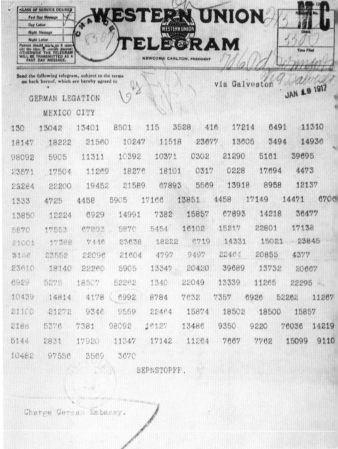

ABOVE LEFT: Arthur Zimmermann was Germany's state secretary
for foreign affairs. Before his attempts to involve Mexico in
World War I, he had tried to encourage rebellion in Ireland by
promising to land 25,000 soldiers and 75,000 rifles in the west
of the country.

ABOVE RIGHT: The telegram was sent by Zimmermann to
Heinrich von Eckardt, the German ambassador to Mexico. It
was intercepted and decoded by British Intelligence.

Stamfordham.

_G.R.I._

ABOVE: _Lord Stamfordham attending to King George V._

OPPOSITE: _A political cartoon of 1917 showed the king sweeping
aside all references to Germany. Apart from the royal surname
change there were many German titles, such as Prince of
Battenburg and Duke of Teck, which were given a British
name. Prince Louis of Battenburg became the Marquis of
Milford Haven._

Lord Stamfordham suggests a new name for the British royal family

(June 1917)

Kings and emperors tend to be known by their first names, and presidents and dictators by their surnames. In the early twentieth century, few people even knew that the British royal family had a surname. Those that did, including the king himself, very much wished it wasn't Saxe-Coburg-Gotha.

It became a source of embarrassment during World War I that the British royal family had a German surname. After the death of Queen Anne in 1714, her Protestant second cousin, George of Hanover, was offered the British throne. Five generations later, George's great great great great niece Queen Victoria married another German, Prince Albert of Schloss Rosenau. She took her husband's surname in the manner of the times, and became Mrs. Albert Saxe-Coburg-Gotha. On her death in 1901 she was succeeded by her son Edward VII, the first British king of this new Saxe-Coburg-Gotha dynasty.

With blood ties to all the royal houses of Europe, the House of Saxe-Coburg-Gotha found itself in a difficult position in the early twentieth century. Edward VII's son George V was king of Britain when war broke out across the continent in 1914. His first cousin Kaiser Wilhelm II was the emperor of Britain's enemy Germany. Another first cousin, Tsar Nicholas II, was forced to abdicate in Russia as a wave of socialism and communism swept across the continent. All in all it was a bad time to be a Saxe-Coburg-Gotha.

When London was attacked in 1917 by German bombers manufactured by the Gotha Wagon Factory, George V decided that it was time to drop the Saxe-Coburg-Gotha connection. He instructed his private secretary Arthur Bigge, Lord Stamfordham, to find a suitable alternative, preferably from somewhere in the historic line. The problem was that many of the king's British predecessors were soured by scandal or blood feuds. The Stuart

monarchs were too Catholic, and had on occasion been beheaded—not a good precedent; the Tudors were too often married (Henry VIII) or too ruthless (Bloody Queen Mary); the Fitzroys far too illegitimate; the Plantagenets too much at war with each other.

The solution came to Bigge while he was consulting the archives at Windsor Castle. The castle was originally built in the eleventh century by England's first *French* king, William the Conqueror (which was better than being German) and had been used frequently as a center of royal entertainment by Queen Victoria. Bigge wrote a letter to the Prime Minister of the day, Herbert Asquith, who had a say in the matter. "I hope," said Bigge, "we may have finally discovered a name which will appeal to you, and that is that Queen Victoria will be regarded as having founded the House of Windsor."

As a genuine surname from the royal family's illustrious pedigree, it was debatable; but as an undeniably British one it fit the bill perfectly. On July 17, 1917 George V announced that "as from the date of this Our Royal Proclamation Our House and Family shall be styled and known as the House and Family of Windsor." The effect was immediate and positive for the popularity of the British monarchy. As one commentator at the time wrote, "Their strong efforts to remove, in every possible way, the German influence and power from the Court will have its fruit in the affection and loyalty of their devoted subjects."

And today, what could be more British than the Windsors.

Siegfried Sassoon sends an open letter to *The Times*

(July 6, 1917)

Siegfried Sassoon, swept up in the surge of patriotism preceeding World War I, enlisted in the British Army before war was declared. He was admired by his fellow soldiers and decorated for bravery. But, disgusted by the senseless slaughter, he took a stand in a letter to his commanding officer.

Sassoon's citation, for which he was awarded the Military Cross, was "for conspicuous gallantry during a raid on the enemy's trenches. He remained for one and a half hours under rifle and bomb fire collecting and bringing in our wounded. Owing to his courage and determination all the killed and wounded were brought in." On another occasion he was cited for the British Army's highest award, the Victoria Cross.

On another he single-handedly captured a German trench with a handful of grenades, and after sixty terrified German infantrymen fled, sat down in the trench to read a book of poetry that he had brought with him. Sassoon was himself a poet, and despite his earlier patriotism, he came to see the war not as a moral crusade but as a jingoistic exercise in imperial vanity. He became one of the great poet-chroniclers of the conflict.

It was while he was recuperating back in England from a bullet wound that he decided he must speak out. He wrote a letter to his commanding officer, headed "A Soldier's Declaration," stating that "I can no longer be a party to prolonging these sufferings for ends which I believe to be evil and unjust.

"I believe," he wrote, "that the war upon which I entered as a war of defence and liberation has now become a war of aggression and conquest." It wasn't, he stressed, the fault of his immediate military superiors— "I am not protesting against the conduct of the war"; and certainly not of his comrades in arms—"I am a soldier, convinced that I am acting on behalf of soldiers." But he now suspected "that the war is being deliberately prolonged by those who have the power to end it."

The patriotic fervor that accompanied the outbreak of war with Germany had made it very difficult to be a conscientious objector. Those who wouldn't fight were branded cowards, isolated and ostracized; deserters could be court-martialed and shot. But as the war took its toll on the youth of the nation, public opinion shifted. Although it was still a defiant act to speak out as Sassoon did, there was some sympathy for such a position.

Sassoon was not shot. He was, after all, a military hero and a nationally known poet. Instead, the War Office diplomatically declared him to be suffering from shellshock. He was sent far away from the public eye, to a convalescent hospital in Edinburgh, where he met another fine war poet, Wilfred Owen. The two became friends, with a mutual admiration for each other's work.

In time, despite their opposition to it, both men returned to the front line in France. Sassoon was injured again and survived again, eventually dying in 1967, at the age of eighty. Owen was killed in action exactly a week before the Armistice ended the fighting. Sassoon would champion Owen's poetry for the postwar generation, and along with Ivor Gurney, Robert Graves, and Rupert Brooke, the war poets' work would represent a lost generation of British youth.

Siegfried Sassoon's open letter to *The Times* newspaper

I am making this statement as an act of wilful defiance of military authority because I believe that the war is being deliberately prolonged by those who have the power to end it. I am a soldier, convinced that I am acting on behalf of soldiers. I believe that the war upon which I entered as a war of defence and liberation has now become a war of agression and conquest. I believe that the purposes for which I and my fellow soldiers entered upon this war should have been so clearly stated as to have made it impossible to change them and that had this been done the objects which actuated us would now be attainable by negotiation.

I have seen and endured the sufferings of the troops and I can no longer be a party to prolonging these sufferings for ends which I believe to be evil and unjust. I am not protesting against the conduct of the war, but against the political errors and insincerities for which the fighting men are being sacrificed.

On behalf of those who are suffering now, I make this protest against the deception which is being practised upon them; also I believe it may help to destroy the callous complacency with which the majority of those at home regard the continuance of agonies which they do not share and which they have not enough imagination to realise.

LEFT: Having won the highest award for bravery the country offered, nobody could accuse Siegfried Sassoon of cowardice.

OPPOSITE: Sassoon's letter was an embarrassment for the British military, who tried to remove him from the public eye.

Adolf Hitler's first anti-Semitic writing, a letter sent to Adolf Gemlich

(September 16, 1919)

The German Empire was broken up at the end of World War I, and the victorious Allies imposed punitive war reparations on the defeated nation. These actions fueled poverty, anger, and resentment among the German population. In more than one returning soldier, that resentment boiled over into hatred.

Germany was on its knees after World War I, and for returning infantrymen like Adolf Hitler, there was little to look forward to. The economy was in ruins and the German Army was being disbanded. Some ex-soldiers formed paramilitary groups to pursue extreme views in the uncertain political climate of the new German Republic.

Hitler was recruited by Karl Mayr, head of an intelligence unit in Munich, to spy on soldiers awaiting demobilization who were suspected of being communists. Mayr, pursuing his own right-wing agenda, saw nationalism as an antidote to communism, which had been gaining support across Europe before and after the Russian Revolution. He sent Hitler for indoctrination on Mayr's so-called "national thinking" courses, and encouraged him to attend meetings of the newly formed German Workers Party (Deutsche Arbeiterpartei—DAP).

Hitler admired the philosophy of the DAP, which was not only nationalist and anti-communist but anti-capitalist and anti-Semitic. He spoke at meetings and showed an aptitude, one might say a vulnerability, for the DAP doctrine, which brought him to the attention of the Party's founder, Dietrich Eckhart.

He became a member of the DAP on September 12, 1919. His way with words persuaded Mayr to delegate to Hitler the job of replying to a letter of enquiry from another soldier, Adolf Gemlich, on a matter of DAP policy. "What," Gemlich had asked, "would they do about the Jewish Question?"

Jews, without a homeland of their own, were always outsiders wherever they settled, and an easy target for those looking for scapegoats for their troubles, just as immigrants and refugees are today. Jews have often shown themselves to be good businessmen and financiers at the heart of many nation's economies. "The Jewish Question" was a euphemism used since the eighteenth century by those who resented their presence and success.

Hitler set about drafting his reply to Gemlich with enthusiasm. Jews, he told Gemlich, kept themselves apart by race, religion, wealth and "thousands of years of the closest kind of inbreeding. … There lives among us a non German, alien race," he reasoned, "which neither wishes nor is able to sacrifice its racial character or to deny its feeling, thinking, and striving." All they wanted was to accumulate the wealth of the nation. "Their dance around the golden calf is becoming a merciless struggle for all those possessions we prize most highly on earth."

To Germans like Hitler and Gemlich, who had lost everything in defeat, this was all too easy to believe. But, Hitler insisted, there was a rational solution to the Jewish Question: "systematic legal combating and elimination of the privileges of the Jews. … The ultimate objective must, however, be the irrevocable removal of the Jews in general."

Hitler became the DAP's chief propagandist only a few months later, when it changed its name to the National Socialist German Workers Party—Nationalsozialistische Deutsche Arbeiterpartei (NSDAP), or, more commonly, the Nazi Party. He demonstrated his Final Solution to the Jewish Question with sickening efficiency during the war that he started twenty years later.

Letter from Adolf Hitler to Adolf Gemlich

Dear Herr Gemlich,

The danger posed by Jewry for our people today finds expression in the undeniable aversion of wide sections of our people. The cause of this aversion is not to be found in a clear recognition of the consciously or unconsciously systematic and pernicious effect of the Jews as a totality upon our nation. Rather, it arises mostly from personal contact and from the personal impression which the individual Jew leaves–almost always an unfavorable one. For this reason, antisemitism is too easily characterized as a mere emotional phenomenon. And yet this is incorrect. Antisemitism as a political movement may not and cannot be defined by emotional impulses, but by recognition of the facts. The facts are these: First, Jewry is absolutely a race and not a religious association. Even the Jews never designate themselves as Jewish Germans, Jewish Poles, or Jewish Americans but always as German, Polish, or American Jews. Jews have never yet adopted much more than the language of the foreign nations among whom they live. A German who is forced to make use of the French language in France, Italian in Italy, Chinese in China does not thereby become a Frenchman, Italian, or Chinaman. It's the same with the Jew who lives among us and is forced to make use of the German language. He does not thereby become a German. Neither does the Mosaic faith, so important for the survival of this race, settle the question of whether someone is a Jew or nonJew. There is scarcely a race whose members belong exclusively to just one definite religion.

Through thousands of years of the closest kind of inbreeding, Jews in general have maintained their race and their peculiarities far more distinctly than many of the peoples among whom they have lived. And thus comes the fact that there lives amongst us a non German, alien race which neither wishes nor is able to sacrifice its racial character or to deny its feeling, thinking, and striving. Nevertheless, it possesses all the political rights we do. If the ethos of the Jews is revealed in the purely material realm, it is even clearer in their thinking and striving. Their dance around the golden calf is becoming a merciless struggle for all those possessions we prize most highly on earth. ...

BBC Internal Circulating Memo

Subject: Mr. Guy Burgess

From :

C.(P)

To :

C.(A)

In a letter which I had from George Trevelyan this morning he writes as follows:

"I believe a young friend of mine, Guy Burgess, late a scholar of Trinity, is applying for a post in the B.B.C. He was in the running for a Fellowship in History, but decided (correctly I think) that his bent was for the great world - politics, journalism, etc. etc. - and not academic. He is a first rate man, and I advise you if you can to try him. He has passed through the communist measles that so many of our clever young men go through, and is well out of it. There is nothing second rate about him and I think he would prove a great addition to your staff."

CGG/GHS

Coleman,

December 5th, 1935.

5.0 Thus. 12ᵗ Dec.

ABOVE: The Oxbridge "old boy network" was evident in Burgess's BBC reference.

RIGHT: Born into a wealthy middle-class family, Guy Francis de Moncy Burgess was educated at Eton College and Trinity College, Cambridge. After working for the BBC, and a short spell at MI6, he joined the Foreign Office in 1944 and became the confidential secretary to the deputy foreign secretary.

Master spy Guy Burgess gets a reference to join the BBC

(December 5, 1935)

All spies need a good cover story, and what better cover could there be than a job with that bastion of broadcasting neutrality, the BBC. A tutor at the University of Cambridge wrote a glowing testimonial for Burgess, assuring his prospective employer that he had turned his back on communism.

Guy Burgess embraced communism while he was a student at Cambridge. The great economic crash of the early 1930s had undermined confidence in capitalism, while the rise of the far right in Hitler's Germany was a cause for public concern. Burgess was a member of the shadowy intellectual group the Cambridge Apostles, as was his fellow spy Anthony Blunt. He met another future member of the Cambridge spy ring, Donald Maclean, at Cambridge University Socialist Society, within which he formed a communist cell.

After a student trip to Moscow in 1934, Burgess and Maclean were recommended for recruitment to spy for the Soviet Union by another Cambridge graduate, Kim Philby.

The rationale behind their recruitment was that the finest student minds in the universities of Oxford and Cambridge tended to become the future leaders of Britain's political and social institutions. It would be easier and more discreet to engage them in espionage at an early stage in their careers.

As a smokescreen for his activities Burgess renounced his membership of the Communist Party and joined the pro-Nazi Anglo-German Fellowship. After a spell as personal assistant to a right-wing Conservative Member of Parliament, his name was put forward for a job as assistant producer in the Talks Department at the BBC.

A letter from the University of Cambridge Appointments Board, which recommended him, reported that "Burgess would appear to be much the likeliest of these three candidates. He seems to have a real gift for friendship in quite a wide circle, including a close friendship with an ex-miner here." (This was a veiled reference to Burgess's lover Jack Hewitt.) "Burgess is a man of considerable self-assurance and a fellow for whom it is easy to feel both admiration and liking."

Following up this splendid character appraisal, the BBC asked Burgess for a reference, and it came in a letter from the respected Cambridge history professor G. M. Trevelyan, an academic of unimpeachable reputation and another Cambridge Apostle. "I believe a young friend of mine, Guy Burgess, late a scholar of Trinity, is applying for a post in the BBC," Trevelyan wrote. "He is a first rate man, and I advise you if you can to try him. He has passed through the communist measles that so many of our clever young men go through, and is well out of it." One wonders whether Trevelyan really thought so, or was covering for a fellow Apostle.

"There is nothing second rate about him," Trevelyan added, "and I think he would prove a great addition to your staff." The reference was impressive, and in July 1936, Burgess started at the BBC.

Work as an assistant producer in the BBC's Talks Department gave him access to high-ranking politicians. He contacted Winston Churchill, then out of favor with the government, asking him to give talks on Mediterranean countries. He cultivated a friendship with David Footman, who his Soviet paymasters knew was an MI6 officer, a contact that eventually led to Burgess being given small jobs for British Intelligence.

Having infiltrated the British counterespionage operations organizations MI5 and MI6, and with high-level access to Foreign Office policymakers he was able to report accurately on British government policy and covert operations. His dissolute lifestyle of promiscuity and alcoholism probably hampered his spy work, although it may also have covered for it. The shocking level at which he had compromised British Intelligence was only exposed after he and Maclean, fearing discovery, fled to Moscow in 1951.

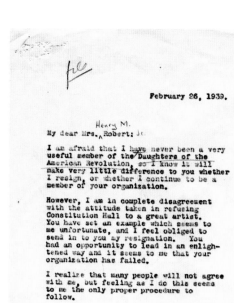

February 26, 1939.

Henry M.

My dear Mrs. Robert: Jr.

I am afraid that I have never been a very useful member of the Daughters of the American Revolution, so I know it will make very little difference to you whether I resign, or whether I continue to be a member of your organization.

However, I am in complete disagreement with the attitude taken in refusing Constitution Hall to a great artist. You have set an example which seems to me unfortunate, and I feel obliged to send in to you my resignation. You had an opportunity to lead in an enlightened way and it seems to me that your organization has failed.

I realize that many people will not agree with me, but feeling as I do this seems to me the only proper procedure to follow.

Very sincerely yours,

LEFT: A draft of the letter sent to the Daughters of the American Revolution.

BELOW: Washington's prominent figures listened to Marian Anderson singing at the Lincoln Memorial, Washington, D.C., April 9, 1939, in front of a crowd of 75,000. Marian Anderson recalled the historic concert: "All I knew then was the overwhelming impact of that vast multitude … I had a feeling that a great wave of goodwill poured out from these people."

Eleanor Roosevelt takes a stand against the DAR

(February 26, 1939)

The Daughters of the American Revolution is an organization set up in 1890 when the Sons of the Revolution refused to admit women. But in 1939, when the Daughters conducted some discrimination of their own, First Lady Eleanor Roosevelt felt that she had to write a strongly worded letter.

Membership of the Daughters of the American Revolution (DAR) was, like many historical groups in the US, established to commemorate the centenary of George Washington's presidency. DAR is exclusive, as its name implies, to women descended from people who helped to create the United States through the Revolution of 1776.

DAR's membership expanded rapidly, and in 1929, it outgrew its original meeting place in Washington, D.C., the Memorial Continental Hall. Next door to it they erected DAR Constitution Hall, a 3,702-seat auditorium that is still the largest of its kind in Washington. DAR held its own meetings there and also leased it for use by other organizations and for performances. The International Monetary Fund has been a regular client in this century, and the venue has been used for video recordings of acts, including Whitney Houston and Chris Rock.

In 1939, DAR turned down an application to rent DAR Constitution Hall to the internationally renowned African American contralto Marian Anderson, on the grounds that her audience would be a mixture of black and white fans. DAR members frowned on racial integration and, since 1932, had barred black performers from the hall.

First Lady Eleanor Roosevelt, herself a Daughter of the American Revolution, wrote to DAR's president general Mrs. Henry Roberts to express her disgust with the decision. Beginning by playing down her own role in the organization, Mrs. Roosevelt soon cut to the chase. "I am in complete disagreement with the attitude taken in refusing Constitution Hall to a great artist. You have set an example which seems to me unfortunate, and I feel obliged to send in to you my resignation. You had an opportunity to lead in an enlightened way and it seems to me that your organization has failed."

Although Mrs. Roberts replied that she wished she had been there "to remove some of the misunderstanding and to have presented to you personally the attitude of the Society," DAR's position was unmoved by Mrs. Roosevelt's resignation. It did not abandon its whites-only rule until 1952, and did not admit African American members until 1977.

Nevertheless, Mrs. Roosevelt's stand, a generation before Martin Luther King, was an important marker in the fight against racial discrimination in the USA. She and her husband found Marian Anderson a new and

better venue to perform from—the steps of the Lincoln Memorial, from which on Easter Sunday 1939 she entertained an open-air crowd of over 75,000—sons and daughters, black and white, and perhaps the parents of a future revolution.

LEFT: Eleanor Roosevelt photographed in 1933. She was First Lady from 1933 to 1945, and after FDR's death in 1945, served as the United States delegate to the United Nations General Assembly from 1945 to 1952. Harry S. Truman called her "the First Lady of the World."

Albert Einstein and Leo Szilárd warn President Franklin D. Roosevelt

(August 2, 1939)

Leo Szilárd is one of science's forgotten heroes. His pioneering early work on the cyclotron led to a Nobel Prize in Physics for Ernest Lawrence. When he heard about German scientists' successful attempt at nuclear fission, he was well aware of the destructive power that could be harnessed by a nuclear weapon.

A list of Leo Szilárd's scientific breakthroughs would fill this page. He invented a linear particle accelerator, a chemostat, and enzyme inhibitors, and he played a part in the first cloning of human cells. He devised a carbon-50 radiotherapy, which he then used to treat his own bladder cancer, and with a colleague he discovered the Szilárd-Chalmers Effect, used to separate medical isotopes. Leo Szilárd had a brilliant mind.

A Hungarian Jew by birth, Szilárd was active in scientific research throughout Europe long before he fled to America in 1937 as the storm clouds of World War II gathered. When, in early 1939, two German scientists achieved nuclear fission for the first time, Szilárd understood instinctively the benefits and the risks of the new technology. Its potential for power generation was obvious. But in Adolf Hitler's dangerous hands it could be a force for the most appalling destruction.

The immediate concern of Szilárd and his colleagues was that Germany should be denied the uranium that it would need to develop an atomic bomb. They planned to write a letter to the king of Belgium, because the Belgian Congo was the source of the best uranium ore. In typically selfless fashion, Szilárd suggested that the letter, dated August 2, 1939, should be signed by his old friend Albert Einstein, who actually knew the king slightly. Einstein and Szilárd had known each other for years, having invented a refrigerator together in the 1920s.

Einstein told Szilárd that he had not even imagined that nuclear power could be turned to such violent ends. He and many other scientists were conducting research in the same field in America. It now seemed more urgent than ever to secure uranium for their efforts—Germany had, alarmingly, already blocked ore sales from the uranium mines that it now controlled in Czechoslovakia. And so a copy of Szilárd's letter, again signed by Einstein, was presented to President Roosevelt on October 11, by another friend of Szilárd's, Alexander Sachs, who had the president's ear.

The letter painted a frightening picture of the potential of an atomic bomb. "A single bomb of this type, carried by boat and exploded in a port, might very well destroy the whole port together with some of the surrounding territory." Szilárd balanced that with the assurance that research was well underway in the US. "In view of this situation you may think it desirable to have some permanent contact maintained between the Administration and the group of physicists working on chain reactions in America."

After Sachs had read the letter to Roosevelt, the president remarked, "Alex, what you are after is to see the Nazis don't blow us up." "Precisely," replied Sachs. FDR wrote a reply to Einstein, saying, "I found this data of such import that I have convened a Board … to thoroughly investigate the possibilities of your suggestion regarding the element of uranium." This was the Advisory Committee on Uranium, which went through a number of changes of title and function before becoming, in June 1942, the Manhattan Project. Germany was unable to develop fission for warfare; and Einstein, a pacifist, later regretted his own role in America's success. "Had I known that the Germans would not succeed in developing an atomic bomb," he told *Newsweek* in 1947, "I would have done nothing."

OPPOSITE: Einstein and Szilárd. Albert Einstein was a personal friend of Queen Elizabeth of Belgium, and Szilárd wanted him to write to the royal family and prevent export of uranium from the Belgian-controlled Congo, where it was mined.

Albert Einstein
Old Grove Rd.
Nassau Point
Peconic, Long Island

August 2nd, 1939

F.D. Roosevelt,
President of the United States,
White House
Washington, D.C.

Sir:

Some recent work by E.Fermi and L. Szilard, which has been communicated to me in manuscript, leads me to expect that the element uranium may be turned into a new and important source of energy in the immediate future. Certain aspects of the situation which has arisen seem
to call for watchfulness and, if necessary, quick action on the part
of the Administration. I believe therefore that it is my duty to bring
to your attention the following facts and recommendations:

In the course of the last four months it has been made probable -
through the work of Joliot in France as well as Fermi and Szilard in
America - that it may become possible to set up a nuclear chain reaction
in a large mass of uranium,by which vast amounts of power and large quant-
ities of new radium-like elements would be generated. Now it appears
almost certain that this could be achieved in the immediate future.

This new phenomenon would also lead to the construction of bombs,
and it is conceivable - though much less certain - that extremely powerful bombs of a new type may thus be constructed. A single bomb of this
type, carried by boat and exploded in a port, might very well destroy
the whole port together with some of the surrounding territory. However,
such bombs might very well prove to be too heavy for transportation by
air.

ABOVE: Economist Alexander Sachs told the Hungarian physicist that if they wrote to Franklin D. Roosevelt, he would make sure it was brought to his attention.

Letter from Benito Mussolini to Adolf Hitler

Concerning the agreement with Russia, I approve of that completely… I have previously told Marshal Goring that a rapprochement between Germany and Russia was necessary to prevent encirclement by the democracies …

I consider it desirable to try to avoid a break or any deterioration in relations with Japan, since that would result in Japan's return to a position close to the democratic powers …

As regards Poland, I have complete understanding for the German position, and for the fact that such strained relations cannot continue permanently.

As for the practical position of Italy, in case of a military collision… If Germany attacks Poland and the conflict remains localized, Italy will afford Germany every form of political and economic assistance requested. If Germany attacks and Poland's allies open a counterattack against Germany, I want to let you know in advance that it would be better if I did not take the initiative in military activities, in view of the present situation of Italian war preparations, which we have repeatedly explained to you …

At our meetings, the war was envisaged for after 1942 and at such time I would have been ready on land, on sea and in the air, according to the plans which had been arranged. …

I consider it my implicit duty as a true friend to tell you the whole truth and inform you about the actual situation in advance. Not to do so might have unpleasant consequences for us all.

Mussolini congratulates Hitler on his pact with Russia

(August 25, 1939)

On August 23, 1939, Hitler concluded a nonaggression pact that ensured that Russia would not intervene if Germany invaded Russia's neighbor Poland in pursuit of *Lebensraum*, or Living Space. Two days later he wrote his Italian ally, Benito Mussolini, about the implications of the pact.

Hitler had made meticulous plans for World War II. "Through these arrangements," he wrote to Mussolini about the pact, "the favorable attitude of Russia in case of any conflict is assured." In truth, his pact with Russia was just a ruse to keep Stalin at bay until Hitler was ready to invade Russia (which he did in 1941). He had deliberately been raising border tensions with Poland as a pretext for invading that country. "In case of an intolerable Polish action, I will act immediately." In fact, he staged just such an "intolerable action" himself using German troops dressed in Polish uniforms, so that he could claim provocation.

Mussolini replied at once. He was delighted with the pact: "a rapprochement between Germany and Russia was necessary to prevent encirclement by the democracies," wrote Il Duce to der Führer, as one dictator to another. "As regards Poland, I have complete understanding for the German position, and for the fact that such strained relations cannot continue permanently."

The two leaders had met several times to discuss Germany's plans for expansion. There was even a timetable of events; and it was in regard to this that Mussolini now sounded a dissenting note. "At our meetings," he pointed out, "the war was envisaged for after 1942 and at such time I would have been ready on land, on sea and in the air."

By jumping the gun, as it were, Hitler could not be assured of the full strength of Italy's support "in case of a military collision." In a simple two-way war between Germany and Poland, "Italy will afford Germany every form of political and economic assistance requested." However, if all those troublesome encircling democracies leaped to Poland's aid with a counterattack on Germany, "I want to let you know in advance that it would be better if I did not take the initiative in military activities."

Italian military capacity had been reduced by Mussolini's own efforts to expand his country's influence around the Mediterranean. The former journalist-turned-politician aspired to be Caesar in a new Roman Empire. Italy had helped Franco to power in Fascist Spain; and it was in the process of colonizing Libya and Ethiopia.

As one of the Axis powers, Italy might in any case have been attacked by the Allies, but Mussolini's ambition and pride drew him into the war less than a year later. Confident that Germany would soon defeat the French without needing much help from Italy, he invaded France from the southwest on June 10, 1940. The assault stalled in the Alps, where more than two thousand Italian troops suffered from frostbite.

Mussolini turned his war effort to North Africa and to the Balkans, where he had rather more success. By 1942, Italy held sway in all the Balkan coastal states and Greece, and controlled parts of British Egypt, along with many of its African colonies. It looked like Mussolini's hesitance to join the war until 1942 had been ill-founded. …

OPPOSITE: *Adolf Hitler with Benito Mussolini in Munich. Neither man had risen above the rank of corporal in the last war yet both would control their country's army, navy, and air force.*

Winston Churchill pens a blunt response to his private secretary

(June 28, 1940)

Between May 27 and June 4, 1940, nearly 340,000 Allied troops were rescued from beaches around Dunkirk in northern France, to which they had been driven by the relentlessly advancing German Army. Despite the heroism of all concerned, it was a body blow to British hopes of victory in Europe.

Winston Churchill gave short shrift to appeasers and defeatists. He became prime minister in a time of emergency, when the diplomatic efforts of his predecessor Neville Chamberlain had failed to secure "peace for our time."

In the days surrounding the Dunkirk evacuation of the defeated British Expeditionary Force, Churchill—only a few weeks into his premiership—gave three of his most stirring speeches to rally national morale: "Blood, sweat, tears and toil," "We shall fight on the beaches" and "This was their finest hour." They collectively created a definition of plucky, isolated, indomitable Britishness, which continues to define Britain's relationship with its enemies and friends in the twenty-first century.

He did not convince everyone. On June 28, he received a letter from Eliot Crawshay-Williams, one of his Parliamentary Private Secretaries. The two men were old acquaintances: Churchill had first employed Crawshay-Williams when he was head of the Colonial Office back in 1906. Crawshay-Williams then briefly entered politics, as an MP for the Liberal Party to which Churchill had recently defected. He had to resign after an extramarital affair was exposed.

Crawshay-Williams served with distinction in Egypt during World War I, and between the wars he wrote plays and novels. It is for the letter he wrote to Churchill that he is best remembered today. "I'm all for winning this war if it can be done," he began, loading that "if" with doubt. And he continued: "An informed view of the situation shows that we've really not got a practical chance of actual ultimate victory."

Referring to the rousing evocations of British Empire and character in Churchill's recent speeches, Crawshay-Williams argued that "no questions of prestige should stand in the way of our using our nuisance value while we have one to get the best peace terms possible. Otherwise, after losing many lives and much money, we shall merely find ourselves in the position of France—or worse. I hope this doesn't sound defeatist; I'm not that. Only realist." Crawshay-Williams may have felt that, with their long association and his current position, his opinion might carry some weight with the prime minister.

Churchill read the letter with due attention and replied immediately, but certainly not in the terms that his private secretary was hoping for. "Dear Eliot," he wrote, "I am ashamed of you for writing such a letter. I return it to you—to burn and forget. Yours sincerely, Winston S. Churchill."

The rest, as they say, is history. Britain, isolated in Europe, held firm against fascism and fought the Axis powers on other fronts in North Africa and the Balkans. After the Japanese attack on Pearl Harbor, America joined the fight; and the successful D-Day landings in Normandy marked the beginning of the end for Hitler's war.

Eliot Crawshay-Williams did not burn either his letter or Churchill's reply, and in 2010, the pair sold at auction for $51,264 (£34,850). He spent the war as chief civil defence officer in Treforest, a Welsh village best known as the birthplace, on June 7, 1940, of singer Tom Jones.

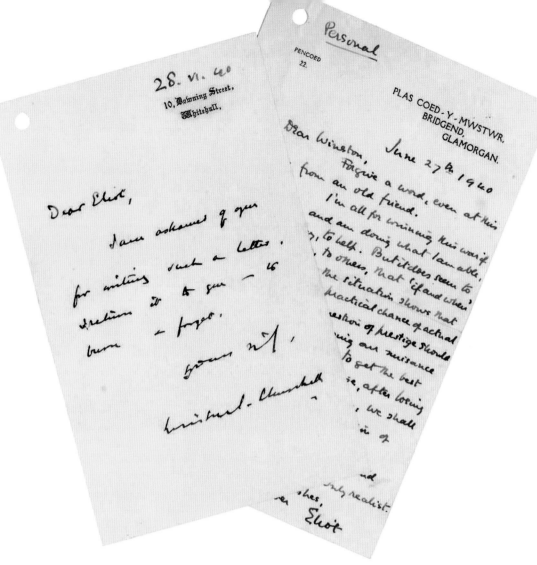

ABOVE: *Winston Churchill's curt response on top of Crawshay-Williams's letter asking him to consider a negotiated settlement with Hitler.*

LEFT: *Eliot Crawshay-Williams, writing in 1940—with no prospect of the United States joining the Allies—told Churchill that the British had no "practical chance of actual ultimate victory."*

Roosevelt sends Churchill the poem that moved Abraham Lincoln

(January 20, 1941)

While Britain weathered the storm in the early years of World War II, America remained publicly neutral, constrained by a series of Neutrality Acts passed in the 1930s. President Roosevelt could see that Britain needed help and sent Churchill a short letter offering moral support.

In the skies above Britain in 1940, the aerial Battle of Britain was fought. While Messerschmitts, Spitfires, and Hurricanes engaged in single combat, Dorniers and Heinkels systematically bombed Britain's centers of population and industry in Hitler's blitzkrieg—"lightning war." Towns and cities, especially the industrial core of Britain, were badly damaged: Clydebank, with its shipbuilding, and Coventry, with its aircraft factories, were particularly hard-hit.

The US, stung by losses in the previous world war and isolationist by nature, stood back from the conflict. Meanwhile, Denmark, Norway, the Netherlands, Belgium, and France fell like dominoes to Germany's military might. Only Britain and neutral Ireland remained unconquered in the waters between Germany and America. Roosevelt began to build up US troop numbers in readiness for the spread of conflict.

On January 20, 1941, he sent British Prime Minister Churchill just the sort of short, friendly letter that anyone would wish to receive from a friend in time of trouble. This was not a communication from president to premier. "Dear Churchill," it began informally, in FDR's own handwriting, not typed. "Wendell Willkie will give you this—he is truly helping to keep politics out over here."

Wendell Willkie was Roosevelt's defeated opponent in the presidential elections of 1940, in which FDR won an unprecedented third term in office. Willkie and Roosevelt agreed on aid for Britain and on the need for a peacetime draft in the US. Thus, the European War had not become an issue during their political campaigns.

Willkie thereafter acted as Roosevelt's unofficial envoy overseas. The letter for which Willkie acted as postman was short. "I think this verse applies to you people as it does to us" was Roosevelt's only comment, after which he copied out the following extract from "The Building of the Ship" by American poet Henry Wadsworth Longfellow:

> Sail on, Oh Ship of State!
> Sail on, Oh Union strong and great.
> Humanity with all its fears
> With all the hope of future years
> Is hanging breathless on thy fate.

The poem, written in 1849, uses a ship called the *Union* as a metaphor for the building of the United States, constructed of "only what is sound and strong." Abraham Lincoln quoted the same lines from it on the eve of the American Civil War, and was so moved by them that he could not speak for some minutes. When he resumed, it was to say, "It's a wonderful gift to be able to stir men like that."

As FDR observed, it might apply to the relationship between the US and the UK just as well. He sealed it in an envelope marked "To a Certain Naval Gentleman," knowing that Churchill, a former First Lord of the Admiralty, would appreciate the poem's nautical metaphor more than most. Churchill told Roosevelt that the letter was an inspiration. He kept it in a frame beside his desk for many years. Besides its uplifting imagery, the letter was written by a president beginning the third of four terms in the White House—on the very day of his inauguration.

TOP: FDR's brief but inspirational letter.

ABOVE: Roosevelt and Churchill finally met up in 1941.

ABOVE: *Virginia Woolf outside Monk's House, her sixteenth-century cottage in the village of Rodmell, East Sussex.*

RIGHT: *The novelist wrote two final letters: one to her sister, Vanessa Bell, and the other to her husband, Leonard Woolf.*

Tuesday.

Dearest,

I feel certain that I am going mad again: I feel we cant go through another of those terrible times. And I shant recover this time. I begin to hear voices, & cant concentrate. So I am doing what seems the best thing to do. You have given me the greatest possible happiness. You have been in every way all that anyone could be. I dont think two people could have been happier till this terrible disease came. I cant fight any longer, I know that I am spoiling your life, that without me you could work. And you will I know. You see I cant even write this properly. I cant read. What I want to say is I owe all the happiness of my life to you. You have been entirely patient with me & incredibly good. I want to say that — everybody knows it. If anybody could

Virginia Woolf writes a final letter to husband Leonard

(March 1941)

Virginia Woolf, leading modernist author at the heart of the bohemian community the Bloomsbury Group, battled with depression her whole life, following a string of close family deaths in her early years. One sad element of her written legacy is the number of letters written when at her lowest.

Virginia's mother died when she was 13; her beloved stepsister when she was 15; her father when she was 22; her brother Thoby when she was 23. It was, as she described it, "a decade of deaths" that blighted her childhood and overshadowed her adult life. She often felt summoned by those beyond the grave, and each new loss prompted a collapse of mental health. She was institutionalized on several occasions and sometimes attempted suicide.

Under the circumstances it is remarkable that she produced such a body of literary work. Woolf herself saw her condition as both a curse and a blessing. By experiencing it, and by trying to understand it, she produced her finest writing. "The only way I keep afloat," she once wrote, "is by working. Directly I stop working I feel that I am sinking down, down. And as usual, I feel that if I sink further I shall reach the truth." Water was a favorite, powerful metaphor for her mental illness.

The only "cure" was complete mental, emotional, and physical inactivity, but these were intolerable sacrifices for Virginia. Work on a new book would often trigger another depressive episode. In March 1941, she had just completed her novel *Between the Acts*, and her recently published biography of the painter and fellow member of the Bloomsbury Group Roger Fry was being poorly received by the critics. Furthermore, as a pacifist, she was very distressed by the continuing conflict of World War II, and by her husband Leonard's decision to join the Home Guard, Britain's civil defense organization. The Blitz had destroyed their London home. A few days before she took her own life, she sat down to write him a letter.

"Dearest," she began, "I feel certain that I am going mad again. I feel we can't go through another of those terrible times." Her recurring bouts of melancholia had taken their toll on all those around her. "I begin to hear voices, and I can't concentrate. So I am doing what seems the best thing to do."

It's hard to imagine how it must feel for a husband to read such a letter from his wife. "You have given me the greatest possible happiness," she wrote. "You have been in every way all that anyone could be. I don't think two people could have been happier than we have been." But without spelling it out, her intention was clear: "I can't go on spoiling your life any longer."

On the morning of March 28, 1941, she left their house in Sussex, filled the pockets of her coat with stones, and walked out into the waters of the nearby River Ouse, where she drowned. Her body was not found for three weeks.

Virginia Woolf's suicide letter was released to the newspapers, where it was sorely and perhaps deliberately misunderstood. At a time when Britain was enduring harsh privations and fighting a lone battle against Germany, her assertion that "I can't fight it any longer" was seen as weakness, a distinct lack of British stiff upper lip. And what could you expect from a pacifist? In the 1970s, however, she was reappraised by a new generation and hailed not only as a fine author but as a beacon of twentieth-century feminism. Nearly eighty years after she put an end to her sorrows, her reputation is secure.

Winston Churchill gets an urgent request from the codebreakers

(October 21, 1941)

Without the codebreaking activities of Bletchley Park, the outcome of World War II might have been very different. Today the work of Alan Turing and his colleagues in cracking the Enigma code is recognized, but at the time the project was desperately starved of resources.

Bletchley's greatest achievement was to decipher the Enigma code used by the German Navy. General Eisenhower described that success as "decisive" in enabling an Allied victory. Turing and his fellow decipherists Gordon Welchman, Hugh Alexander, and Stuart Milner-Barry certainly understood the importance and urgency of the work in which they were engaged. But at the time their pleas for extra support staff were ignored by their managing officers.

Workers were in short supply. Able-bodied men left their jobs to join the armed forces, and women left their jobs to do those vacated by the men. The team's efforts to break Enigma generated a lot of data, which had to be recorded and processed, but without extra administrative staff they had to do it all themselves, leaving them less time to do the analysis. Exhausted and frustrated, they decided to bypass their immediate superiors and go straight to the top. They addressed a letter to the leader of the country, Winston Churchill.

In a letter headed *Secret and Confidential—Prime Minister Only* they wrote: "We think you ought to know that this work is being held up, and in some cases is not being done at all, principally because we cannot get sufficient staff to deal with it." Churchill had visited Bletchley Park only a few weeks earlier, and they thought he understood the importance of the work. They told him that their colleague Mr. Freeborn was so overstretched by the shortage of staff that he "has had to stop working night shifts. The effect of this is that the finding of the naval keys [to the Enigma code, which changed regularly] is being delayed at least twelve hours every day."

Twenty unskilled clerks would solve this problem, they told Churchill. Another twenty would fix another shortfall: coded messages from the Middle East were going undecoded "owing to the shortage of trained typists and the fatigue of our present decoding staff." They acknowledged that "there is a tremendous demand for labour of all kinds and that its allocation is a matter of priorities." It was because their needs were relatively low, they believed, that their requests for more staff were overlooked. "It is absolutely vital that our wants, small as they are, should be promptly attended to."

It was a bold letter to a leader whose mind was already full of the endless daily decisions required for the continued defense of Britain. Even bolder, the group decided that it must be delivered in person, to be sure of getting Churchill's attention. Milner-Barry was given the job of traveling to London, taking a taxi to 10 Downing Street and knocking on the prime minister's door.

Although he didn't meet Churchill in person, he did have the opportunity to impress on Churchill's private secretary the urgency of the contents of the letter. Unknown to him or the rest of the team, Churchill's response was immediate and commanding: "ACTION THIS DAY. Make sure they have all they want on extreme priority and report to me that this has been done."

Milner-Barry recalled forty-five years later that "almost from that day the rough ways began miraculously to be made smooth. The flow of bombes [computers used to help decipher Enigma] was speeded up, the staff bottlenecks were relieved, and we were able to devote ourselves uninterruptedly to the business in hand."

ABOVE: Alan Turing became the best-known codebreaker, but it was Stuart Milner-Barry who delivered the vital letter to Churchill.

TOP: A wartime photo of Bletchley Park. The job of codebreaking took place in the many hastily erected huts within its grounds.

RIGHT: A German Enigma machine.

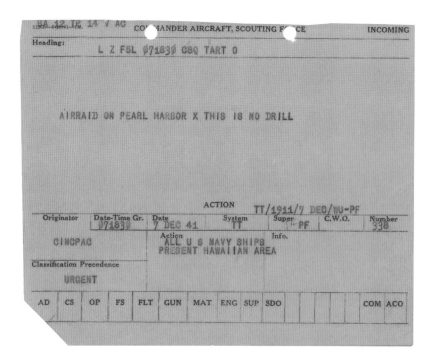

Heading:

L Z F5L 071830 C8Q TART 0

AIRRAID ON PEARL HARBOR X THIS IS NO DRILL

ACTION   TT/1911/7 DEC/WU-PF

Originator	Date-Time Gr.	Date	System	Super	C.W.O.	Number
	071830	7 DEC 41	TT	PF		338

CINCPAC

Action
ALL U S NAVY SHIPS
PRESENT HAWAIIAN AREA

Info.

Classification Precedence

URGENT

AD	CS	OP	FS	FLT	GUN	MAT	ENG	SUP	SDO				COM	ACO

Telegram reports that
Pearl Harbor is under attack

(December 7, 1941)

The attack on Pearl Harbor took place on the morning of Sunday, December 7, 1941. The war in the Pacific started with one of the oldest military tactics: a surprise attack. It ended with the deployment of terrifying new technology that has the potential to end human life on earth.

While the attack on Pearl Harbor was unexpected (conspiracy theories that US officials had advance warning have been widely discounted), tensions between Japan and the United States had been building to a head since Japan's invasion of Manchuria in 1931. The US wanted to thwart Japan's expansionist ambitions in the Pacific region and negotiations between the two parties had long been strained. Admiral Isoroku Yamamoto, commander of Japan's Combined Fleet, had been overseeing preparations for a preemptive strike on American forces and other targets since the spring of 1941.

Part of a wave of simultaneous Japanese attacks across the South Pacific region, the Pearl Harbor raid started shortly before 8 a.m. Japanese pilots initiated the attack using the code words "Tora tora." The two-hour attack hit army, navy, and marine airfields, and then naval assets at Pearl Harbor.

More than 2,400 sailors were killed and 20 American ships were destroyed or damaged, as were more than 300 airplanes. It was a devastating attack but one which failed in its primary objective to destroy the Pacific fleet. Not one US aircraft carrier was present in Pearl Harbor at the time of the raid and the bombing missed much of the port's infrastructure.

The disastrous news was conveyed to the rest of the US Navy in the most undramatic of terms. Written by Lieutenant Commander Logan Ramsey, marked "Urgent," and sent to all US Navy ships in the Hawaii area, this briefest of telegrams announced the start of a chain of events that changed the course of World War II.

The message announcing Japan's attack was only eight words long: "AIRRAID ON PEARL HARBOR X THIS IS NO DRILL."

The next day, the United States declared war on Japan and, shortly afterward, its Axis ally Germany declared war on the United States. President Franklin D. Roosevelt famously broadcast that December 7, 1941 was a date "which will live in infamy." It certainly convinced the previously reluctant American people to go to war with Japan and heralded the onset of internment for many Japanese Americans.

The assets destroyed and lives lost at Pearl Harbor were considerable but those that survived the attack enabled the US forces to recover quickly. This would prove significant in 1942, when the US defeated the Imperial Navy at the Battle of Midway, an event which many historians regard as a decisive turning point for the war in the Pacific theater. Three years later, the war in the Pacific was effectively finished when American B-29 planes dropped the Little Boy and Fat Man atomic bombs on Hiroshima and Nagasaki.

When he sent his brief telegram, Lieutenant Commander Logan Ramsey could not have known what would follow. However, the conflict started at Pearl Harbor ended over Hiroshima with what Japan's Emperor Hirohito called a "new and most cruel bomb."

OPPOSITE TOP: Having witnessed a Japanese plane drop a bomb at Ford Island, Lieutenant Commander Logan C. Ramsey urgently ordered this telegram to be sent to all ships in the area.

OPPOSITE: The USS Shaw ablaze and exploding after the Japanese attack.

ABOVE: "Pam," the fictitious girlfriend of the fictitious major, whose photograph was included in his wallet.

TOP: The crew of HMS Seraph photographed in December 1943. Commanding officer Lieutenant Norman Jewell is second from right.

RIGHT: Part of the "wallet litter" was a reference from Louis Mountbatten.

In reply, quote S.R.1924/43

COMBINED OPERATIONS HEADQUARTERS,
1A, RICHMOND TERRACE,
WHITEHALL. S.W.1.

Telephone
Whitehall 9777

21st April,
1 9 4 3.

Dear Admiral of the Fleet,

I promised V.C.I.G.S. that Major Martin would arrange with you for the onward transmission of a letter he has with him for General Alexander. It is very urgent and very "hot" and as there are some remarks in it that could not be seen by others in the War Office, it could not go by signal. I feel sure that you will see that it goes on safely and without delay.

I think you will find Martin the man you want. He is quiet and shy at first, but he really knows his stuff. He was more accurate than some of us about the probable run of events at Dieppe and he has been well in on the experiments with the latest barges and equipment which took place up in Scotland.

Let me have him back, please, as soon as the assault is over. He might bring some sardines with him - they are "on points" here!

yours sincerely

Louis Mountbatten

Admiral of the Fleet Sir A.B. Cunningham, C.C.B.,D.S.O.,
Commander in Chief Mediterranean,
Allied Force H.Q.,
Algiers.

General Nye sends General Alexander a misleading letter … by submarine

(1943)

A high point for British skulduggery during World War II, Operation Mincemeat used a tramp's corpse to hoodwink Hitler and change the course of the war. Other unlikely participants included a Spanish fisherman, an angry bank manager, and Ian Fleming, the creator of the James Bond novels.

The object of the operation was to convince the Germans that the Allies were preparing to open a second front by making troop landings in Sardinia and Greece. To do this they proposed to plant a letter with highly sensitive military information on the body of a corpse and drop it into Spanish waters. The letter would be addressed to General Sir Harold Alexander, commander of the Anglo-American 18th Army Group in Algeria and Tunisia.

The tactical deception was originally suggested in the Trout memo written in 1939 by Rear Admiral John Godfrey, director of naval intelligence, and his personal assistant, later the Bond novelist, Lieutenant Commander Ian Fleming. The memo compared wartime espionage with trout fishing and suggested several methods for hooking the enemy with false information. Setting a trap with a dead body was one of them.

Inspired by the Trout memo, British Intelligence officers Charles Cholmondeley and Ewen Montagu set out to deceive their German espionage counterparts who were known to be working in neutral Spain. Glyndwr Michael, a homeless Welshman who had died after eating rat poison several months earlier, was selected. The body of Michael was spirited from a morgue and given a fictitious identity as Major William Martin of the Royal Marines. Michael/Martin was equipped with documents—"wallet litter" in spy lingo—detailing his false backstory. These included love letters, a photo of his girlfriend, a receipt for an engagement ring, and an overdraft demand from an irate bank manager.

Many drafts of the letter were attempted but none seemed natural. In order to make it as authentic as possible, the letter setting out the bogus invasion plans was written by Lieutenant General Sir Archibald Nye, an officer well aware of military planning. The core document was supported by an introductory letter containing a deliberately bad pun on sardines and Sardinia; the hope being that this dreadful example of the much-vaunted British humor would further validate the story. It also touched on sensitive subjects, such as the award of Purple Heart medals by US forces to British servicemen serving with them in North Africa.

Michael's corpse was manicured and dressed in a Royal Marine uniform, which Cholmondeley wore for three weeks so it looked suitably broken in. Unfortunately, rationing meant that there was a shortage of army-issue underwear so the corpse was given a second-hand pair of woollen pants. An inconsistency that happily failed to ring alarm bells later.

Given the time that had elapsed since Glyndwr Michael's death and the date of deployment of the corpse, it was important to keep the body as fresh as possible as it traveled south by submarine to the Spanish coast. Major Martin, with briefcase attached to his wrist by a leather-covered chain, had supposedly drowned after an aircraft accident. Set adrift off the coast of Huelva, the body was netted by a Spanish fisherman. The now rapidly decomposing corpse was swiftly interred and the documents were passed to Adolf Clauss, a German agent who was operating in neutral Spain.

Encouraged by the fact that British agents seemed desperate to recover the documents, they were passed up the German chain of command to Hitler. The highly sensitive information it contained prompted Hitler to deploy his forces in readiness for an attack on the German-held Sardinia and Greece. The success of the operation was confirmed by messages decoded at Bletchley Park, and when the Allies invaded their real target, Sicily, the Allied forces were met with very little resistance.

Oppenheimer gets the go-ahead to research an atomic bomb

(February 25, 1943)

In a curiously worded joint letter, James B. Conant and General Leslie R. Groves authorized Robert Oppenheimer to develop the atomic bomb. Though the most curious thing of all was that the phrase "atomic bomb" did not appear in it.

General Groves was in charge of the Manhattan Project, America's effort to devise nuclear weaponry. He was notoriously single-minded in getting what he wanted, and he wanted the Bomb. Such was his determination to get it that, having decided that Robert Oppenheimer was the man for the job, he willingly overlooked Oppenheimer's communist connections and low security clearance to appoint him—in a letter of February 25, 1943—as director of the Manhattan Project's Los Alamos facility in New Mexico.

James Conant was President Roosevelt's scientific adviser. He had experience in creating scientific weapons of a new and frightening nature; he had invented poisonous gases for the US Army during World War I. Having recognized the theoretical possibility of atomic weapons he was enthusiastic that America should lead the development of them. But he also recognized the dangerous risk of an arms race. Conant had taught Oppenheimer chemistry at Harvard University.

J. Robert Oppenheimer was a brilliant, impatient physicist, with distinctly left-leaning sympathies as a student. Although he himself was probably not a member of the Communist Party, many of his friends and associates were, and the FBI built a large file on him throughout his time on the Manhattan Project. Oppenheimer wrote in his Manhattan Security Questionnaire: "member of just about every Communist Front organization on the West Coast," but Groves ordered, only a few months after appointing him to Los Alamos, "that clearance be issued to Julius Robert Oppenheimer without delay irrespective of the information which you have concerning Mr. Oppenheimer. He is absolutely essential to the project."

The joint letter from Conant and Groves sets out Oppenheimer's duties and responsibilities as their new Scientific Director at Los Alamos. Secrecy and security are stressed, to the extent that there are no explicit references to the work in hand, only "the development and final manufacture of an instrument of war." The work is to be in two parts:

"A. Certain experimental studies in science, engineering and ordnance; and
B. At a later date, large-scale experiments involving difficult ordnance procedures and the handling of highly dangerous material."

The letter notes that although the first part will be a civilian operation, the second will certainly not, and any civilians wishing to continue on the project will be offered military commissions. It stresses the need for cooperation between military and civilian participants: "Such a cooperative attitude now exists on the part of Dr. Conant and General Groves and has so existed since General Groves first entered the project."

The Los Alamos facility conducted the world's first nuclear detonation a little over two years later, on July 16, 1945, in a desert area of New Mexico called Jornada del Muerto—literally "journey of the dead man." Three weeks later, Boeing B-29 Superfortress *Enola Gay* dropped its bomb, Little Boy, on Hiroshima and 30 percent of the Japanese city's inhabitants and almost 70 percent of its buildings were destroyed. As Oppenheimer remarked after the test, "Now I am become Death, the destroyer of worlds."

OFFICE FOR EMERGENCY MANAGEMENT

OFFICE OF SCIENTIFIC RESEARCH AND DEVELOPMENT
1530 P STREET NW.
WASHINGTON, D. C.

VANNEVAR BUSH
Director

~~SECRET~~

February 25, 1943

CLASSIFICATION CANCELLED

Dr. J. R. Oppenheimer
University of California
Berkeley, California

Per DOC

By D.C. Bradley

Dear Dr. Oppenheimer:

     We are addressing this letter to you as the Scientific Director of the special laboratory in New Mexico in order to confirm our many conversations on the matters of organization and responsibility. You are at liberty to show this letter to those with whom you are discussing the desirability of their joining the project with you; they of course realizing their responsibility as to secrecy, including the details of organization and personnel.

     I. The laboratory will be concerned with the development and final manufacture of an instrument of war, which we may designate as Projectile S-1-T. To this end, the laboratory will be concerned with:

     A. Certain experimental studies in science, engineering and ordnance; and

     B. At a later date large-scale experiments involving difficult ordnance procedures and the handling of highly dangerous material.

The work of the laboratory will be divided into two periods in time: one, corresponding to the work mentioned in section A; the other, that mentioned in section B. During the first period, the laboratory will be on a strictly civilian basis, the personnel, procurement and other arrangements being carried on under a contract arranged between the War Department and the University of California. The conditions of this contract will be essentially similar to that of the usual OSRD contract. In such matters as draft deferment, the policy of the War Department and OSRD in regard to the personnel working under this contract will be practically identical. When the second division of the work is entered upon (mentioned in B), which will not be earlier than January 1, 1944, the scientific and engineering staff will be composed of commissioned officers. This is necessary because of the dangerous nature of the

ABOVE: The letter of appointment to construct an "instrument of war." Groves saw in Oppenheimer an ambitious man who was frustrated that his contribution to theoretical physics had not brought him recognition. This would be his chance.

LEFT: J. Robert Oppenheimer with General Leslie Groves. In his book about the Manhattan Project, Groves later wrote: "Oppenheimer had two major disadvantages—he had had almost no administrative experience of any kind, and he was not a Nobel Prize winner." Despite their difference in style, the pair made an effective team.

J. Edgar Hoover receives "The Anonymous Letter"

(August 7, 1943)

During World War II, Director of the FBI J. Edgar Hoover had his hands full keeping tabs on German and Japanese spies, along with a host of suspected Nazi sympathizers. Then he was sent an anonymous letter detailing an entire network of Soviet spies. But who had sent it, and why … ?

Despite being allies in the war against Germany, there was little warmth or trust between the Soviet Union and the United States in the 1940s. The two nations were ideologically opposed and each hoped to shape the new world order which would follow Hitler's defeat. Each spied on the other and no doubt assumed that the other was spying on them.

In 1943, J. Edgar Hoover, the director of the FBI, was responsible for policing America's potential enemies at home. The United States was at war to the East and to the West, in Europe and in the Pacific, and keenly aware of threats from German and Japanese sympathizers within its borders. But an anonymous letter received at FBI offices and postmarked August 7 claimed to expose a network of Russian spies at work in the US.

Hoover cannot have believed his luck. The letter named thirteen senior agents of the Soviet espionage effort in the US and Canada. It not only exposed them but made accusations against the group's leaders, Vasily and Elizabeth Zarubin: they were, the letter claimed, double agents acting for America's enemies Japan and Germany, as well as its ally Russia.

Was the information trustworthy? Some of the names were already linked to an investigation into communist infiltration of a top-secret military project—so secret that even the FBI did not know what was being infiltrated. (It was the Manhattan Project to develop the atomic bomb.) It appeared that the anonymous letter-writer was a KGB insider, and the FBI began to monitor the activities of the alleged spies.

In 1944, the mystery took an unexpected turn. In Moscow, Josef Stalin received a letter from one of those named in the FBI's letter, Vasily Mironov. Mironov, whose US cover was as Second Secretary in the Soviet embassy in Washington, D.C., again accused the

Zarubins of being double agents, this time for the FBI. Moscow, incredulous but aware that its American agents were being investigated, recalled Mironov, the Zarubins, and several other agents and began its own investigation into Mironov's allegations.

In the course of those enquiries the Zarubins were completely exonerated and Mironov was found to be schizophrenic. He had a particular dislike of his superior Vasily Zarubin, of whose "crudeness, general lack of manners, use of street language and obscenities, carelessness in his work, and repugnant secretiveness" he had previously complained to Moscow. Although it has never been definitively confirmed, it seems likely that Mironov wrote the anonymous letters to Stalin and to Hoover, including himself in the list of Russian spies he gave to America.

Zarubin, his cover blown, was appointed deputy chief of foreign intelligence. Mironov was sentenced to hard labor and, when he tried to smuggle more information to the US embassy in Moscow, shot as a traitor to his country.

RIGHT: The "Anonymous Letter" which revealed the extent of wartime Soviet spying in the US.

LEFT: Vasily Zarubin became the chief KGB officer in the United States in the fall of 1941. In 1943, he traveled to California with a view to placing sympathetic Communist Party members in industries engaged in important war production.

Copy No. 10
Copy 7's 7th CIA 5/6:

Mr. HOOVER,

Exceptional circumstances impel us to inform you
of the activities of the so-called director of the Soviet
Intelligence in this country. This "Soviet" intelligence
officer genuinely occupies a very high post in the GPU (now NKVD),
enjoys to a vast extent the confidence of the Soviet Government,
but in fact, as we know very accurately, works for Japan himself,
while his wife (works) for Germany. Thus, under cover of the name
of the USSR, he is a dangerous enemy of the USSR and the U.S.A.
The vast organisation of permanent staff [KADROVYE] workers of
the NKVD under his command in the U.S.A. does not suspect that,
thanks to the treachery of their director, they are also
inflicting frightful harm on their own country. In this same
false position is also their whole network of agents, among
whom are many U.S. citizens, and finally BROWDER himself, who
has immediate contact with them. BROWDER passes on to him
very important information about the U.S.A., thinking that all
this goes to MOSCOW, but, as you see, it all goes to the
Japanese and Germans. ⊕ The "Director of the Soviet Intelligence"
here is ZUBILIN, Vasilij, 2nd secretary in the embassy of the
USSR, his real name is ZARUBIN, V., deputy head of the Foreign
Intelligence Directorate [UPRAVLENIE] of the NKVD. He personally
deals with getting agents into and out of the U.S.A. illegally,
organises secret radio-stations and manufactures forged documents.
His closest assistants are:
1. His wife, directs political intelligence here, has a vast
network of agents in almost all ministries including the State
Department. She sends false information to the NKVD and
everything of value passes on to the Germans through a certain
Boris MOROZ (HOLLYWOOD). Put her under observation and you will
very quickly uncover the whole of her network.
2. KLARIN, Pavel, vice-consul in NEW YORK. Has a vast network of agents among Russian emigrés, meets them almost openly,
brings agents into the U.S.A. illegally. Many of his agents
work in very high posts in American organisations, they are all
Russian.
3. KhEJFETs - vice-consul in SAN FRANCISCO, deals with
political and military intelligence on the West Coast of the U.S.A.
has a large network of agents in the ports and war factories,
collects very valuable strategic material, which is sent by
ZUBILIN to Japan. Has a radio station in the consulate.
He himself is a great coward, on arrest will quickly give away
all the agents to save himself and remain in this country.
4. KVASNIKOV, works as an engineer in AMTORG, is ZUBILIN's
assistant for technical intelligence, through SEMENOV - who also
works in AMTORG, is robbing the whole of the war industry of
America. SEMENOV has his agents in all the industrial towns
of the U.S.A., in all aviation and chemical war factories and
in big institutes. He works very brazenly and roughly, it would
be very easy to follow him up and catch him red handed. He would
just be glad to be arrested as he has long been seeking a reason
to remain in the U.S.A., hates the NKVD but is a frightful coward
and loves money. He will give all his agents away with pleasure
if he is promised an American passport. He is convinced that he
is working for the USSR, but all his materials are going via
Z. to Japan, if you tell him about this, he will help you find
the rest himself.

[Continued overleaf]

DECLASSIFIED BY S.P2.CLCG-4M
ON 7-10-56

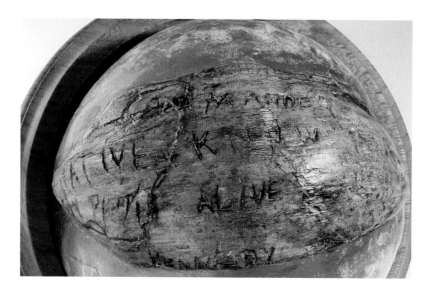

TOP LEFT: Lieutenant Kennedy onboard the PT-109 patrol boat.

TOP RIGHT AND ABOVE: The coconut shell installed in a heavy paperweight and prominent on the presidential desk in the Oval Office.

The shipwrecked JFK sends a vital message with two Solomon Islanders

(August 1943)

During his brief presidency, John Fitzgerald Kennedy kept a fragment of a coconut shell on his desk in the Oval Office. He used it as a paperweight, but prior to its life as desk furniture, the coconut had played a more important role for JFK. It had helped save his life.

In 1943, the man who would later become the thirty-fifth president of the United States of America was a twenty-six-year-old lieutenant in the US Navy. He was the commander of patrol torpedo boat PT-109, and his boat was part of a force ordered to strike a convoy of Japanese ships off the coast of the Solomon Islands in the South Pacific. The attack failed, and in the early hours of August 2, PT-109 was rammed by the *Amagiri*, a Japanese destroyer. The impact and subsequent explosion killed two men, injured others, and pitched the crew into the fuel-covered sea.

With the patrol boat sinking, Kennedy marshaled the surviving ten men to swim the three and a half miles to tiny Plum Island. A former member of the Harvard swim team, Kennedy pulled an injured man to safety by gripping the strap of his life jacket between his teeth.

Although the coconuts on Plum provided some sustenance, it was a spit of land, barely 330 feet across. Kennedy and his crew would have slowly starved had they stayed. Acutely aware that they were unlikely to be rescued from such a small, remote spot, Kennedy made several exploratory swims in the open sea, hoping to spot a more suitable island or, even better, a US Navy boat.

As a result of his scouting missions, the crew made another grueling swim to Olasana, a larger, but still uninhabited island. While there, the group was spotted by two Solomon Islanders, Eroni Kumana and Biuku Gasa, who had been passing in a canoe. Fortunately for the crew of PT-109, the locals were friendly to the Allied forces rather than to the Japanese.

Despite neither party speaking each other's language, Kennedy managed to communicate that Kumana and Gasa had to get a message to the US base on the island of Rendova. Using a knife, he scored a message onto a coconut shell and entrusted it to the two locals. Short and to the point, the message read: "NAURO ISL. COMMANDER. NATIVE KNOWS POS'IT. HE CAN PILOT. 11 ALIVE. NEED SMALL BOAT. KENNEDY."

At great personal risk, Kumana and Gasa carried the message to Rendova, and a boat was sent to rescue Kennedy and his crew. Although Kennedy never again saw the islanders, the trio did exchange letters, and Kumana and Gasa lived to a ripe old age. For his part in the episode, Kennedy was hailed a hero and awarded the Navy and Marine Corps Medal as well as a Purple Heart. He kept the fragment of coconut shell as a more personal memento of the episode.

Kennedy's war record considerably boosted his appeal during the 1960 presidential election, but in person, he played down his wartime feats. If people asked him how he became a hero, he would say, "It was involuntary. They sank my boat."

Marshal Tito warns Stalin to stop sending assassination squads

(1948)

Having fought in World War I and led the communist Partisans that helped expel the Axis powers in World War II, Yugoslavia's president Josip Broz Tito was no stranger to conflict. Refusing to let Yugoslavia be a satellite state of the USSR, he determined to forge the country's own path to socialism.

Much like the famously fractured politics of the Balkan countries, relations between the USSR and other communist states tended to be complicated and tense. This was especially the case between Yugoslavia and the USSR after World War II. At the time, Yugoslavia was its own union of Slavic states, made up of what would become Bosnia-Herzegovina, Croatia, Macedonia, Slovenia, and Serbia. Tito held them together with an iron grip.

By 1948, the USSR and Yugoslavia were denouncing each other for assorted ideological heresies and, when not contemplating an invasion, Stalin was lining up killers to send to Belgrade. Stalin's successor, Nikita Khrushchev, reported that Stalin had once said, "It's enough for me to move my little finger, and Tito will be no more." Some sources claim that Russian agents were behind twenty-two plots to kill Tito. As well as bombs and bullets, Soviet intelligence also discussed plans to kill Tito with poison gas and even bubonic plague.

One document has turned up. When the Soviet dictator Joseph Stalin died in 1953, a message was found among his personal effects. Sent by Tito, president of Yugoslavia, it read:

> "Stalin: Stop sending people to kill me! We've already captured five of them, one with a bomb and another with a rifle. If you don't stop sending killers, I'll send one to Moscow, and I won't have to send another."

Tito's letter demonstrates a certain bravura. The Russian leader was not known for calmly talking through his differences with his enemies, or indeed his friends: much simpler to just kill them. Whether through state-directed famine, harsh conditions in the gulags, the effects of collectivization, or simple judicial execution,

"Uncle Joe" was terrifyingly good at killing people—up to 20 million of them according to some estimates.

However, he appeared to have met his match in the iron will of Tito. After his wartime exploits, Tito held together the separate ethnicities that made up Yugoslavia with an astute combination of diplomacy and force. He was certainly not averse to suppressing or even liquidating dissidents but he could also balance the competing demands of Yugoslavia's various factions. Stalin was ruthless but Tito was wily.

As it turned out, Tito outlived Stalin by 27 years. Having reached a respectable 87, Tito expired in 1980 due to a gangrene-related infection in his left leg, perhaps not the most pleasant way to die but surely better than bubonic plague or an assassin's bullet. In the light of the Balkan conflicts of the late twentieth century, which tore Yugoslavia apart, there are many in the former Yugoslavia who miss Tito's diplomatic skills.

ABOVE: After the death of Stalin in 1953, Tito had a much better relationship with his successor Nikita Khrushchev, who had little objection to the Yugoslav form of market socialism.

LEFT: Josip Broz Tito with fellow communist leader Ho Chi Minh in Belgrade.

OPPOSITE: A wartime photo of Marshal Tito, who led one of the most effective World War II guerilla forces, the Partisans.

Lillian Hellman sends a letter and a message to Senator McCarthy

(May 19, 1952)

Lillian Hellman was an acclaimed dramatist who made no secret of her left-wing views. Like many working in the entertainment industry, she was called to testify before the House Un-American Activities Committee (HUAC) during the anti-communist witch hunts of Senator Joe McCarthy.

As the end of World War II loomed, America and Russia jostled for position and influence in the new world order. Empires crumbled and newly liberated countries became targets for the competing political systems of the two superpowers. Each fomented mistrust of the other.

In the US, fear of communism rose with the growing influence of the USSR around the world and the high-profile 1945 defections to the West of two Soviet spies, who revealed the extent of Russian espionage in America. The rise to power of Mao Zedong's Communist Party in China in 1949 heightened already high levels of paranoia about socialist ideologies.

After President Truman introduced "loyalty" tests for civil service employees in 1947, based on political memberships, the search for communist sympathizers became a national obsession. The creative industries, especially movie, television, and literature, have always been the home of free and radical thinkers, and they became a particular target. Individuals were accused of subversive activity and forced to denounce fellow "conspirators" in an atmosphere of near hysteria.

Those convicted on the hearsay of others, desperate to clear their own names, could find themselves blacklisted and unable to work, or worse, imprisoned. They included hundreds of the biggest names in entertainment—singer Paul Robeson, actor Edward G. Robinson, and composer Leonard Bernstein to name just three. Lillian Hellman's sympathies were well-known, and by the time she was called to testify before the HUAC, she knew what to expect. She refused to cooperate, as she explained in a letter to the chairman of the committee, John Wood.

"I am not willing, now or in the future, to bring bad trouble to people who, in my past association with them, were completely innocent of any talk or any action that was disloyal or subversive," she wrote to Wood. "But to hurt innocent people whom I knew many years ago in order to save myself is, to me, inhuman and indecent and dishonorable."

Recognizing the witch hunts as a craze more than a considered democratic process, she declared: "I cannot and will not cut my conscience to fit this year's fashions." Hellman insisted that, far from being un-American, she was "raised in an old-fashioned American tradition ... to try to tell the truth, not to bear false witness, not to harm my neighbor, to be loyal to my country and so on."

The Fifth Amendment preserves the right of the accused not to incriminate themselves. But Hellman offered "to waive the privilege against self-incrimination and to tell you anything you wish to know about my views or actions if your committee will agree to refrain from asking me to name other people."

HUAC refused to refrain, and Hellman was obliged therefore to cite the Fifth Amendment. She was blacklisted for her implied guilt of the "crime" of communism, and her friends and her movements were monitored by the FBI. The ironic echoes of life in the Soviet Union under Stalin were inescapable. She was buoyed up by a remark from a journalist, which she overheard after she took the Fifth: "Thank God someone finally had the guts to do it."

OPPOSITE TOP: A carbon copy of part of the letter Hellman sent to the HUAC. McCarthy wanted her to name Hollywood names and the feisty Hellman was not going to start.

OPPOSITE: Lillian Hellman in 1937 discussing script changes with movie director William Wyler on the set of Dead End.

May 19, 1952

Honorable John S. Wood
Chairman
House Committee on
 Un-American Activities
Room 226 Old House Office Building
Washington 25, D. C.

Dear Mr. Wood:

        As you know, I am under subpoena to appear before
your Committee on May 21, 1952.

        I am most willing to answer all questions about
myself. I have nothing to hide from your Committee and
there is nothing in my life of which I am ashamed. I have
been advised by counsel that under the Fifth Amendment I
have a constitutional privilege to decline to answer any
questions about my political opinions, activities and
associations, on the grounds of self-incrimination. I do
not wish to claim this privilege. I am ready and willing
to testify before the representatives of our Government as
to my own opinions and my own actions, regardless of any
risks or consequences to myself.

        But I am advised by counsel that if I answer the
Committee's questions about myself, I must also answer
questions about other people and that if I refuse to do so,
I can be cited for contempt. My counsel tells me that if
I answer questions about myself, I will have waived my rights
under the Fifth Amendment and could be forced legally to
answer questions about others. This is very difficult for a
layman to understand. But there is one principle that I do
understand: I am not willing, now or in the future, to bring
bad trouble to people who, in my past association with them,
were completely innocent of any talk or any action that was
disloyal or subversive. I do not like subversion or disloyalty
in any form and if I had ever seen any I would have considered
it my duty to have reported it to the proper authorities. But
to hurt innocent people whom I knew many years ago in order to
save myself is, to me, inhuman and indecent and dishonorable.

William Borden identifies J. Robert Oppenheimer as a Soviet spy

(November 7, 1953)

J. Robert Oppenheimer may have led the team developing the atomic bomb, but in the postwar years of communist witch hunts and the growing threat of the Soviet Union, any past links to the Communist Party could be inflated and used against an individual.

Julius Robert Oppenheimer is known as the "father of the atomic bomb." He was the first choice to oversee the development of the devices that were dropped on Hiroshima and Nagasaki at the end of World War II. General Groves of the Manhattan Project willingly turned a blind eye to his known associations with communists in order to grant him the necessary security clearance.

In 1943, being a communist was less important than ending the war. The bombing of Japan made national heroes of the scientists involved in the Manhattan Project. Oppenheimer became a celebrity. But fast-forward ten years: in 1953 the Cold War of espionage and counterespionage was raging between America and Russia, and Joe McCarthy's paranoid anti-communist witch hunt was raging, supported by J. Edgar Hoover's Federal Bureau of Investigation (FBI).

Communism was no longer something to be swept under the carpet but a grievous sin to be exposed. "This letter concerns J. Robert Oppenheimer," began William Borden, a director of the Joint Committee on Atomic Energy, writing to Hoover to expose the physicist. Borden was writing because "more probably than not J. Robert Oppenheimer is an agent of the Soviet Union."

In 1949, the Soviet Union had become the second nation to detonate an atomic bomb, confirming American fears that it had access to US military know-how. What was alarming to military intelligence was how rapidly the Soviets had progressed. Oppenheimer had access to the highest level of secrets, so Borden's unsupported accusation ran; he must be the spy "[b]ecause the scope of his access may well be unique … he is and for some years has been in a position to compromise more vital and detailed information

affecting the national defense and security than any other individual in the United States."

In the febrile atmosphere of McCarthyism, there was no distinction between being a communist and being a communist spy. Oppenheimer's communism was a matter of record, which Borden merely restated as his evidence of espionage. His proof was entirely circumstantial: "his wife and younger brother were Communists; … he had at least one Communist mistress; … he either stopped contributing funds to the Communist Party or else made his contributions through a new channel not yet discovered."

For Borden, the most damning evidence was Oppenheimer's reaction to the bombing of Japan. Having developed the bombs, Oppenheimer was horrified by their effect and, as Borden put it, "personally urged each senior individual working in this field to desist." Oppenheimer was an outspoken opponent of the further development of the hydrogen bomb after the war, which Borden saw as proof that he was trying to slow down US progress in favor of the USSR's.

Borden concluded that "more probably than not, J. Robert Oppenheimer was a sufficiently hardened communist that he volunteered espionage information to the Soviets; more probably than not, he has since been functioning as an espionage agent; more probably than not, he has since acted under a Soviet directive in influencing United States military, atomic energy, intelligence and diplomatic policy." It was a comprehensive list of accusations, all without any direct evidence.

Like many victims of McCarthyism, Robert Oppenheimer was never a spy. But he was stripped of his security clearance in 1954 and never worked for the government again.

Letter from William Borden to J. Edgar Hoover

November 7, 1953

Dear Mr. Hoover:

This letter concerns J. Robert Oppenheimer.

As you know, he has for some years enjoyed access to various critical activities of the National Security Council, the Department of State, the Department of Defense, the Army, Navy and Air Force, the Research and Development Board, the Atomic Energy Commission, the Central Intelligence Agency, the National Security Resources Board, and the National Sciences Foundation. His access covers most new weapons being developed by the Armed Forces, war plans at least in comprehensive outline, complete details as to atomic and hydrogen weapons and stockpile data, the evidence on which some of the principal CIA Intelligence estimates is based, United States participation in the United Nations and NATO and many other areas of high security sensitivity.

Because the scope of his access may well be unique, because he has had custody of an immense collection of classified papers covering military, intelligence, and diplomatic as well as atomic energy matters, and because he also possesses a scientific background enabling him to grasp the significance of classified data of a technical nature, it seems reasonable to estimate that he is and for some years has been in a position to compromise more vital and detailed information affecting the national defense and security than any other individual in he United States.

While J. Robert Oppenheimer has not made major contributions to the advancement of science, he holds a respected professional standing among the second rank of American physicists. In terms of his mastery of Government affairs, his close liaison with ranking officials, and his ability to influence high level thinking, he surely stands in the first rank, not merely among scientists but among all those who have shaped postwar decisions in the military, atomic energy, intelligence, and diplomatic fields. ...

ABOVE: The text of Borden's letter. The final paragraph reveals his antipathy toward Oppenheimer.

LEFT: A photograph taken at Albert Einstein's 70th birthay celebration in 1949. From left: I. I. Rabi, Einstein, R. Ladenburg, and J. Robert Oppenheimer. After the 1954 hearings, fellow physicist and Nobel Prize winner I. I. Rabi commented caustically: "… it didn't seem to me the sort of thing that called for this kind of proceeding … against a man who has accomplished what Dr. Oppenheimer has accomplished. There is a real positive record. … We have an A-bomb and a whole series of it, and we have a whole series of super bombs, and what more do you want, mermaids?"

Telephone
MUrray Hill 2-0500

Chock full o' Nuts

425 LEXINGTON AVENUE

New York 17, N. Y.

THE WHITE HOUSE

MAY 14 11 36 AM '58

RECEIVED

May 13, 1958

The President
The White House
Washington, D. C.

My dear Mr. President:

I was sitting in the audience at the Summit Meeting of Negro
Leaders yesterday when you said we must have patience. On
hearing you say this, I felt like standing up and saying, "Oh
no! Not again."

I respectfully remind you sir, that we have been the most
patient of all people. When you said we must have self-
respect, I wondered how we could have self-respect and remain patient considering the treatment accorded us through
the years.

17 million Negroes cannot do as you suggest and wait for the
hearts of men to change. We want to enjoy now the rights
that we feel we are entitled to as Americans. This we cannot do unless we pursue aggressively goals which all other
Americans achieved over 150 years ago.

As the chief executive of our nation, I respectfully suggest
that you unwittingly crush the spirit of freedom in Negroes
by constantly urging forbearance and give hope to those pro-
segregation leaders like Governor Faubus who would take
from us even those freedoms we now enjoy. Your own experience with Governor Faubus is proof enough that forbearance and not eventual integration is the goal the pro-
segregation leaders seek.

In my view, an unequivocal statement backed up by action
such as you demonstrated you could take last fall in deal-

MAY 26 1958

*ABOVE: The headed notepaper Robinson used was from a New York coffee
company, of which he was a vice president.*

OPPOSITE: Jackie Robinson played for the Dodgers before they headed west.

Jackie Robinson tells Eisenhower his people are tired of waiting

(May 13, 1958)

During World War II, many black Americans fought abroad for the principles of freedom and democracy. That they were denied similar rights at home, almost a century after the Civil War had abolished slavery, was a bitter, unjust irony that baseball star Jackie Robinson wanted to pursue.

A former soldier, Jackie Roosevelt Robinson helped to break down segregation in 1947 when he broke the color barrier and became the first black man to play in Major League Baseball rather than the racially segregated Negro League. He bore the abuse that followed with a stoicism and grace that made him a symbol of hope and change across the color divide.

The civil rights movement of the fifties and sixties harnessed a growing sense of frustration with continuing discrimination and called for equal rights. During and after his baseball career, Robinson wrote to every president who held office between 1956 and 1972, asking why equality was taking so long to achieve. His most famous letter was to Eisenhower in May 1958, after the president had urged African Americans to be patient.

Reminding the president that black Americans had already been the "most patient of people," the central thrust of Robinson's letter was direct and eloquent: "17 million Negroes cannot do as you suggest and wait for the hearts of men to change. We want to enjoy now the rights that we feel we are entitled to as Americans."

Robinson was right to protest. Powerful forces, such as the governor of Arkansas, Orval Faubus, were already fighting to preserve the status quo and nullify any changes in the law. In September 1957, in defiance of a recent Supreme Court decision to desegregate schools, Faubus had ordered the National Guard to stop nine African American

students taking their rightful place in Little Rock Central High School.

Eisenhower did not believe it was possible to "change the hearts of men with laws" and favored a gradual approach to change. Nonetheless, he sent federal troops to protect the students, safeguard their entry to the school, and uphold the decision of the Supreme Court.

The Arkansas episode fueled Robinson's argument that Eisenhower's "own experience with Governor Faubus is proof enough that forbearance and not eventual integration is the goal the pro-segregation leaders seek."

In Robinson's view, Eisenhower would "unwittingly crush the spirit of freedom in Negroes by constantly urging forbearance and give hope to those pro-segregation leaders like Governor Faubus who would take from us even those freedoms we now enjoy."

Urging Eisenhower to back his words with actions if necessary, as at Arkansas, he concluded that this "would let it be known that America is determined to provide—in the near future—for Negroes—the freedoms we are entitled to under the constitution."

Born into a Georgian sharecropping family in 1919, Robinson saw great change before he died in 1972. Though had he lived into the twenty-first century, he may still have had cause to write to every incumbent of the White House.

Wallace Stegner composes a paean to the American wilderness

(December 3, 1960)

In the late 1950s, the Outdoor Recreation Resources Review Commission (ORRRC) was established to examine how America's wild spaces could best be managed. In 1960, Pulitzer Prize-winning novelist and early environmentalist Wallace Stegner expressed his views in a letter to the commission.

Beautifully written and passionately argued, "A Word for Wilderness" is much more than a straightforward plea to preserve wild spaces for recreation. Instead, Stegner deftly links the abstract idea of wilderness, "an intangible and spiritual resource," with the equally abstract concept of America. For Stegner, the wilderness shaped American history, its character and even its soul. While the pioneers were "slashing and burning and cutting our way through a wilderness continent, the wilderness was working on us." It must be preserved "because it was the challenge against which our character as a people was formed."

To fail in the mission would be to fail America's people. Or, as he puts it, "something will have gone out of us as a people if we ever let the remaining wilderness be destroyed." Pitching his letter at the patriotic instincts of his countrymen, he warns that if we let the wilderness be polluted then "never again will Americans be free in

their own country from the noise, the exhausts, the stinks of human and automotive waste."

For Stegner, the wilderness is a source of regeneration, rebirth, and purity: "an American … is a civilized man who has renewed himself in the wild." By contrast, progress is, at best, a mixed blessing that "threatens now to become the Frankenstein that will destroy us." At worst, it pollutes. In fact, "American technological culture … has dirtied a clean continent and a clean dream."

The solution? "One means of sanity is to retain a hold on the natural world," he reckons. Moreover, "We need the spiritual refreshment that being natural can produce."

According to Stegner, the wilderness is so powerful that "the reminder and the reassurance that it is still there is good for our spiritual health even if we never once in ten years set foot in it." His childhood memories of vast prairies and arid deserts still sustain and nourish him. They are "close to whatever God you want to see in them." For readers of a more humanist bent, Stegner's wildernesses are places where people can "look as deeply into themselves as anywhere I know."

Ideas of spiritual refreshment seldom influence government policy but Stegner's letter did. It was picked up by the Secretary of the Interior and used for a speech to a wilderness conference; newspapers reprinted it, and it appeared in the ORRRC report. Shortly afterward, President Lyndon Johnson signed the Wilderness Act, which led to the National Wilderness Preservation System.

Composing the letter distilled the experience of Stegner's lifetime. Generations of past, present, and future Americans have benefited from it and enjoyed the wild country or what Stegner terms "the geography of hope."

Letter from Wallace Stegner to David E. Pesonen at the Wildland Research Center, California

Dear Mr. Pesonen:

I believe that you are working on the wilderness portion of the Outdoor Recreation Resources Review Commission's report. If I may, I should like to urge some arguments for wilderness preservation that involve recreation, as it is ordinarily conceived, hardly at all. Hunting, fishing, hiking, mountain-climbing, camping, photography, and the enjoyment of natural scenery will all, surely, figure in your report. So will the wilderness as a genetic reserve, a scientific yardstick by which we may measure the world in its natural balance against the world in its man-made imbalance.

What I want to speak for is not so much the wilderness uses, valuable as those are, but the wilderness idea, which is a resource in itself. Being an intangible and spiritual resource, it will seem mystical to the practical minded—but then anything that cannot be moved by a bulldozer is likely to seem mystical to them. I want to speak for the wilderness idea as something that has helped form our character and that has certainly shaped our history as a people. It has no more to do with recreation than churches have to do with recreation, or than the strenuousness and optimism and expansiveness of what the historians call the "American Dream" have to do with recreation. Nevertheless, since it is only in this recreation survey that the values of wilderness are being compiled, I hope you will permit me to insert this idea between the leaves, as it were, of the recreation report.

Something will have gone out of us as a people if we ever let the remaining wilderness be destroyed; if we permit the last virgin forests to be turned into comic books and plastic cigarette cases; If we drive the few remaining members of the wild species into zoos or to extinction; if we pollute the last clear air and dirty the last clean streams and push our paved roads through the last of the silence, so that never again will Americans be free in their own country from the noise, the exhausts, the stinks of human and automotive waste. And so that never again can we have the chance to see ourselves single, separate, vertical and individual in the world, part of the environment of trees and rocks and soil, brother to the other animals, part of the natural world and competent to belong in it. Without any remaining wilderness we are committed wholly, without chance for even momentary reflection and rest, to a headlong drive into our technological termite-life, the Brave New World of a completely man-controlled environment. …

OPPOSITE: *Growing up in Utah, Wallace Stegner experienced some of the United States' most dramatic wilderness areas. In recognition of his legacy at the University of Utah, the Wallace Stegner Prize in Environmental Humanities was established in 2010 and is administered by the University of Utah Press.*

Letter from Neson Mandela to Prime Minister Hendrik Verwoerd

I REFER YOU TO MY LETTER of 20 April 1961, to which you do not have the courtesy to reply or acknowledge receipt. In the letter referred to above I informed you of the resolutions passed by the All-In African National Conference in Pietermaritzburg on 26 March 1961, demanding the calling by your Government before 31 May 1961 of a multiracial and sovereign National Convention to draw up a new nonracial and democratic Constitution for South Africa.

The Conference Resolution which was attached to my letter indicated that if your Government did not call this Convention by the specific date, countrywide demonstrations would be staged to mark our protest against the White Republic forcibly imposed on us by a minority. The Resolution further indicated that in addition to the demonstrations, the African people would be called upon not to co-operate with the Republican Government, or with any Government based on force.

As your Government did not respond to our demands, the All-In African National Council, which was entrusted by the Conference with the task of implementing its resolutions, called for a General Strike on the 29th, 30th and 31st of last month. As predicted in my letter of 20 April 1961, your Government sought to suppress the strike by force. You rushed a special law in Parliament authorizing the detention without trial of people connected with the organization of the strike. The army was mobilized and European civilians armed. More than ten thousand innocent Africans were arrested under the pass laws and meetings banned throughout the country.

Long before the factory gates were opened on Monday, 29 May 1961, senior police officers and Nationalist South Africans spread a deliberate falsehood and announced that the strike had failed. All these measures failed to break the strike and our people stood up magnificently and gave us solid and substantial support. Factory and office workers, businessmen in town and country, students in university colleges, in the primary and secondary schools, rose to the occasion and recorded in clear terms their opposition to the Republic.

The Government is guilty of self-deception if they say that non-Europeans did not respond to the call. Considerations of honesty demand of your Government to realize that the African people who constitute four-fifths of the country's population are against your Republic. ...

ABOVE: *A photo of Nelson Mandela taken outside the Johannesburg law courts. From 1952, Mandela and Oliver Tambo operated the first legal firm with black partners in South Africa. Both were indicted for treason in 1956, but while Tambo left the country, Mandela remained, and in 1961, was cleared of the charge.*

Nelson Mandela sends the South African prime minister an ultimatum

(June 26, 1961)

By 1961, Nelson Mandela had emerged as a vigorous and active leader of the campaign against apartheid in South Africa. When the country's prime minister Hendrik Verwoerd declared the creation of the Republic of South Africa, Mandela gave him the chance to make it a new, multiracial state.

The dawn of the 1960s was a turbulent time in South Africa. As a part of the British Commonwealth, it had to endure Harold Macmillan's implied criticism of its apartheid policies in his "Wind of Change" speech to the country's parliament. In 1960, global condemnation followed when sixty-nine Africans were killed in the Sharpeville Massacre during a demonstration. Many around the world began to boycott South African goods and services.

The minority European population of what was then the Union of South Africa felt threatened and besieged by the world. In a referendum, they voted to withdraw from the Commonwealth and become a republic. Mandela organized the All-In African National Conference in March 1961 to discuss the anti-apartheid response to the government decision, which was widely seen as a political maneuver to perpetuate the minority regime. He wrote to Verwoerd in April to convey the Conference's call for "a multiracial and sovereign National Convention to draw up a new nonracial and democratic Constitution for South Africa."

He must have had little expectation of success. The inauguration of the new republic took place on May 31, 1961, without any national convention and with the violent suppression of a strike called to mark the occasion. And so Mandela wrote a second letter to the prime minister on June 26, noting the continued oppression of 80 percent of the country's population. "Your Government sought to suppress the strike by force," he reminded Verwoerd. "The Army was mobilized and European civilians armed. More than ten thousand innocent Africans were arrested under the pass laws and meetings banned throughout the country."

Mandela laid out the ANC's response. "Failure by your government to call the Convention makes it imperative for us to launch a full-scale and country-wide campaign for non-co-operation with your Government." And he presented Verwoerd with a choice: He could still call the convention. "By pursuing this course and abandoning the repressive and dangerous policies of your Government you may still save our country from economic dislocation and ruin and from civil strife and bitterness.

"Alternatively," Mandela continued, "you may choose to persist with the present policies which are cruel and dishonest and which are opposed by millions of people here and abroad." Mandela knew what the future held. "We know that your Government will once again unleash all its fury and barbarity to persecute the African people. But … history punishes those who resort to force and fraud to suppress the claims and legitimate aspirations of the majority of the country's citizens."

Mandela was now secretly organizing Umkhonto we Sizwe ("Spear of the Nation"), the armed wing of the ANC. "We are resuming active opposition against your regime," he warned Verwoerd. Spear of the Nation began a sabotage campaign in December, bombing not people but state facilities. In August the following year, he and fellow activists were arrested and given a show trial.

After his inevitable conviction Mandela served twenty-seven years in prison, while the world beyond his bars changed. Verwoerd was assassinated by a rogue member of the South Africa Communist Party in 1966. Mandela lived to see an end to apartheid and to serve as the first president of the fully representative multiracial democracy of South Africa.

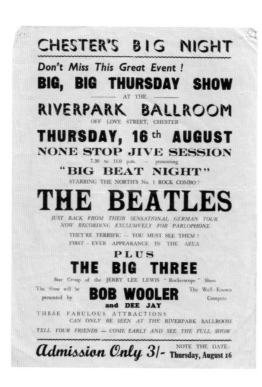

CHESTER'S BIG NIGHT

Don't Miss This Great Event !

BIG, BIG THURSDAY SHOW

—— AT THE ——

RIVERPARK BALLROOM

OFF LOVE STREET, CHESTER

THURSDAY, 16th AUGUST

NONE STOP JIVE SESSION

7.30 to 11.0 p.m. — presenting

"BIG BEAT NIGHT"

STARRING THE NORTH'S No. 1 ROCK COMBO !

THE BEATLES

JUST BACK FROM THEIR SENSATIONAL GERMAN TOUR
NOW RECORDING EXCLUSIVELY FOR PARLOPHONE

THEY'RE TERRIFIC — YOU MUST SEE THEM !

FIRST - EVER APPEARANCE IN THE AREA

PLUS

THE BIG THREE

Star Group of the JERRY LEE LEWIS "Rockerscope" Show

The Show will be presented by **BOB WOOLER** and **DEE JAY** The Well-Known Compere

THESE FABULOUS ATTRACTIONS

CAN ONLY BE SEEN AT THE RIVERPARK BALLROOM

TELL YOUR FRIENDS — COME EARLY AND SEE THE FULL SHOW

Admission Only 3/- NOTE THE DATE: Thursday, August 16

LEFT: A poster advertising a critical Beatles gig on August 16, 1962, in Chester. It was the day that drummer Pete Best was sacked by the band. Cavern Club deejay Bob Wooler had told Brian Epstein that he was too popular with the fans to be fired.

BELOW: Best (seated) originally agreed to play at the Chester gig and then pulled out, leaving the drummer from The Big Three to stand in on the night. On August 18, Ringo Starr took over the drummer's stool.

OPPOSITE RIGHT: Brian Epstein photographed outside one of his NEMS record stores in the Liverpool suburbs.

Decca sends a rejection letter to Beatles' manager Brian Epstein

(February 10, 1962)

On New Year's Eve 1961, four pop musicians from Liverpool drove to London in their road manager's old van. The next day they auditioned for one of Britain's biggest record companies, Decca. Was this their big break? Decca kept their manager waiting for nearly six weeks before delivering its verdict.

Decca's A&R (artists and repertoire) officer Mike Smith had traveled to Liverpool a few weeks earlier to witness the Beatles performing in the famous Cavern Club. The lineup included their original drummer, Pete Best. Smith was impressed enough to book them in for a one-hour audition at 11 a.m. on New Year's Day 1962, at Decca's studios in London. The journey took the Beatles ten hours because their road manager, Neil Aspinall, got lost in a snow storm. Their manager, Brian Epstein, wisely traveled separately by train.

The session did not begin on time. Mike Smith arrived late and a little the worse for wear after a late New Year's Eve party; and he insisted on the band using the studio's amplifiers instead of their own familiar equipment, which Smith considered to be inferior.

Once they were set up, the Beatles rattled through a fifteen-song set that Epstein had selected to show their talent to best effect. It included three Lennon–McCartney compositions ("Like Dreamers Do," "Hello Little Girl" and "Love of the Loved") and a range of songs by the finest songwriters of the day, including Carole King, Phil Spector, Leiber & Stoller, and Chuck Berry.

The audition went well. Smith foresaw no problems and promised Epstein that they would hear from Decca within a few weeks. The session was recorded at the request of Epstein, and Decca went so far as to make an acetate of "Like Dreamers Do" to play to Decca's

decision makers. Finally, in mid-February, Epstein received a letter from Mike Smith's boss, Dick Rowe.

The letter—which in today's currency of pop memorabilia would rival a minor Van Gogh—is now lost, but we have Epstein's recollection of its contents. "Not to mince words, Mr. Epstein, we don't like your boys' sound. Groups are out; four-piece groups with guitars particularly are finished. The Beatles have no future in show business."

The letter has been a source of embarrassment for Rowe and Decca ever since. Often cited as the worst business decision ever, it could not have been more wrong in its opinion. Brian Epstein used the Decca demo tapes, which he had paid for, to hawk the Beatles around other recording companies, and eventually the group signed with Parlophone, a subsidiary of EMI Records. No other group before or since has sold so many records or had such a profound and lasting influence on popular music.

On that fateful New Year's Day, Mike Smith also auditioned Brian Poole and the Tremeloes, and Decca decided to sign them instead, because they were from Dagenham, closer to London, and therefore easier and cheaper to deal with. However, after the Beatles had signed to EMI and proved that groups with guitars were definitely not on the way out, Dick Rowe didn't make a similar mistake with a five-piece band reviving classic American R&B numbers—they were the Rolling Stones.

LS NO. 46118
T-85/T-94
Russian

[Embossed Seal of the USSR]

Dear Mr. President:

I have received your letter of October 25. From your letter I got the feeling that you have some understanding of the situation which has developed and a sense of responsibility. I appreciate this.

By now we have already publicly exchanged our assessments of the events around Cuba and each of us has set forth his explanation and his interpretation of these events. Therefore, I would think that, evidently, continuing to exchange opinions at such a distance, even in the form of secret letters, would probably not add anything to what one side has already said to the other.

I think you will understand me correctly if you are really concerned for the welfare of the world. Everyone needs peace: both capitalists, if they have not lost their reason, and all the more, communists--people who know how to value not only their own lives but, above all else, the life of nations. We communists are against any wars between states at all, and have been defending the cause of peace ever since we came into the world. We have always regarded war as a calamity, not as a game or a means for achieving particular purposes, much less as a goal in itself. Our goals are clear, and the means of achieving them is work. War is our enemy and a calamity for all nations.

This is how we Soviet people, and together with us, other peoples as well, interpret questions of war and peace. I can say this with assurance at least for the peoples of the Socialist countries, as well as for all progressive people who want peace, happiness, and friendship among nations.

His Excellency
    John Kennedy,
        President of the United States of America

SECRET

DECLASSIFIED
State Dept. Guidelines
E.O. 11652, Sec. 3(E) and 5(D) or (E)
By _____, NARS, Date 2/22/74

GPO-818994

---

*ABOVE: The first page of Khrushchev's
October 26 letter to Kennedy.*

On the brink of war, Khrushchev sends a conciliatory letter to Kennedy

(October 26, 1962)

The Cuban Missile Crisis of 1962 brought the world to the brink of nuclear war. With the memory of Hiroshima still fresh in people's minds, it was a tense thirteen days for politicians and populations on all sides. Letters from all three protagonists reveal hot heads and cool diplomacy.

After the US-attempted invasion of Cuba at the Bay of Pigs in 1961, Fidel Castro was convinced that President Kennedy would try again before long. In a secret meeting between Castro and Soviet leader Nikita Khrushchev in July 1962, the USSR agreed to station some of its nuclear missiles on Cuba, only ninety miles from the American mainland, as a deterrent to any US invasion plans.

In August, construction work began on the Cuban launch sites. In September, under cover of night, the first nuclear warheads arrived by sea. And finally, on October 14, an American U-2 spy plane captured incontrovertible proof: photographs of a medium-range ICBM launch site in western Cuba.

America decided on October 22 to impose a blockade on Cuban ports, to prevent further military hardware from arriving on the island. Russia accused the US of piracy on the high seas; America prepared to retaliate against any missile attack from Cuba; and over the space of four days of rhetoric and refusals to back down, tensions in the region became frighteningly high.

This was now a high-powered standoff between the US and the USSR, and Fidel Castro's Cuba was caught in the middle. Convinced, with some justification, that another invasion attempt was on the cards, Castro wrote a letter to Khrushchev on October 26, urging him to strike first. "[I]f they manage to carry out an invasion of Cuba … then that would be the moment to eliminate this danger forever … However harsh and terrible the solution, there would be no other." He was advocating nothing less than a Soviet first nuclear strike against the US.

Had his ally Khrushchev heeded Castro's hotheaded call, nuclear war would have broken out. Mercifully, on the same day that Castro wrote to Khrushchev, Khrushchev wrote a remarkably personal, late-night letter to Kennedy. Making allowances for political posturing, it was a frank reflection on the horrors of war and on the duty of the two leaders to avoid it if at all possible.

"I have participated in two wars," he reminded Kennedy, "and know that war ends when it has rolled through cities and villages, everywhere sowing death and destruction." Only lunatics or suicides, he said, would start a nuclear war of mutually assured obliteration. Instead he argued for "the peaceful coexistence of the two different socio-political systems" and proposed a simple trade-off: the withdrawal of Soviet missiles in return for a guarantee of no invasion of Cuba.

"Mr. President," Khrushchev ended his letter, "we and you ought not now to pull on the ends of the rope in which you have tied the knot of war, because the more the two of us pull, the tighter that knot will be tied. … If there is no intention to tighten that knot and thereby to doom the world to the catastrophe of thermonuclear war, then let us not only relax the forces pulling on the ends of the rope, let us take measures to untie that knot. We are ready for this."

US intelligence deemed the letter to be genuine and its sentiments were very much those in which you would like to believe. But as tensions rose even higher over the following hours, it wasn't until the following evening that Kennedy drafted a reply. The world was on a knife's edge.

Kennedy replies to Khrushchev as tensions ease

(October 27, 1962)

The siting of Soviet nuclear missiles on Cuba, only ninety miles off the coast of Florida, was an act of self-defense as far as Fidel Castro was concerned, but an aggressive provocation in American eyes. Despite his advisers favoring an invasion of Cuba to solve the crisis, Kennedy followed his own path.

Once it became aware of the construction of Soviet missile sites on Cuba, the United States discussed its options—diplomacy, a preemptive airstrike, or a preemptive invasion. The Joint Chiefs of Staff favored the latter, believing that the USSR would abandon Cuba to its fate in such circumstances. Kennedy, however, argued that "they can't, after all their statements, permit us to take out their missiles, kill a lot of Russians, and then do nothing. If they don't take action in Cuba, they certainly will in Berlin." Instead, on October 22, the US Navy had begun a blockade of the island.

Tensions rose when Kennedy told the American people (and the world) that any attack from Cuba would be seen as an attack by the USSR. Khrushchev accused America of outright piracy by stopping its ships, while China weighed in with a promise that 650 million Chinese men and women were standing by the Cuban people. American B-52 bombers were kept airborne around the world in readiness for an attack on the USSR itself, while more than 500 US fighter planes were stationed in preparation for an assault on Cuba. No one was backing down.

Khrushchev's very personal letter to Kennedy about the folly of war was followed by another more formal one the next morning, containing an expanded Soviet offer for peace, now addressing US missile sites on Turkey's border with the USSR as well as the Soviet ones in Cuba. The Soviet leader offered to withdraw Cuban missiles if Kennedy would withdraw Turkish ones, and promised not to invade Turkey if Kennedy would not invade Cuba.

The Joint Chiefs of Staff decided to ignore the Turkish angle of Khrushchev's second letter and did not relay this new offer to Kennedy for over twenty-four hours. Instead, Kennedy wrote a letter to Khrushchev accepting the lesser terms of his first. "As I read your letter, the key elements of your proposals … are as follows: 1) you would agree to remove these weapons systems from Cuba … 2) We, on our part, would agree … (a) to remove promptly the quarantine measures now in effect and (b) to give assurances against an invasion of Cuba …" He added that "a prolonging of this discussion concerning Cuba by linking these problems to the broader questions of European and world security would surely lead to an intensified situation on the Cuban crisis and a grave risk to the peace of the world."

Khrushchev immediately accepted the lesser deal. But when Kennedy learned of the second letter's Turkish element, he is reported to have said, "Most people will think this is a rather even trade and we ought to take advantage of it." Despite opposition from his advisers and from Turkey, Kennedy ordered the removal of missiles based there. Meanwhile, the blockade of Cuban ports monitored the removal of missiles from Cuba and was finally lifted on November 20.

To prevent future nuclear alarms, a hotline was established between the White House and the Kremlin. For at least a few years following the Cuban Missile Crisis, tensions between the USSR and the US were greatly reduced and the crisis, so nearly a global disaster, became instead an example of the benefits of wise diplomacy and prompt, honest letter writing.

No. 10

LETTER FROM PRESIDENT KENNEDY TO PREMIER

KHRUSHCHEV -   OCTOBER 27, 1962

- - - - - - -

Dear Mr. Chairman:

I have read your letter of October 26th with great care and welcomed the statement of your desire to seek a prompt solution to the problem. The first thing that needs to be done, however, is for work to cease on offensive missile bases in Cuba and for all weapons systems in Cuba capable of offensive use to be rendered inoperable, under effective United Nations arrangements.

Assuming this is done promptly, I have given my representatives in New York instructions that will permit them to work out this week end -   in cooperation with the Acting Secretary General and your representative -- an arrangement for a permanent solution to the Cuban problem along the lines' suggested in your letter of October 26th. As I read your letter, the key elements of your proposals -- which seem generally acceptable as I understand them -- are as follows:

1. You would agree to remove these weapons systems from Cuba under appropriate United Nations observation and supervision; and undertake, with suitable safeguards, to halt the further introduction of such weapons systems into Cuba.

2. We, on our part, would agree -- upon the establishment of adequate arrangements through the United Nations to ensure the carrying out and continuation of these commitments-- (a) to remove promptly the quarantine measures now in effect and (b) to give assurances against an invasion of Cuba and I am confident that other nations of the Western Hemisphere would be prepared to do likewise.

If you will give your representative similar instructions there is no reason why we should not be able to complete these arrangements and announce them to the world within a couple of days. The effect of such a settlement on easing world tensions would enable us to work toward a more general arrangement regarding "other armaments", as proposed in your

ABOVE: Kennedy's reply to the Khrushchev letter signaled the end of the political impasse.

Letter from Martin Luther King Jr. to seven local clergymen

16 April 1963

My Dear Fellow Clergymen:
While confined here in the Birmingham city jail, I came across your recent statement calling my present activities "unwise and untimely." Seldom do I pause to answer criticism of my work and ideas. If I sought to answer all the criticisms that cross my desk, my secretaries would have little time for anything other than such correspondence in the course of the day, and I would have no time for constructive work. But since I feel that you are men of genuine good will and that your criticisms are sincerely set forth, I want to try to answer your statement in what I hope will be patient and reasonable terms. ...

I am in Birmingham because injustice is here. Just as the prophets of the eighth century B.C. left their villages and carried their "thus saith the Lord" far beyond the boundaries of their home towns, and just as the Apostle Paul left his village of Tarsus and carried the gospel of Jesus Christ to the far corners of the Greco Roman world, so am I compelled to carry the gospel of freedom beyond my own home town. Like Paul, I must constantly respond to the Macedonian call for aid.

Moreover, I am cognizant of the interrelatedness of all communities and states. I cannot sit idly by in Atlanta and not be concerned about what happens in Birmingham. Injustice anywhere is a threat to justice everywhere. We are caught in an inescapable network of mutuality, tied in a single garment of destiny. Whatever affects one directly, affects all indirectly. Never again can we afford to live with the narrow, provincial "outside agitator" idea. Anyone who lives inside the United States can never be considered an outsider anywhere within its bounds.

You deplore the demonstrations taking place in Birmingham. But your statement, I am sorry to say, fails to express a similar concern for the conditions that brought about the demonstrations. ...

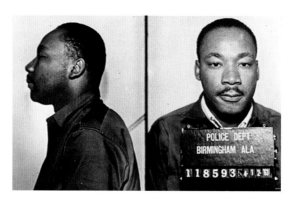

LEFT: The Birmingham Police Department photo of Dr. King after he was arrested.

Martin Luther King Jr. sends a letter from Birmingham City Jail

(April 16, 1963)

In 1963, Martin Luther King Jr. was thrown into jail for taking part in protests in Birmingham, Alabama. In his cell, someone brought him a copy of a newspaper in which seven local ministers, all white, condemned the protests. There and then he began drafting a reply in the margins of the paper.

It was a long letter. When he ran out of newspaper, he relied on scraps of paper smuggled to him by a fellow prisoner until finally his lawyer was allowed to bring him a notepad. "It would have been much shorter," he apologized to his clerical critics, "if I had been writing from a comfortable desk; but what else can one do when he is alone in a narrow jail cell, other than write long letters, think long thoughts and pray long prayers?

"Birmingham," Dr. King wrote, "is probably the most thoroughly segregated city in the United States. Its ugly record of brutality is widely known. … There have been more unsolved bombings of Negro homes and churches in Birmingham than in any other city in the nation." When accused of being an outsider and less entitled to join the protests than a local, he replied that "I am in Birmingham because injustice is here. … Injustice anywhere is a threat to justice everywhere." He had been arrested on a charge of parading without a permit—under an unjust law hurriedly passed less than a week earlier to suppress the coordinated actions of the Birmingham campaign.

The seven ministers, while sympathetic to the cause of desegregation, argued that it should be fought in the courts, not on the streets. That, as King pointed out, was easy for them to say, lacking the urgency that 340 years of slavery and discrimination gave the black American. When white men suggested that "colored people will receive equal rights eventually, but it is possible that you are in too great a religious hurry," he countered that "the time is always ripe to do right."

In one powerful paragraph within his letter, Martin Luther King Jr. spelled out for the white men just what being black in a segregated society meant. "When you have seen vicious mobs lynch your mothers and fathers at will and drown your sisters and brothers at whim,

when you have seen hate-filled policemen curse, kick and even kill your black brothers and sisters … when you seek to explain to your six-year-old daughter why she can't go to the public amusement park that has just been advertised on television, and see tears welling up in her eyes when she is told that Funtown is closed to colored children … there comes a time when the Cup of Endurance runs over."

Much of the letter was a defense of nonviolent civil disobedience: "We have not made a single gain in civil rights without determined legal and non-violent pressure. … Privileged groups seldom give up their privileges voluntarily." Civil disobedience could be found in the Bible, where Shadrach, Meshach, and Abednego broke Nebuchadnezzar II's laws; and in America's own origins at the Boston Tea Party. Hitler's outrages were legal in Germany; were men wrong to resist them?

King very directly expressed his disappointment with the nation's white religious leaders: "the white moderate who is more devoted to 'order' than to justice. … I have heard many ministers say 'those are social issues, with which the Gospel has no real concern.' … Is organized religion too inextricably bound to the status quo to save our nation and the world?"

It is, as you might expect from Martin Luther King Jr., an impassioned letter, full of his trademark oratorical skills, rooted in the Bible, and given insistence by his use of repeated phrases and questions. The circumstances of its writing give it an immediacy and an anger that fly off the page. It has become a standard text for students of American society and politics, appearing in over fifty anthologies in the decades after King felt moved to write it.

Profumo's resignation puts an end to British politics' biggest sex scandal

(June 4, 1963)

Politics and sex scandals are so often splashed across the press that they no longer end a politician's career. Back in 1960s Britain, however, exposure was a source of disgrace and shame that lost people their careers and, in some cases, their lives.

John Profumo was a distinguished British politician. During World War II, he was simultaneously a Member of Parliament and a serving officer who fought in both North Africa and in the D-Day landings in Normandy. Rising through the ranks of the Conservative Party, in 1960 he was appointed Secretary of State for War by Prime Minister Harold Macmillan.

Profumo was married to the actress Valerie Hobson. Her greatest moments on screen were in David Lean's version of *Great Expectations* and the classic Ealing Studios black comedy *Kind Hearts and Coronets*. Being married to a prominent politician allowed her to continue to enjoy life in the spotlight, and she gave up acting when she married Profumo. Her farewell stage appearance was in *The King and I* opposite Herbert Lom.

Her husband had a brief affair in 1961 with Christine Keeler, a call girl he met at a high-society pool party. It lasted only a few weeks before Profumo brought it to an end. But in 1962, two other men with whom Keeler had had relationships were involved in a shooting. She became the object of prying press attention and details emerged, not only of her affair with Profumo but of another one with a Naval attaché at the Soviet embassy in London, Yevgeny Ivanov.

The affairs had overlapped, and Ivanov had been at the pool party with Keeler and Profumo. This potential breach of security from war minister to Soviet agent rang alarm bells in the corridors of power, but in those days the British press exercised a certain discreet restraint about the private lives of public figures. It was only when a political opponent used the cloak of parliamentary immunity (freedom from libel prosecution) to accuse Profumo of compromising state secrets that the affair was openly discussed.

Profumo denied it, but as journalists dug deeper, it emerged that the minister, although an honorable man, was no stranger to injudicious casual affairs. Before the war, and his marriage, he had conducted an affair with a German model who later worked for German intelligence in Paris after the fall of the French capital. His affair with Keeler was confirmed. Lying to fellow Members of Parliament was in those days seen as a cardinal sin, and Profumo decided that he must write a letter to his prime minister.

"You will recollect," he wrote, "that on 22 March, following certain allegations made in Parliament, I made a personal statement. In my statement I said there had been no impropriety in this association. To my very deep regret I have to admit that this was not true, and that I misled you and my colleagues and the House." John Profumo felt that he had no option but to resign from government, a resignation that Harold Macmillan gratefully accepted.

An inquiry found no evidence of damage to the security of the country, but John Profumo spent the rest of his life trying to atone for his folly through charitable work. His wife stood by him. The government was rocked by the very public scandal, and Macmillan himself resigned later in the year. Ivanov was recalled to Moscow. Keeler was hounded by the press, and after two short marriages, withdrew from public life and lived alone. She died in 2017. Simon Ward, the man accused of being Keeler's pimp and introducing her to both Profumo and Ivanov, committed suicide during his trial.

Top Secret and Personal

19th June, 1963.

Rec: 19.6.63.

Dear Arthur,

John Dennis PROFUMO

showed you recently a PF on Gisela Hendrina KLEIN about whom our two offices corresponded before the war, e.g. your L.260(123)B.2b of 5th July, 1938, and our   of 21st July, 1938.

2. Although it is not particularly relevant to the current notorious case, Geoffrey thought you might like to have for your files, the attached copy of a report from our representative   dated 2nd October 1950, which makes mention of an association between Gisela KLEIN and PROFUMO which began ca. 1933 and had apparently not ceased at the time of this report. The report was based on information from four different sources in   The non-PROFUMO items were included in our letter dated 5th December, 1951 to C.W. CAIN of your office.

3. On 17th January 1952 our representative   wrote to P.C.D. in connection with the application of Mrs. Gisela Hendrina WINEGARD or WEINGARD (nee KLEIN) for a visa to visit the U.K. This letter contains the following paragraphs:

"Mrs. WINEGARD refuses to give any definite reference in the U.K. where she says she has a "great many friends".

"We have good reason to believe that Mr. & Mrs. WINEGARD have recently engaged in blackmailing activities and now think it possible that their intended visit to the U.K. may be connected with this affair."

Yours ever

Cyril Mackay.

for

THIS IS A COPY
ORIGINAL DOCUMENT RETAINED
IN DEPARTMENT UNDER SECTION
3(4) OF THE PUBLIC RECORDS
ACT 1958 DECEMBER 2016

A. S. Martin, Esq.,
M.I.5.

Top Secret and Personal

TOP: Secretary of State for War, John Profumo.

ABOVE: Christine Keeler.

LEFT: After his resignation it was revealed that MI5 already had a file on Profumo from an earlier dalliance with a German model.

Che Guevara tells Fidel Castro he wants to continue the fight

(April 1, 1965)

Marxist revolutionary Ernesto "Che" Guevara was second-in-command to Fidel Castro during the overthrow of the Cuban dictator, the US-backed Fulgencio Batista. After the establishment of their communist state, Che took his leave of Fidel in a letter that reviewed their partnership.

Che Guevara wanted to export the successful Cuban Revolution to countries around the world, while Castro preferred to stay and lead his country. Fidel was the Cuban after all; Che was an Argentinian drawn to Marxism by the poverty and disease, induced by capitalism, which he saw all over South America.

In 1954, he had witnessed the CIA toppling the socialist government of Guatemala at the request of a private American corporation, the United Fruit Company, whose work practices—and profits—the government was restricting. The company had been accustomed to running Guatemala as its own private banana republic. Guevara met Castro in Mexico City later that year and forged a revolutionary friendship that would ultimately topple the US-backed Cuban government. A defeated Batista fled Cuba on New Year's Day 1959.

Che's contributions to the new Cuba included a literacy program and agricultural reforms. His tactical genius helped repel the disastrous US invasion at Cuba's Bay of Pigs, and he was instrumental in installing the Soviet nuclear warheads that precipitated the Cuban Missile Crisis. He acted as an international ambassador for Cuba's brand of socialism, and this, combined with his earlier travels in South America, convinced him of the need for global revolution.

In 1965, he left Cuba to kick-start revolutionary change abroad, at first in the Congo and later in Bolivia. Before his departure, he wrote Castro a farewell letter, which he intended to be made public in the event of his death. He expected to die for the revolutionary cause. As he recalled in the letter: "One day they came by and asked who should be notified in case of death, and the real possibility of it struck us all. Later we knew it was true, that in a revolution one wins or dies."

He explained his departure: "Other nations of the world summon my modest efforts of assistance. I can do that which is denied you due to your responsibility as the head of Cuba, and the time has come for us to part." Privately, his exit may also have had something to do with the failure of his industrial reform program, and his admiration for the Chinese brand of communism over Castro's preferred Soviet version. But in this letter, intended for publication, he was fulsome in his praise for Castro.

"My only serious failing [during the revolution] was not having … understood quickly enough your qualities as a leader and a revolutionary. I have lived magnificent days," he reflected. "I carry to new battlefronts the faith that you have taught me. … Wherever I am I will feel the responsibility of being a Cuban revolutionary."

In the letter he resigned from his political and military offices and renounced his Cuban citizenship, symbolically aligning himself with a more global community of communism. Guevara's efforts at sparking revolution in the Congo failed. "There is no will to fight," he complained—and in 1966, he traveled to Bolivia in search of a more fruitful revolutionary movement. There, he had rather more success, but he was captured by government forces backed by the CIA. He was hastily executed to avoid the international attention that would be focused on any formal trial. After his death he became an icon of the antiestablishment movement of the 1960s, the idealistic revolutionary face on a million T-shirts and posters.

Che Guevara's resignation letter to Fidel Castro

At this moment I remember many things: when I met you in Maria Antonia's house, when you proposed I come along, all the tensions involved in the preparations. One day they came by and asked who should be notified in case of death, and the real possibility of it struck us all. Later we knew it was true, that in a revolution one wins or dies (if it is a real one). Many comrades fell along the way to victory.

Today everything has a less dramatic tone, because we are more mature, but the event repeats itself. I feel that I have fulfilled the part of my duty that tied me to the Cuban revolution in its territory, and I say farewell to you, to the comrades, to your people, who now are mine.

I formally resign my positions in the leadership of the party, my post as minister, my rank of commander, and my Cuban citizenship. Nothing legal binds me to Cuba. The only ties are of another nature—those that cannot be broken as can appointments to posts.

Reviewing my past life, I believe I have worked with sufficient integrity and dedication to consolidate the revolutionary triumph. My only serious failing was not having had more confidence in you from the first moments in the Sierra Maestra, and not having understood quickly enough your qualities as a leader and a revolutionary.

I have lived magnificent days, and at your side I felt the pride of belonging to our people in the brilliant yet sad days of the Caribbean [Missile] crisis. Seldom has a statesman been more brilliant as you were in those days. I am also proud of having followed you without hesitation, of having identified with your way of thinking and of seeing and appraising dangers and principles.

Other nations of the world summon my modest efforts of assistance. I can do that which is denied you due to your responsibility as the head of Cuba, and the time has come for us to part.

You should know that I do so with a mixture of joy and sorrow. I leave here the purest of my hopes as a builder and the dearest of those I hold dear. And I leave a people who received me as a son. That wounds a part of my spirit. I carry to new battlefronts the faith that you taught me, the revolutionary spirit of my people, the feeling of fulfilling the most sacred of duties: to fight against imperialism wherever it may be. …

JAMES W. McCORD, JR.
7 WINDER COURT
ROCKVILLE, MARYLAND 20850

TO: JUDGE SIRICA   March 19, 1973

Certain questions have been posed to me from your honor through the probation
officer, dealing with details of the case, motivations, intent and mitigating
circumstances.

In endeavoring to respond to these questions, I am whipsawed in a variety of
legalities. First, I may be called before a Senate Committee investigating
this matter. Secondly, I may be involved in a civil suit, and thirdly there may
be a new trial at some future date. Fourthly, the probation officer may be
called before the Senate Committee to present testimony regarding what may
otherwise be a privileged communication between defendant and Judge, as I
understand it; if I answered certain questions to the probation officer, it is
possible such answers could become a matter of record in the Senate and therefore available for use in the other proceedings just described. My answers
would, it would seem to me, to violate my fifth amendment rights, and possibly
my 6th amendment right to counsel asxpossibixyxmtherxmxtxx and possibly other rights.

On the other hand, to fail to answer your questions may appear to be non-cooperation, and I can therefore expect a much more severe sentence.

There are further considerations which are not to be lightly taken. Several
members of my family have expressed fear for my life if I disclose knowledge of
the facts in this matter, either publicly for to any government representative.
Whereas I do not share their concerns to the same degree, nevertheless, I do
believe that retaliatory measures will be taken against me, my family, and my
friends should I disclose such facts. Such retaliation could destroy careers,
income, and reputations of persons who are innocent of any guilt whatever.

Be that as it may, in the interests of justice, and in the interests of restoring
faith in the criminal justice system, which faith has been severely damaged in
this case, I will state the following to you at this time which I hope may be
of help to you in meting out justice in this case:

1. There was political pressure applied to the defendants to plead guilty and
   remain silent.

2. Perjury occurred during the trial in matters highly material to the very
   structure, orientation, and impact of the government's case, and to the
   motivation and intent of the defendants.

3. Others involved in the Watergate operation were not identified during the
   trial, when they could have been by those testifying.

ABOVE: The letter from McCord that reignited the Watergate case and ultimately led to a president's downfall.

LEFT: James McCord testifying to the Senate Watergate Committee on April 22, 1973, with one of the bugging devices used to eavesdrop on the Democrats.

James McCord writes to Judge John Sirica after the Watergate trial

(March 19, 1973)

The White House Plumbers was a secret group of security experts set up by the White House, as their name implies, to stop damaging leaks, such as the Pentagon Papers. Rule one when you're a secret organization: don't put your name on the door of your office.

It was a joke by one of the group, G. Gordon Liddy, putting a sign on the door that read "The Plumbers"; and although it was quickly taken down, the name caught on. The Plumbers' first dirty job was to try to discredit Daniel Ellsberg, the former military strategist who had leaked the Pentagon Papers about the conduct of the Vietnam War to the national press.

In 1972, as President Nixon sought a second term, the Plumbers became involved in the Campaign to Re-elect the President (CRP). Liddy, a lawyer and former FBI agent, proposed to bug the offices of the Democratic National Committee in Washington's Watergate buildings. The bugging, disguised as a burglary, was carried out by a team of Plumbers under James McCord, the CRP security coordinator.

Only after the "break-in" on May 28 did the Plumbers discover that the taps they'd installed weren't working properly. A second burglary was undertaken in the early hours of June 18, which went badly wrong. An alert night watchman noticed that locks had been tampered with and called the police. The Plumbers' lookout didn't notice the arrival of the police because the officers were dressed as hippies, having come from an undercover street crime patrol. They caught five Plumbers red-handed, including McCord—complete with lock picks, cameras, and bundles of large-denomination cash—like a bunch of cartoon cat burglars.

The White House distanced itself from the crime, hinting at CIA and Cuban involvement. Despite the known connections of the perpetrators to the CRP, Nixon was reelected by a massive landslide. All five burglars, along with Liddy and another ex-CIA Plumber Howard Hunt, were tried in January 1973, and convicted ten days after President Nixon's second inauguration.

The Plumbers' *omertà*, or vow of silence, had successfully avoided any linkage with the Nixon campaign.

Then in March 1973, one of the convicted, James McCord, wrote a letter to Judge John Sirica, who had tried him and who suspected that a high-level conspiracy was behind the Watergate break-ins. McCord prefaced his letter with concern for his own legal position, livelihood, and life. "I do believe that retaliatory measures will be taken against me, my family, and my friends." Nevertheless, "in the interests of restoring faith in the criminal justice system … I will state the following, which I hope may be of help to you in meting out justice in this case."

McCord had decided to set the record straight. "There was political pressure applied to the defendants to plead guilty and remain silent," he began. "Perjury occurred during the trial. … Others involved," hinted McCord, "were not identified during the trial when they could have been by those testifying." Above all, he flatly rebutted the White House's version of events. "The Watergate operation was not a CIA operation. The Cubans may have been misled by others into believing that it was a CIA operation. I know for a fact that it was not."

Nine months after the break-ins, McCord's letter reignited public interest in Watergate, which the White House had hoped was being forgotten. Renewed press investigations, especially by the *Washington Post*'s Bob Woodward and Carl Bernstein, exposed a vipers' nest of dirty tricks sanctioned by Richard "Tricky Dickie" Nixon. He resigned on August 9, 1974, to avoid impeachment, and was pardoned a month later by his former vice president and successor Gerald Ford—a case of painting rather than plumbing, perhaps. So much for "no whitewash at the White House."

APPLE COMPUTER COMPANY
PARTNERSHIP AGREEMENT

TO WHOM IT MAY CONCERN: **AMENDMENT**

By virtue of a re-assessment of understandings by and between all parties
to the Agreement of April 1, 1976, WOZNIAK, JOBS, and WAYNE, the
following modifications and amendments are herewith appended to the said
Agreement, and made a part thereof. These modifications and amendments,
having been concluded on this 12th day of April, 1976, hereby supercede, and
render void, all contrary understandings given in the Agreement of April 1, 1976.

ARTICLE A:
As of the date of this amendment, WAYNE shall hereinafter cease to function in
the status of "Partner" to the aforementioned Agreement, and all obligations,
responsibilities, agreements, and understandings of the Agreement of April 1,
1976, are herewith terminated. It is specifically understood, and agreed to,
by all of the parties to the original agreement, and the amendments hereto
appended, WOZNIAK, JOBS, and WAYNE, that that portion of all financial
obligations incurred by WAYNE, on the part of the COMPANY, prior to the
date of this amendment, is herewith terminated, and that WAYNE's portion
of obligations (10%) to the creditors of the COMPANY are herewith assumed,
jointly and equally, by the remaining partners to the original agreement,
namely, WOZNIAK and JOBS. It is further mutually understood, and agreed,
that WAYNE shall incur no obligations or responsibilities in, or for, the
COMPANY, nor shall WAYNE be held liable in any litigation, initiated by or
instituted against, the COMPANY, with regard to the conduct of the COMPANY's
business with any creditor, vendor, customer, or any other party, nor with
reference to or arising from any product of the COMPANY, as of the first day
of April, 1976.

ARTICLE B:
In consideration of the relinquishment of WAYNE's former percentage of
ownership, and for all efforts thusfar conducted in honor of the aforementioned
agreement during its term of activity, the remaining parties to the partnership,
WOZNIAK, and JOBS, agree to pay and deliver to WAYNE, as their sole obligations
under the terms of this amendment, the sum of eight hundred dollars ($800.00).

IN WITNESS WHEREOF: These amendments have been appended to the original
Agreement and made a part thereof, and have been executed by each of the parties
hereto, on this 12th day of April, 1976.

Mr. Stephen G. Wozniak (WOZNIAK)

Mr. Steven P. Jobs (JOBS)

Mr. Ronald G. Wayne (WAYNE)

*ABOVE: Ronald Wayne bowed out of the company by
signing this letter of agreement. He even lost out when
he sold the document.*

Ronald Wayne sells his 10 percent share in Apple for $800

(April 12, 1976)

Regret is generally a futile emotion. Former Atari employee Ronald Wayne has expressed few regrets about a financial decision he made back in 1976, which has left him $100 billion poorer than he might have been.

In 1976, Ronald Wayne was designing documentation systems for arcade game pioneers Atari, where among his fellow workers were two guys called Steve—surnames Jobs and Wozniak. Wayne had an engineer's mind, insightful and adept at problem-solving. His colleagues were young men—Woz was sixteen years younger than Wayne, and Jobs was almost half Wayne's age. Wayne, then forty-one years old, had life experience where the Steves had the uninhibited ambition of youth.

Wayne had lived enough to know his limitations. Five years earlier he had tried to move beyond employment to set up his own business, selling slot machines to amusement arcades. The venture failed, and as he recalled later, "I discovered very quickly that I had no business being in business. I was far better working in engineering." The failure traumatized Wayne, who insisted on paying back his investors over the course of the following year.

At Atari, Jobs and Wozniak argued about the future of computers and sometimes turned to the older, more experienced man for his opinion on points of contention. On one such evening after work, they all went back to Wayne's place to thrash out the topic of the day. It was clear that Wozniak and Jobs were going places, and that night they talked about setting up a new company to develop their ideas. They knew that they would argue about the way forward—it was how they operated—and so they invited Wayne to be a third cofounder, to settle any disputes. It was a generous offer, which Wayne accepted. He would get 10 percent of the profits, Steve and Steve 45 percent each.

Ronald Wayne played a full part in setting up the company. He drafted the articles of partnership between the three of them and wrote the manual for the Apple I, the company's first product. Wayne also designed Apple's original logo—a picture of Sir Isaac Newton sitting under an apple tree in the style of an old-fashioned woodcut. This retro image didn't really suit a company about to transform the future and it was replaced within a year by a rainbow version of the more familiar Apple motif.

Wayne, however, was anxious about the role he had taken on as a partner. Partners were liable to equal shares of losses incurred by the company—but young Jobs and Wozniak had no assets to speak of, and Wayne was afraid that he would have to bear the burden of any shortfall. At his age, and in the wake of his slot machine failure, he had worked too hard for what he had to risk losing it all again.

On April 12, 1976, less than two weeks after the formal creation of Apple Computers, he wrote a letter to the company registrar's office ending his association with the company and relinquishing his 10 percent stake, which was valued at $800. It was, he said later, "the best decision with the information available to me at the time." A year later Jobs and Wozniak attracted new investors and paid Wayne a further $1,500 against any future claims on the company. In total therefore, Ronald Wayne got $2,300 for his 10 percent. In 2018, that $2,300 was worth a little over $10,000, allowing for inflation. In the same year, Apple Inc.'s net value topped one trillion dollars, 10 percent of which was $100 million.

Wayne's only regret today is selling his original Apple contract. He got $500 for it in 2000, but in 2011, the document, countersigned by his partners, sold at auction for $1.26 million.

Bill Gates writes an open letter to computer hobbyists who are ripping off his software

(February 3, 1976)

Media piracy is nothing new. People had been taping records since Philips invented the cassette tape. Illegal copying has become a lot easier in the digital age, as Bill Gates found to his cost in the early days of Microsoft.

In their early days, home computers were a niche product for geeks, nerds, and techno-wizards, not for general use. These pioneers of the digital age were known as hobbyists, and they formed clubs to share their experimentation with hardware, software, and programming.

When the Altair 8800 microcomputer was launched in the January 1975 edition of *Popular Electronics* magazine, Bill Gates and Paul Allen saw an opportunity. With the help of Monte Davidoff, they wrote a version of BASIC (Beginner's All-purpose Symbolic Instruction Code) for use with the new model. MITS, the manufacturers of the Altair 8800, licensed the software, and in April 1975, Gates and Allen founded Microsoft together to develop Altair BASIC. They spent the rest of the year improving it and adding new features.

MITS promoted their products in a customized camper that they toured round computer clubs and stores. When the MITS roadshow visited the Homebrew Computer Club in Palo Alto, someone stole a tape of Altair BASIC and made fifty copies, which were distributed at the next meeting of the club. By the end of the year, thousands of Altair 8800s were being sold each month but only hundreds of copies of Altair BASIC. Piracy was rampant.

Frustrated and out of funds, Bill Gates wrote an open letter to America's computer hobbyists, which was circulated to clubs and computing magazines around the country. "The feedback we have gotten from the hundreds of people who say they are using BASIC has all been positive," he began. But he noted that less than 10 percent of all Altair owners had bought BASIC and that the royalties from sales to hobbyists made the time spent on Altair BASIC worth less than $2 an hour. Gates compared this with the $40,000 of computer time they had paid for to develop the software.

He was understandably critical of the prevailing attitude of its users. "As the majority of hobbyists must be aware, most of you steal your software. Hardware must be paid for, but software is something to share. Who cares if the people who worked on it get paid?" This was a stinging rebuke to these early enthusiasts who, in the absence of much commercially available software, were quite accustomed to sharing their own programming for the good of all.

But, of course, Gates had a point. "One thing you do do is prevent good software from being written," he argued. "Who can afford to do professional work for nothing? What hobbyist can put 3-man years into programming, finding all bugs, documenting his product and distribute for free?" Microsoft was, he announced, developing new software, "but there is very little incentive to make this software available to hobbyists." He was blunt. "Most directly, the thing you do is theft."

Bill Gates's letter was provocative. Computer magazines with an eye to the future of the hobby were in general supportive of him. But hobbyists themselves were angry. They questioned the $200 cost of Altair BASIC and the $40,000 cost of developing it. If Microsoft was losing out, they said, then the fault was with Microsoft's business model. In another open letter, in the February 1976 edition of the Homebrew Computer Club's newsletter, member Mike Hayes noted with some bitterness, "By the way, calling all your potential future customers thieves is perhaps 'uncool' marketing strategy."

To me, the most critical thing in the hobby market right now is the lack of good software courses, books and software itself. Without good software and an owner who understands programming, a hobby computer is wasted. Will quality software be written for the hobby market?

Almost a year ago, Paul Allen and myself, expecting the hobby market to expand, hired Monte Davidoff and developed Altair BASIC. Though the initial work took only two months, the three of us have spent most of the last year documenting, improving and adding features to BASIC. Now we have 4K, 8K, EXTENDED, ROM and DISK BASIC. The value of the computer time we have used exceeds $40,000.

The feedback we have gotten from the hundreds of people who say they are using BASIC has all been positive. Two surprising things are apparent, however. 1) Most of these "users" never bought BASIC (less than 10% of all Altair owners have bought BASIC), and 2) The amount of royalties we have received from sales to hobbyists makes the time spent on Altair BASIC worth less than $2 an hour.

Why is this? As the majority of hobbyists must be aware, most of you steal your software. Hardware must be paid for, but software is something to share. Who cares if the people who worked on it get paid?

Is this fair? One thing you don't do by stealing software is get back at MITS for some problem you may have had. MITS doesn't make money selling software. The royalty paid to us, the manual, the tape and the overhead make it a break-even operation. One thing you do do is prevent good software from being written. Who can afford to do professional work for nothing? What hobbyist can put 3-man years into programming, finding all bugs, documenting his product and distribute for free? The fact is, no one besides us has invested a lot of money in hobby software. We have written 6800 BASIC, and are writing 8080 APL and 6800 APL, but there is very little incentive to make this software available to hobbyists. Most directly, the thing you do is theft.

What about the guys who re-sell Altair BASIC, aren't they making money on hobby software? Yes, but those who have been reported to us may lose in the end. They are the ones who give hobbyists a bad name, and should be kicked out of any club meeting they show up at.

I would appreciate letters from any one who wants to pay up, or has a suggestion or comment. Just write me at 1180 Alvarado SE, #114, Albuquerque, New Mexico, 87108. Nothing would please me more than being able to hire ten programmers and deluge the hobby market with good software.

Bill Gates

Bill Gates
General Partner, Micro-Soft

ABOVE: *The letter from a twenty-year-old Bill Gates indicated that he was unlikely to have a future in customer relations.*

LEFT: *Bill Gates (seated) with partner Paul Allen in the early days of Microsoft.*

Michael Schumacher crosses out "the" and becomes world champion

(August 22, 1991)

When a young Michael Schumacher got the sudden opportunity to drive in the Belgian Grand Prix, the Jordan Grand Prix team wanted the German to commit to a long-term contract if things worked out. In his letter of agreement Schumacher made an important last-minute change to the wording.

In the early 1990s, the Mercedes sports car team had three hotshot drivers piloting their C11 sports car: Karl Wendlinger, Heinz-Harald Frentzen, and Michael Schumacher. It was Frentzen who most pundits thought was the major motorsport talent and had already moved into single-seater F3000 cars, the category below the very top formula, F1.

Charismatic Irishman Eddie Jordan was a shrewd team owner. A racer himself, he had moved into running F3000 cars, and then with the help of F1 supremo Bernie Ecclestone, started his own F1 team. However, after an argument with a London taxi driver, Bertrand Gachot, one of his two drivers for 1991, was unexpectedly imprisoned for using tear gas on the cabbie.

The Belgian Grand Prix was next on the F1 calendar, and suddenly, Jordan had an empty seat to fill. Mercedes were keen to get a German driver on the F1 grid and agreed to pay the £150,000 ($200,000) per race that Jordan was asking to put Schumacher in the car for the rest of 1991, plus $3.5m for 1992 and 1993.

Jordan was just as keen to have Schumacher in his fledgling team. His other driver, Andrea de Cesaris, was the journeyman of F1 pilots; accident-prone, at the end of his career, and given a seat thanks to the sponsorship he brought with him. If Schumacher was as good as some in the racing pit reckoned he was, then that would haul the team into contention, attract more sponsorship, and Jordan wouldn't have to rely on "pay drivers."

Jordan sent the German a driver agreement, and Schumacher replied:

"I confirm that if you enter me in the 1991 Belgian Grand Prix I will sign ~~the~~ *a* driver agreement with you prior to Monza in respect of my services in 1991, 1992, 1993 and subject to Mercedes' first option, 1994."

The crucial part of the letter was that he had crossed out "the" and inserted "a."

Time was short before the Belgian Grand Prix, and Schumacher needed a seat fitting and some brief running in the car at Silverstone before tackling what is F1's most demanding circuit, with the fearsome Eau Rouge corner. Jordan didn't insist he send another letter.

At the race, Schumacher started from seventh, equalling Jordan's best grid position of the season, while Andrea de Cesaris was 0.7 seconds slower back in eleventh. The race was a disappointment because Schumacher's clutch broke at the start, but he had already shown so much promise that other teams on the grid were starting to show interest in signing the German.

However, Jordan had an agreement. Or so he thought. Schumacher's manager, Willi Weber, argued that they had agreed to sign "a" contract, not "the" contract, and that "a contract" could be anything, such as a contract to visit his factory two times a year. The courts agreed, and so Michael Schumacher was free to join the Benetton team.

Jordan struggled in the two years that followed with an underperforming, unreliable engine. Had Schumacher been obliged to stay with the team, then his career might have terminally stalled. Not everyone on the Benetton team had wanted Schumacher there. As it was, a year later Schumacher won the Belgian Grand Prix and became world champion in 1994, and is a seven-times world champion. Tragically, he was incapacitated by a skiing accident in 2014.

Eddie Jordan is phlegmatic about the turn of events. "It is incredible that big things in F1 can come down to the difference between using the word 'a' in a contract when it should have been 'the,'" he told *Motorsport News*, "but that's motor racing sometimes. It made me very conscious of every document after that."

22 August 1991

For the attention of Eddie Jordan

Dear Eddie

I confirm that if you enter me in the 1991 Belgian Grand Prix I will sign ~~the~~ driver agreement with you prior to Monza in respect of my services in 1991, 1992, 1993 and subject to Mercedes' first option, 1994. ~~The driver agreement will be substantially in the form of the agreement produced by you with only mutually agreed amendments.~~

I understand that PP Sauber ~~AG~~ Ltd will pay you £150,000 per race for 1991.

I also understand that you require US$ 3.5 million for both 1992 and 1993 and if I or my backers are unable to find this money you will be entitled to retain my services in those years.

Yours sincerely

Michael Schumacher

LEFT: The letter sent to team boss Eddie Jordan had an important change from its first draft.

BELOW: After his one race with Jordan Grand Prix, Michael Schumacher went on to become a seven-time world champion (five of them with Ferrari) and has won the most F1 grands prix.

Boris Yeltsin admits running Russia was tougher than he expected

(December 31, 1999)

Originally a protégé of Mikhail Gorbachev, in 1987 Boris Yeltsin became the first man to resign from the politburo, the USSR's ruling body. This act established him as a popular rebel at a time when the Soviet Union's internal authority was crumbling. Everyone loves an outsider.

As the central authority of the Communist Party dwindled, and iron curtains and Berlin walls fell, Moscow's power extended little farther than the Russian Republic within the Soviet Union. Yeltsin, a former mayor of Moscow with a reputation for drunken public appearances, was hugely popular in the capital, where in 1989, he received 92 percent of the vote to become Moscow's delegate on the USSR's Congress of People's Deputies.

The following year he was elected president of the Russian Republic, where his popularity often put him at odds with the leaders of the Soviet Union (including his former mentor, Gorbachev). In August 1991, Gorbachev was fatally weakened when Yeltsin had to step in and save him from a military coup. Russia under Yeltsin seceded from the USSR, and at the end of year, Gorbachev resigned and signaled the break-up of the Soviet Union. Yeltsin became the president of the Russian Federation.

Yeltsin found out, just as every other populist politician has found, that it's much easier to be swept to power in protest at current conditions than it is to change those conditions once you're in the hot seat. By the time he resigned a second time, on the last day of the twentieth century, he had to admit that "what we thought would be easy turned out to be painfully difficult."

Yeltsin's rush to liberalize the Russian economy resulted in high prices followed by a depression as Russian factories, unable to compete in the free world, closed down. Hoping to spread wealth throughout the population, his reforms instead concentrated it in the hands of a few oligarchs. Corruption was rife, and by the time of his resignation, his popularity had slumped from that high of 92 percent to just 2 percent.

He delivered his resignation in the form of a letter, which he read out on state television on New Year's Eve 1999. "Dear friends, my dears," he began, "Today I am addressing you for the last time as Russian president. ...Today, on the last day of the outgoing century, I am retiring." Recent elections to the Duma, the Russian Parliament, had seen a new generation of politicians enter the fray, and Yeltsin must have felt that time was running out for him. "Russia must enter the new millennium with new politicians, new faces, new intelligent, strong and energetic people."

Yeltsin's health was poor, and in 1996, he had undergone quintuple heart bypass surgery. Despite this he insisted that "I am not leaving because of my health, but because of all the problems taken together." He, like others, had believed "that we would be able to jump from the grey, stagnating, totalitarian past into a bright, rich and civilized future in one go. ... I was too naïve."

In one final bid to control the direction of Russian politics, he nominated a successor, his prime minister, the relatively unknown Vladimir Putin. "Why hold on to power for another six months," he said, "when the country has a strong person, fit to be president? ... Why should I stand in his way?" Presidential elections were in any case due in three months' time. "I have no doubt what choice you will make at the end of March 2000."

And he was right. Putin was elected in March and remains president to this day, with a mixture of free-market practices, corruption, and authoritarianism that seem to suit a people accustomed to the old certainties of the Communist state. Boris Yeltsin died of congestive heart failure in 2007.

Resignation letter from Boris Yeltsin to the Russian people

Dear Russians, very little time remains to a momentous date in our history. The year 2000 is upon us, a new century, a new millennium.

We have all measured this date against ourselves, working out—first in childhood, then after we grew up—how old we would be in the year 2000, how old our mothers would be, and our children. Back then it seemed such a long way off to the extraordinary New Year. So now the day has come.

Dear friends, my dears, today I am wishing you New Year greetings for the last time. But that is not all. Today I am addressing you for the last time as Russian president. I have made a decision. I have contemplated this long and hard. Today, on the last day of the outgoing century, I am retiring.

Many times I have heard it said: Yeltsin will try to hold on to power by any means, he won't hand it over to anyone. That is all lies. That is not the case. I have always said that I would not take a single step away from the constitution, that the Duma elections should take place within the constitutional timescale. This has happened.

And likewise, I would have liked the presidential elections to have taken place on schedule in June 2000. That was very important for Russia. We were creating a vital precedent of a civilized, voluntary handover of power; power from one president of Russia to another, newly elected one.

And yet, I have taken a different decision. I am standing down. I am standing down earlier than scheduled. I have realized that I have to do this. Russia must enter the new millennium with new politicians, new faces, new intelligent, strong and energetic people. As for those of us who have been in power for many years, we must go.

Seeing with what hope and belief people voted during the Duma elections for a new generation of politicians, I understood that I had done the main job of my life. Russia will never return to the past. Russia will now always be moving forward. …

LEFT: *In March 1999, Boris Yeltsin (right) promoted Vladimir Putin to the post of secretary of the Security Council of the Russian Federation. The former KGB officer became acting president after Yeltsin's resignation, a position confirmed in May 2000.*

Dear Mr. Lay,

Has Enron become a risky place to work? For those of us who didn't get rich over the last few years, can we afford to stay?

Skilling's abrupt departure will raise suspicions of accounting improprieties and valuation issues. Enron has been very aggressive in its accounting—most notably the Raptor transactions and the Condor vehicle....

We have recognized over $550 million of fair value gains on stocks via our swaps with Raptor, much of that stock has declined significantly.... The value in the swaps won't be there for Raptor, so once again Enron will issue stock to offset these losses. Raptor is an LJM entity. It sure looks to the layman on the street that we are hiding losses in a related company and will compensate that company with Enron stock in the future.

I am incredibly nervous that we will implode in a wave of scandals. My 8 years of Enron work history will be worth nothing on my resume, the business world will consider the past successes as nothing but an elaborate accounting hoax. Skilling is resigning now for "personal reasons" but I think he wasn't having fun, looked down the road and knew this stuff was unfixable and would rather abandon ship now than resign in shame in 2 years.

Is there a way our accounting gurus can unwind these deals now? I have thought and thought about how to do this, but I keep bumping into one big problem—we booked the Condor and Raptor deals in 1999 and 2000, we enjoyed a wonderfully high stock price, many executives sold stock, we then try and reverse or fix the deals in 2001 and it's a bit like robbing the bank in one year and trying to pay it back 2 years later....

I realize that we have had a lot of smart people looking at this and a lot of accountants including AA & Co. have blessed the accounting treatment. None of this will protect Enron if these transactions are ever disclosed in the bright light of day....

The overriding basic principle of accounting is that if you explain the "accounting treatment" to a man on the street, would you influence his investing decisions? Would he sell or buy the stock based on a thorough understanding of the facts?

My concern is that the footnotes don't adequately explain the transactions. If adequately explained, the investor would know that the "Entities" described in our related party footnote are thinly capitalized, the equity holders have no skin in the game, and all the value in the entities comes from the underlying value of the derivatives (unfortunately in this case, a big loss) AND Enron stock and N/P....

The related party footnote tries to explain these transactions. Don't you think that several interested companies, be they stock analysts, journalists, hedge fund managers, etc., are busy trying to discover the reason Skilling left? Don't you think their smartest people are pouring [sic] over that footnote disclosure right now? I can just hear the discussions—"It looks like they booked a $500 million gain from this related party company and I think, from all the undecipherable ½ page on Enron's contingent contributions to this related party entity, I think the related party entity is capitalized with Enron stock."…. "No, no, no, you must have it all wrong, it can't be that, that's just too bad, too fraudulent, surely AA & Co. wouldn't let them get away with that?"

LEFT: Sherron Watkins sent this letter anonymously to Enron chairman Kenneth Lay after the abrupt departure on August 14, 2001, of Chief Executive Officer Jeffrey Skilling.

BELOW: On February 26, 2002, Sherron Watkins (far left), Jeffrey Skilling (center), and Jeffrey McMahon testified before the United States Senate Committee on Commerce, Science, and Transportation.

Sherron Watkins sends a letter criticizing Enron's dubious accounting

(August 2001)

From its 1930s origins as a gas distribution company, Enron grew rapidly in the mid-1980s when Kenneth Lay became its CEO. From the start he expanded the corporation's interests far beyond its roots, overstretching its capacity with questionable dealings. It was a bubble just waiting to burst.

In 1990, Lay was joined at Enron by Jeff Skilling, from the failed First City National Bank of Houston, and Andrew Fastow from the failed Continental Illinois National Bank and Trust Company. The three men bought or created a multinational maze of interdependent companies, among which they hid debts and exaggerated profits. They created a business culture at the company's Houston headquarters in which its directors and accountants went along with the trio's dubious practices, tolerating the sometimes illegal conflicts of interest instead of challenging them.

What was behind the glamorous veneer of multinational expansion and spectacular profit levels was a fraudulent accounting system that concealed losses in artificial subsidiaries. By this practice Enron deliberately misled shareholders into the belief that the company could deliver good returns on their investment, ensuring that money would continue to flow into the company—and into the pockets of its executives.

In August 2001, however, Jeff Skilling resigned from Enron; and Sherron Watkins, vice president for corporate development in the corporation, began to voice concerns about its accounting systems. Her letter to Lay was initially sent anonymously. She had formerly worked at Arthur Andersen, Enron's accountants, and knew what she was talking about. "I am incredibly nervous," she admitted, "that we will implode in a wave of accounting scandals."

Skilling's sudden departure from a company in such supposedly good financial condition looked suspicious.

"I would think," wrote Watkins, "he wasn't having fun, looked down the road and knew this stuff was unfixable and would rather abandon ship now than resign in shame in two years." She was thinking particularly of two schemes, Condor and Raptor, which were due to mature in 2002 and 2003 and would not deliver on promised returns. "It's a bit like robbing the bank in one year and trying to pay it back two years later," she told Lay. "We are under too much scrutiny and there are probably one or two disgruntled 'redeployed' employees who know enough about the 'funny' accounting to get us in trouble."

Her questions to Kenneth Lay triggered quiet panic in the offices of both Enron and its accountants; executives ditched share holdings, and Arthur Andersen shredded documents while insisting that Enron was in robust good health.

The facade crumbled, and on December 2, Enron became the largest corporate bankruptcy in American history. Arthur Andersen, one of the five largest accounting firms in the world at the time, also collapsed. Skilling was released in February 2019 after serving twelve years of a twenty-four-year sentence for felony. Fastow—convicted of fraud, money laundering, and conspiracy—reduced his sentence by turning state's evidence and was released in 2006. Lay was convicted on ten counts but died of a heart attack before sentencing. Sherron Watkins speaks at conferences on the dangers of US corporate culture.

Dr. David Kelly admits he was the source for critical BBC report

(June 30, 2003)

In 2002, the British government commissioned a dossier assessing the weapons of mass destruction (WMDs) held by Iraq. It was intended to support Britain's planned participation in an invasion of Iraq to topple its leader Saddam Hussein. It proved to be the flimsiest of excuses for going to war.

What became known as "the dodgy dossier" included the claim that Iraq was capable of firing chemical and biological weapons within forty-five minutes of any order by President Saddam Hussein. Dr. David Kelly, an expert in biological warfare, was asked to proofread the dossier, and he disagreed with some of the claims, including the one about the forty-five-minute response time.

The joint US-UK invasion of Iraq, with the express aim of removing its weapons of mass destruction and ending its support of terrorism, followed in March 2003. Invading troops found no evidence of WMDs. In an off-the-record interview with the BBC journalist Andrew Gilligan in May 2003, Dr. Kelly expressed his reservations about the dossier. He told Gilligan that he believed it had been "sexed up" by Prime Minister Tony Blair's combative director of communications, Alastair Campbell, to encourage public support for the invasion.

Gilligan then repeated the accusation in his broadcast report, naming Campbell but not his source, Kelly. Opponents of the invasion seized on it as proof that Blair had deliberately falsified the reasons for going to war. British lives had been lost, Iraq had been thrown into chaos with no postwar planning, and the principle reason for prosecuting the war did not exist. Pressure grew on the BBC to reveal its source, and so Dr. Kelly decided to write to his line manager in the Ministry of Defence, admitting confidentially that he had met with Gilligan.

He denied that he had discussed the dossier, although he had talked about his own experiences as a weapons inspector in Iraq. "I did not even consider that I was the source of Gilligan's information, until a friend said she recognized that some of the comments were the sort I would make about Iraq's chemical and biological capacity." Kelly felt that "Gilligan has considerably embellished my meeting with him; he has met with other individuals who truly were intimately associated with the dossier; or he has assembled comments from multiple sources for his articles."

The ministry took the same view and announced only that an employee had admitted to meeting Gilligan. However, it was possible to deduce Kelly's identity from the details in the announcement, and he was soon uncovered as the journalist's source. Many believe that he was deliberately identified by the government in an effort to discredit Gilligan's report.

David Kelly came under intense pressure from both supporters and critics. A mild, soft-spoken man, he was aggressively interrogated in hearings by two parliamentary committees on consecutive days, July 15 and 16. His answers were so quiet at times, he could barely be heard. The experiences shook him deeply. On the afternoon of July 17, he left his home, walked to a favorite nearby woodland, took an overdose of painkillers, and cut his wrist. His body was found the following morning.

Conspiracy theorists suggested that Kelly might have been murdered by government agents. But a government inquiry into his death concluded that the government was not to blame for any pressure that resulted in Kelly's suicide. Andrew Gilligan resigned from the BBC in the wake of the inquiry, which questioned the accuracy of his report. Although the Blair government subsequently won another term in power, Tony Blair and Alistair Campbell were permanently tainted by the belief that they had tampered with the dossier in order to take the country into an unpopular and illegal war.

LEFT: Former UN weapons inspector Dr. David Kelly photographed as he arrives at the House of Commons on July 15, 2003, two days before he took his own life.

BELOW: Protestors hold up placards outside the Royal Courts of Justice in London. British Prime Minister Tony Blair was due to give evidence to the Hutton Inquiry, which investigated Dr. Kelly's death and the much-criticized dossier that set Britain on the path to the Iraq war. There are placards for Defence Secretary Geoff Hoon, Blair, and Foreign Secretary Jack Straw.

Bobby Henderson asks Kansas to acknowledge the Spaghetti Monster

(January 2005)

In 2005, Kansas State Board of Education discussed the introduction of intelligent design teaching in schools. Intelligent design suggests that the world is too complex to have evolved on its own and that a higher being must have been involved—specifically, the Christian God. Not everyone agreed.

Creationists and religious conservatives wanted to teach that the theory of evolution was flawed and proposed that the curriculum should give equal time to alternative theistic theories. Scientists were appalled.

Presenting as a "concerned citizen," physics graduate Bobby Henderson wrote an open letter to the Kansas School Board in which he voiced his disingenuous worry that "students will only hear one theory of intelligent design." According to the letter from the twenty-five-year-old from Oregon, there were many theories of intelligent design; and, along with "many others around the world," he was "of the strong belief that the universe was created by a Flying Spaghetti Monster."

He set out his theological stall in very equitable fashion. Taking into account how important it was for students "to hear multiple viewpoints so they can choose for themselves," Henderson advocated that schools should teach students about the Flying Spaghetti Monster's involvement in intelligent design. After all, he continued, "if the intelligent design theory is not based on faith, but instead another scientific theory, as is claimed, then you must also allow our theory to be taught, as it is also based on science, not on faith."

Interweaving his own hoax scientific theories with familiar religious tropes about an omnipotent deity, Henderson satirized the arguments of intelligent design and wittily undermined the legitimacy of its claims to be recognized as a science.

Creationists have long sought to discredit carbon dating by pointing out statistically insignificant anomalies in the science. Henderson also argued against carbon dating, but he blamed any inconvenient figures on the Flying Spaghetti Monster "changing the results with His Noodly Appendage." And besides,

"the overwhelming scientific evidence pointing toward evolutionary processes is nothing but a coincidence." According to "Pastafarians" such as Henderson, it was a coincidence that has been "put in place by Him [the Flying Spaghetti Monster]."

According to creationists, natural disasters such as Noah's flood were a godly punishment on disbelievers. Using the same pseudologic, Henderson's letter argued that "global warming, earthquakes, hurricanes, and other natural disasters are a direct effect of the shrinking numbers of pirates since the 1800s." A deliberately nonsensical graph illustrated his theories. His underlying point that correlation is not causation is one that has been made at much greater length by prominent atheists such as Richard Dawkins.

While the Flying Spaghetti Monster generated lots of headlines (and real-life Pastafarian adherents) and added some much-needed levity to the discussion, it was a change in the power balance between Republicans and Democrats on the Kansas State Board of Education which ensured that intelligent design did not become a permanent part of the curriculum.

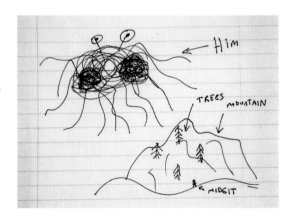

Statement regarding Traditional Pastafarian Headgear:

Allow me to confirm that the wearing of a Colander is a tradition in the Pastafarian faith. Not all followers dress so formally, but it is a common practice for us to do so while making official identification documents.

As you know, religion plays a serious part in many people's lives, including the wearing of specific clothing. Believers over the years have sometimes unfortunately experienced resistance, mockery, or even discrimination for simply following the guidelines of their religion.

Thankfully case law has repeatedly affirmed that believers have a constitutionally-protected right to wear such clothing in nearly all public situations including: work, school, while taking identification photos, even in the courtroom — provided that the clothing does cause undo harm. That is to say, that religious clothing is with very few exceptions a protected right.

We, the Church of the Flying Spaghetti Monster, are not a litigious group but of course we, along with the ACLU and others, have an interest in defending the individual rights and liberties guaranteed by the Constitution and the laws of the United States.

Thank you for your cooperation and May You Be Touched by His Noodly Appendage.

Sincerely,

Bobby Henderson, Church of the Flying Spaghetti Monster

TOP: *A further edict from the Church of the Flying Spaghetti Monster.*
For twenty-five dollars you can become a Pastafarian minister.

ABOVE: *The FSM has inspired great art, such as* Touched by His Noodly
Appendage, *a work by Arne Niklas Jansson.*

OPPOSITE: *Some not-so-great art: a figurative drawing by Bobby Henderson.*

Chelsea Manning writes to Wikileaks with a data dump

(February 3, 2010)

Chelsea Manning's story is—depending on your sympathies—one of treason, or the failure of the military, or a story of gender identity. One thing is certain: hoping that the masculine environment of the US Army would "cure" her femininity was a mistake.

Chelsea was christened Bradley and raised as a boy. Her mother was an alcoholic during and after the pregnancy, and Chelsea's older sister, Casey, provided most of her early care. Her mother attempted suicide when Chelsea was eleven, and her parents divorced when she was thirteen.

Her femininity in an outwardly male body made her the target of bullying at school. By the age of seventeen, she was identifying as a gay man, but her moods were unpredictable—sometimes locked down, on another occasion attacking her stepmother with a knife. In 2007, she joined the US Army, where the relentless physical life and further bullying drove her to a breakdown. She transferred to intelligence analysis, for which she was well suited—computer savvy, sharp-witted, and thoughtful.

In this capacity she had access to all manner of sensitive information. She was beginning to think of herself as female, but the army's policy of "Don't Ask, Don't Tell" was still in force. Isolated, frustrated, the pressure was building inside her. Her emotional instability was a cause for concern, and she was referred to a mental health counselor; but despite a risk of her being a danger to herself and others, in 2009 her skills as an analyst got her posted to Baghdad.

Unhappy about her identity and her role in a war that she opposed, she turned to the internet for comfort and found Wikileaks, an organization dedicated to making private records public. In early January 2010, she copied nearly 500,000 army files about the wars in Iraq and Afghanistan onto an SD card so that she could smuggle them back to the US in her camera next time she was on leave.

Intending to offer them to the *Washington Post*, she added a cover letter in the form of a readme.txt file.

"Items of historic significance of two wars Iraq and Afghanistan," she wrote. "You might need to sit on this information for 90 to 180 days, to best send and distribute such a large amount of data to a large audience and protect the source." Empowered by what she was doing she added, "This is one of the most significant documents of our time removing the fog of war and revealing the true nature of 21st century asymmetric warfare. Have a good day."

When neither the *Post* nor the *New York Times* showed any interest in her offer of information, she sent it to Wikileaks. Over the next three months she passed on further files, including damning video of a US helicopter attack on civilians and the press. The release of that video by Wikileaks is considered to have cemented the organization's reputation for exposing suppressed truth.

It is possible that Chelsea Manning wanted to be caught. She pointed out to a superior that the helicopter video was a copy of one stored in the network on which she worked. In May 2010, she had a series of online chats with Adrian Lamo, a hacker-turned-journalist, in which she confessed to everything she'd done. Lamo thought that she was endangering lives and reported her to army counterintelligence. She was arrested on May 26, and after pleading guilty she was sentenced to thirty-five years in prison.

President Obama commuted Manning's sentence in January 2017 as he left the Oval Office, but incoming President Trump tweeted that she was an "ungrateful TRAITOR. Terrible!" In 2019, she was imprisoned once again, for refusing to testify against Wikileaks founder Julian Assange.

Chelsea Manning's letter to Wikileaks (in the form of a readme.txt file)

Items of historic significance of two wars Iraq and Afghanistan. You might need to sit on this information for 90 to 180 days, to best send and distribute such a large amount of data to a large audience and protect the source. This is one of the most significant documents of our time removing the fog of war and revealing the true nature of 21st century asymmetric warfare. Have a good day.

ABOVE: Born Bradley Edward Manning, Chelsea Elizabeth Manning was imprisoned from 2010 to 2017 for releasing 750,000 documents to Wikileaks. She was imprisoned again in March 2019 for contempt of court after refusing to testify before a grand jury investigating Wikileaks founder Julian Assange. Manning argued that she had revealed everything she knew at her court-martial.

US astronauts' open letter to Barack Obama

...The design and the production of the flight components and infrastructure to implement this vision was well underway. Detailed planning of all the major sectors of the programme had begun. Enthusiasm within NASA and throughout the country was very high.

When President Obama recently released his budget for NASA, he proposed a slight increase in total funding, substantial research and technology development, an extension of the International Space Station operation until 2020, long range planning for a new but undefined heavy lift rocket and significant funding for the development of commercial access to low earth orbit.

Although some of these proposals have merit, the accompanying decision to cancel the Constellation programme, its Ares 1 and Ares V rockets, and the Orion spacecraft, is devastating.

America's only path to low Earth orbit and the International Space Station will now be subject to an agreement with Russia to purchase space on their Soyuz (at a price of over $50m per seat with significant increases expected in the near future) until we have the capacity to provide transportation for ourselves. The availability of a commercial transport to orbit as envisioned in the president's proposal cannot be predicted with any certainty, but is likely to take substantially longer and be more expensive than we would hope.

Scott Carpenter	Bob Crippen	Jim McDivitt	Bruce McCandless
Neil Armstrong	Michael D. Griffin	Gene Kranz	Frank Borman
James Lovell	Ed Gibson	Joe Kerwin	Paul Weitz
Eugene Cernan	Jim Kennedy	Fred Haise	George Mueller
Chris Kraft	Alan Bean	Gerald Carr	Harrison Schmitt
Jack Lousma	Alfred M. Worden	Jake Garn	Dick Gordon
Vance Brand	Glynn Lunney	Charlie Duke	

LEFT: *The Lunar Rover helped astronauts Eugene Cernan and Harrison Schmitt collect rock samples from a far greater distance than early Apollo missions, during the United States' final visit to the moon's surface, Apollo 17.*

Astronauts lament America's lack of a space delivery system

(April 14, 2010)

Veteran astronauts were appalled when the United States lost its ability to send either spacemen or satellites into orbit and became totally reliant on the Russians, the nation they had beaten so convincingly in the space race.

NASA's Constellation program had been inaugurated in 2004 in response to President George W. Bush's interest in further space exploration. Its mission statement was "to establish an extended human presence on the Moon as a stepping stone for deeper space journeys to Mars and beyond."

Following the expected completion of the International Space Station (ISS), and the planned retirement of NASA's Space Shuttle vehicles, Constellation was to be an exciting new phase of space travel, and its creation was cheering news for veterans of the original moon landings. Neil Armstrong, the first astronaut to walk on the Moon had earlier observed, "I fully expected that, by the end of the century, we would have achieved substantially more than we actually did." The space program launched by President Kennedy in 1962 had ended in 1972 with Apollo 17. Armstrong's colleague Eugene Cernan complained, "I'm quite disappointed that I'm still the last man on the Moon."

After the shuttle, NASA began to develop the next generation of space vehicles for inner and outer space travel, using new Ares I and heavy-lifting Ares V rockets. "Enthusiasm within NASA and throughout the country," noted Armstrong, Cernan, and Jim Lovell, "was very high." But during Barack Obama's presidency, two reviews found that Constellation was "over budget, behind schedule, and lacking in innovation." In his 2010 budget, he extended the life of the International Space Station but axed Constellation completely.

Three veteran space commanders—Armstrong (Apollo 11), Lovell (Apollo 13), and Cernan (Apollo 17) added their names to an open letter to the American public deploring the decision. Without Ares, and with the end of the Space Shuttle in sight, "America's only path to low Earth orbit and the International Space Station will now be subject to an agreement with Russia to purchase space on their Soyuz ..."

The loss of time and money spent in Constellation research and development, and in recreating it, if and when the program was reinstated, was—the former astronauts agreed—a terrible waste of the $10 billion so far invested in it. Of the country that won the space race in 1969, they predicted that "to be without carriage to low Earth orbit and with no human exploration capability to go beyond Earth orbit for an indeterminate time into the future, destines our nation to become one of second or even third rate stature."

The Apollo program of which the three men had been part was a painstaking process of incremental learning, with each new mission building on the lessons and discoveries of earlier ones. There was, the open letter argued, no substitute for real, practical space travel. "Without the skill and experience that actual spacecraft operation provides, the USA is far too likely to be on a long downhill slide to mediocrity."

The future, self-evidently, remains to be seen. The United States was indeed reliant on Russian *Soyuz* craft and now also uses the inner space vehicles of entrepreneurs like Elon Musk. NASA still has an ongoing program of deep space probes with which it is exploring our own solar system and beyond. And although the Ares rocket family has been cancelled, NASA is still developing the Orion spacecraft, which they were to have carried. Meanwhile, other nations, including China, are actively pursuing the idea of a moon base from which to take the next leap into space.

Letter to Slavoj Žižek from Nadezhda Tolokonnikova

Dear Slavoj,

In my last letter, written in haste as I worked in the sewing shop, I was not as clear as I should have been about the distinction between how "global capitalism" functions in Europe and the US on the one hand, and in Russia on the other. However, recent events in Russia—the trial of Alexei Navalny, the passing of unconstitutional, anti-freedom laws—have infuriated me. I feel compelled to speak about the specific political and economic practices of my country. The last time I felt this angry was in 2011 when Putin declared he was running for the presidency for a third time. My anger and resolve led to the birth of Pussy Riot. What will happen now? Time will tell.

Here in Russia I have a strong sense of the cynicism of so-called first-world countries towards poorer nations. In my humble opinion, "developed" countries display an exaggerated loyalty towards governments that oppress their citizens and violate their rights. The European and US governments freely collaborate with Russia as it imposes laws from the middle ages and throws opposition politicians in jail. They collaborate with China, where oppression is so bad that my hair stands on end just to think about it. What are the limits of tolerance? And when does tolerance become collaboration, conformism and complicity?

To think, cynically, "let them do what they want in their own country", doesn't work any longer, because Russia and China and countries like them are now part of the global capitalist system.

Russia under Putin, with its dependence on raw materials, would have been massively weakened if those nations that import Russian oil and gas had shown the courage of their convictions and stopped buying. Even if Europe were to take as modest a step as passing a "Magnitsky law" [the Magnitsky Act in the US allows it to place sanctions on Russian officials believed to have taken part in human-rights violations], morally it would speak volumes. A boycott of the Sochi Winter Olympics in 2014 would be another ethical gesture. But the continued trade in raw materials constitutes a tacit approval of the Russian regime—not through words, but through money. It betrays the desire to protect the political and economic status quo and the division of labour that lies at the heart of the world economic system.

You quote Marx: "A social system that seizes up and rusts ... cannot survive." But here I am, working out my prison sentence in a country where the 10 people who control the biggest sectors of the economy are Vladimir Putin's oldest friends. He studied or played sports with some, and served in the KGB with others. Isn't this a social system that has seized up? Isn't this a feudal system?

I thank you sincerely, Slavoj, for our correspondence and can hardly wait for your reply.
Yours,
Nadya

ABOVE: Transcript of a letter from Nadezhda (Nadya) Tolokonnikova to Slavoj Žižek.

LEFT: Nadezhda Tolokonnikova (left), Yekaterina Samutsevich, and Maria Alyokhina in the dock at their 2012 court appearance. Samutsevich was freed on probation after two months.

Pussy Riot singer trades philosophies with Slavoj Žižek

(January–July 2013)

Pussy Riot is an all-female Russian collective punk band who gained notoriety for staging impromptu street performances in support of women's and LGBT rights in Russia. They were in direct opposition to the policies of President Vladimir Putin. A clash with the latter was inevitable.

On February 21, 2012, the group held one of their flash mob gigs inside the Cathedral of Christ the Savior in Moscow in protest at Putin's links with the patriarchs of the Russian Orthodox Church. The performance was eventually stopped by church security guards amid cries from the priests of sacrilege. Two weeks later three members of the group—Nadezhda (Nadya) Tolokonnikova, Yekaterina Samutsevich, and Maria Alyokhina—were arrested. On August 17, they were convicted of "hooliganism motivated by religious hatred" and sentenced to two years' imprisonment.

Although they attracted less sympathy in Russia, their sentence was considered to be unduly harsh to the rest of the world. Amnesty International declared them to be prisoners of conscience. They were sent to separate jails and roughly treated by both their jailers and their fellow prisoners.

Beginning in January 2013, the magazine *Philosophie* facilitated an exchange of letters between Nadezhda Tolokonnikova and Slavoj Žižek, professor of philosophy at Ljubljana University. His ideas straddle high and low cultures, and have earned him the nickname "the Elvis of Cultural Theory." The correspondence revealed a punk singer who was, in Žižek's words, "an equal partner in a theoretical dialogue." Nadezhda and Žižek traded critiques of capitalism and discussed the value of protest in publicly criticizing the status quo even if it has no easy answers to offer in exchange.

"We are a part of this force that has no final answers or absolute truths," wrote Nadezhda, in Russian, "for our mission is to question." Although Žižek questioned demonstrations that were "a purely negative gesture of angry rejection," he praised Pussy Riot because "beneath the dynamics of their acts there is the inner stability of a firm ethico-political attitude." In other words, it was based on a considered philosophical position. In the erratic unstable world of capitalism, Pussy Riot's challenge to society ironically offered it a form of stability.

Nadezhda expressed her anger at regressive restrictions on freedom being introduced in Russia. "The last time I felt this angry was in 2011 when Putin declared he was running for the presidency for a third time. My anger and resolve led to the birth of Pussy Riot." And she was highly critical of the UK and the US, who by trading with Russia and China tacitly expressed approval of their oppressive regimes—"not through words, but through money." Žižek had been amused to note that "all hearts were beating for you as long as you were perceived as just another version of the liberal-democratic protest against the authoritarian state. The moment it became clear that you rejected global capitalism, reporting on Pussy Riot became much more ambiguous."

This was not the sort of exchange you might expect between a punk singer and a professor. It clearly benefited both parties, comforting Tolokonnikova during her incarceration and enlightening Žižek. "You make visible," said Žižek, "the hidden continuity between Stalin and contemporary global capitalism."

After twenty-one months, Tolokonnikova and Alyokhina were released on December 23, 2013, cynically just over a month before the world's attention was to be focused on Russia's Sochi Winter Olympics. The women called for an international boycott of the event, to the fury of many Russians. They were beaten up in a fast food outlet on one occasion and horsewhipped on another by Cossacks acting as security guards in Sochi. They continue to speak out.

Edward Snowden has a shocking revelation for the German press

(October 31, 2013)

When whistleblower Edward Snowden leaked sensitive documents from the intelligence agencies of the USA and their allies to the world's press, he described it as an "act of political expression." Most shocking of all, he revealed that the US had been bugging the German chancellor, Angela Merkel.

From 2006 to 2013, Snowden worked in cyber counterintelligence for a succession of America's security services—the Central Intelligence Agency (CIA), the National Security Agency (NSA), and the Defense Intelligence Agency (DIA)—either directly or for companies that supplied services to them.

In the course of his work he participated in some security operations which stretched the definitions of national and international legality to breaking point. In 2012, he began to download documents about the US government's spying activities. Increasingly disaffected, he would later claim that the last straw came when he watched the Director of National Intelligence, James Clapper, lying to Congress during a testimony under oath.

He set about gathering as much evidence as possible for the abuses he saw, before fleeing to Hong Kong on May 20, 2013. From there he released thousands of secret documents to the *Guardian* in Britain and the *Washington Post* in the US. They appeared to show that America was routinely harvesting information about millions of ordinary phone users, online gamers, and clients of corporations like Google and Yahoo all over the world—in effect almost anything done on the internet. The NSA's so-called black budget for this activity in 2013 was $52 billion.

This was large-scale mission creep. Snowden also revealed the extent of the spying activity that the US was engaged in—not against enemies but against its closest allies. Thirty-five world leaders were shown to be victims of US surveillance in Australia, Canada, Scandinavia, and Europe. The personal cell phone of German Chancellor Angela Merkel was being monitored, which prompted her to complain to President Obama that "spying among friends is not acceptable."

In June 2013, Snowden's US passport was revoked and he fled from Hong Kong to Moscow. When Germany began a formal investigation into Snowden's evidence, he dared not leave the relative safety of Russia to testify to it. Instead, he wrote an open letter to the German chancellor, Parliament, and state prosecutors, defending his "act of political expression."

He listed the US agencies for which he had worked. "In the course of my service to these organizations," he wrote, "I believe I witnessed systemic violations of law by my government that created a moral duty to act." Snowden noted that his revelations had been welcomed by many both high and low and that they had "resulted in the proposal of many new laws and policies to address formerly concealed abuses of the public trust."

He continued: "Though the outcome of my efforts has been demonstrably positive, my government continues to treat dissent as defection, and seeks to criminalize political speech with felony charges that provide no defense. However, speaking the truth is not a crime."

In the light of Snowden's truth, Obama ordered a review of America's surveillance activities, which recommended some forty-six changes of policy and found no evidence that such mass snooping had prevented any acts of terrorism. Apart from the specific practices that Snowden exposed, he revealed the extent to which we are all vulnerable to unscrupulous prying in our use of the internet. Edward Snowden remains in asylum at a secret location in Moscow.

OPPOSITE: Snowden's dossier revealed surveillance information that may well have surprised the intelligence agencies of some of America's closest NATO partners.

To whom it may concern,

I have been invited to write to you regarding your investigation of mass surveillance.

I am Edward Joseph Snowden, formerly employed through contracts or direct hire as a technical expert for the United States National Security Agency, Central Intelligence Agency, and Defense Intelligence Agency.

In the course of my service to these organizations, I believe I witnessed systemic violations of law by my government that created a moral duty to act. As a result of reporting these concerns, I have faced a severe and sustained campaign of persecution that forced me from my family and home. I am currently living in exile under a grant of temporary asylum in the Russian Federation in accordance with international law.

I am heartened by the response to my act of political expression, in both the United States and beyond. Citizens around the world as well as high officials - including in the United States - have judged the revelation of an unaccountable system of pervasive surveillance to be a public service. These spying revelations have resulted in the proposal of many new laws and policies to address formerly concealed abuses of the public trust. The benefits to society of this growing knowledge are becoming increasingly clear at the same time claimed risks are being shown to have been mitigated.

Though the outcome of my efforts has been demonstrably positive, my government continues to treat dissent as defection, and seeks to criminalize political speech with felony charges that provide no defense. However, speaking the truth is not a crime. I am confident that with the support of the international community, the government of the United States will abandon this harmful behavior. I hope that when the difficulties of this humanitarian situation have been resolved, I will be able to cooperate in the responsible finding of fact regarding reports in the media, particularly in regard to the truth and authenticity of documents, as appropriate and in accordance with the law.

I look forward to speaking with you in your country when the situation is resolved, and thank you for your efforts in upholding the international laws that protect us all.

With my best regards,

Edward Snowden
31 October 2013

SIGNED

WITNESSED

The whistleblowers appeal to future whistleblowers

(December 11, 2013)

He was the Edward Snowden of a nondigital age, Daniel Ellsberg was the man responsible for leaking what became known as the "Pentagon Papers" to the New York Times in 1971, which lifted the lid on US government deception during the Vietnam War.

The "Pentagon Papers" was, in fact, a lengthy report commissioned by the US Department of Defense, on the history of the United States' political and military involvement in Vietnam from 1945 to 1967. Ellsberg had worked on the study and had been concerned by some of the revelations. The report showed that the US had secretly enlarged its mandate for operations in the Vietnam War with the bombings of nearby Cambodia and Laos and unreported raids on North Vietnam.

Press reaction was damning, the *New York Times* said that the Pentagon Papers revealed the Johnson administration to have "systematically lied, not only to the public but also to Congress."

Like Edward Snowden, Ellsberg was pilloried by the establishment for his actions. On January 3, 1973, he was charged under the Espionage Act of 1917. Combined with other charges of theft and conspiracy, he faced a total maximum sentence of 115 years for his crimes against the state.

However, to his advantage, it was discovered that the "Plumbers" had been at work on his case (see page 183). The Plumbers were an illegal agency employed by the Nixon White House to bug the Democratic Party convention at the Watergate Hotel, and they had also been tasked with illegal evidence gathering in the Ellsberg case. On May 11, 1973, due to governmental misconduct and this illegal evidence gathering, and the defense by Leonard Boudin and Harvard Law School professor Charles Nesson, Judge William Matthew Byrne Jr. dismissed all charges against Ellsberg. In June 2011, the entirety of the Pentagon Papers was declassified and publicly released.

Following the worldwide attention of the Edward Snowden case, Ellsberg, along with other whistleblowers, decided to write an open letter to leading free-thinking newspapers around the world. They argued that whistleblowers were working on behalf of the public who were being deceived by their governments—and that people like Edward Snowden were heroic by helping call them to account. They did not want to see that effort diminished or other potential whistleblowers inhibited or stymied by face-saving politicians.

ABOVE: Daniel Ellsberg photographed in 2004.

Open letter to future whistleblowers

At least since the aftermath of September 2001, western governments and intelligence agencies have been hard at work expanding the scope of their own power, while eroding privacy, civil liberties and public control of policy. What used to be viewed as paranoid, Orwellian, tin-foil hat fantasies turned out post-Snowden, to be not even the whole story.

What's really remarkable is that we've been warned for years that these things were going on: wholesale surveillance of entire populations, militarization of the internet, the end of privacy. All is done in the name of "national security", which has more or less become a chant to fence off debate and make sure governments aren't held to account— that they can't be held to account—because everything is being done in the dark. Secret laws, secret interpretations of secret laws by secret courts and no effective parliamentary oversight whatsoever.

By and large the media have paid scant attention to this, even as more and more courageous, principled whistleblowers stepped forward. The unprecedented persecution of truth-tellers, initiated by the Bush administration and severely accelerated by the Obama administration, has been mostly ignored, while record numbers of well-meaning people are charged with serious felonies simply for letting their fellow citizens know what's going on.

It's one of the bitter ironies of our time that while John Kiriakou (ex-CIA) is in prison for blowing the whistle on US torture, the torturers and their enablers walk free.

Likewise WikiLeaks-source Chelsea (née Bradley) Manning was charged with—amongst other serious crimes—aiding the enemy (read: the public). Manning was sentenced to 35 years in prison while the people who planned the illegal and disastrous war on Iraq in 2003 are still treated as dignitaries.

Numerous ex-NSA (National Security Agency) officials have come forward in the past decade, disclosing massive fraud, vast illegalities and abuse of power in said agency, including Thomas Drake, William Binney and Kirk Wiebe. The response was 100% persecution and 0% accountability by both the NSA and the rest of the government. Blowing the whistle on powerful factions is not a fun thing to do, but despite the poor track record of western media, whistleblowing remains the last avenue for truth, balanced debate and upholding democracy—that fragile construct which Winston Churchill is quoted as calling "the worst form of government, except all the others." ...

LEFT: Albert Einstein shared his thoughts about God and religion in a 1954 letter. "The word God is for me nothing more than the expression and product of human weaknesses, the Bible a collection of honorable but still primitive legends. No interpretation, no matter how subtle, can (for me) change anything about this." Estimated to fetch between $1 and $1.5 million it sold at Christie's in New York in 2018 for $2,892,500.

BELOW: An unpublished letter from J.R.R. Tolkien discussing the difficulties of completing the third part of The Lord of the Rings *trilogy, sold at Bonhams, London, in 2014 for £10,625 ($13,800).*

Letters–the next investment boom to follow art?

(2017–)

Recent sales of original letters from key moments in history have commanded extraordinarily high prices. The excitement of holding the very piece of paper on which history was made or recorded is, it seems, worth paying for. Might it therefore also be worth investing in?

In July 2017, a group of letters typed and hand-signed by the great scientist Albert Einstein sold for $210,000 at an auction in Israel. The original recipients included fellow scientist David Bohm; and illusionist Uri Geller was one of the buyers. The auction house had originally estimated a sale price of around $46,000. If they were pleased with the eventual result, it was nothing compared to another Einstein letter sale in the city later that year.

A note from Einstein to a bellboy in Tokyo's Imperial Hotel was sold in Israel in October 2017 for a breathtaking $1.7 million. A number of things contributed to the price. It was handwritten, and on headed notepaper from a hotel (later demolished) designed by celebrated architect Frank Lloyd Wright. The circumstances of its writing were interesting—lacking the money to tip the boy, Einstein wrote him the note in the hope that his fame would make it more valuable than the tip would have been. And its provenance was good because it was being sold by a direct descendant of the bellboy.

The content of the note was exceptional too. In it Einstein expressed his theory, not of relativity, but of happiness. It reads:

> "A calm and modest life brings more happiness than the pursuit of success combined with constant restlessness.
> Albert Einstein
> November 1922, Tokyo"

It's an interesting possibility that letters from history may be the shrewd investment commodities of the future. Fewer and fewer paintings by the great artists come up for sale; an early Van Gogh offered for sale in Paris in June 2019 was the first to be auctioned there in twenty years. By contrast the market in significant correspondence is expanding.

There are now dealers who specialize in historical manuscript documents, and the major auction houses hold regular sales of books and manuscripts, in which they include letters of significance. In just one month, June 2019, Sothebys offered a letter written in 1948 by Mao Zedong, with an estimate of $300,000–$400,000; and Christie's devoted an entire sale to the letters of the songwriter Leonard Cohen to his muse Marianne Ihlen. Also in 2019, a pair of letters from 1969 concerning the imminent break-up of the Beatles was offered for sale at $550,000.

The twenty-first century has seen barriers broken in bids to own a handwritten piece of history. In 2017, spurred on by the success of the stage musical *Hamilton*, Sothebys New York sold a collection of letters and other documents from the writing desk of Alexander Hamilton for $2.6 million. That pales beside the highest price ever paid for a letter at auction. In 2013, a letter from Francis Crick, one of the team that discovered DNA, to his son Michael was sold by Christie's New York for $6,098,500. Written in 1953, it described the discovery and included a hand-drawn diagram of the DNA helix.

As we write fewer letters every year, and emails can be deleted at the accidental touch of a keyboard, perhaps old paperwork of all kinds will become more valuable than ever. Hard-copy correspondence is a medium, and a voice, from the past. Maybe, if you can find it, there's a precious letter from history in those old boxes of your grandparents.

Women in the entertainment industry demand change

(January 1, 2018)

On the first of January 2018, the *New York Times* published an open letter signed by more than three hundred women working in the entertainment industry. There had been a surge in women accusing male, film industry executives of sexual abuse. The letter was calling time on sexual harassment and gender inequality.

The letter proclaimed solidarity with all women at risk, from "every house keeper who has tried to escape an assaultive guest" to "every domestic worker or home health aide forcibly touched by a client." It was at pains to avoid criticism that only elite Hollywood women might have the power and temerity to complain about abuse. It spoke, it claimed, for "women in every industry who are subjected to indignities and offensive behavior that they are expected to tolerate in order to make a living."

The signatories demanded that "the struggle for women to break in, to rise up the ranks and to simply be heard and acknowledged in male-dominated workplaces must end. Time's up on this impenetrable monopoly." The open letter sent a shiver down the spine of many a man who previously thought their sexual misconduct would never come to light. The phrase "Time's Up" became both shorthand for the campaign and the umbrella name of several organizations founded to implement its objectives.

The catalyst for the movement was the growing number of sexual assault allegations being made in 2017 against the Hollywood mogul Harvey Weinstein. New York police charged him with several offenses in May 2018 and he was released on a million dollars' bail and ordered to wear a tracking device. He insists on his innocence.

Whatever the outcome of his case, Weinstein's reputation is in tatters, his name indelibly associated with sexual misconduct. The phrase "the Weinstein effect" was coined to describe the subsequent rapid spread of women coming forward with allegations of sexual abuse by powerful and famous men across the world.

While accusations of sexual assault captured headlines, the letter pointed out that this was a symptom of a wider problem: "systemic gender-inequality and imbalance of power fosters an environment that is ripe for abuse and harassment against women." It went on to call for "a significant increase of women in positions of leadership and power across industries" and "equal representation, opportunities, benefits and pay for all women workers."

Making change happen requires resources, and the Time's Up letter set out plans for this. A legal fund was established "to help survivors of sexual assault and harassment across all industries, challenge those responsible for the harm against them and give voice to their experiences." In a little over a year, it had raised more than $20 million.

Time's Up did not happen in isolation. The equally high profile MeToo hashtag is used to draw attention to the ubiquity of sexual violence in dozens of countries. Its French variation—#BalanceTonPorc or Denounce Your Pig—has a nice sense of revulsion to it. Both are part of a wider movement in many countries to realign the balance of power between the genders, a long-overdue next step in the march of civil rights for women.

Time's Up has already changed at least one thing. The letter argued that women, even powerful Hollywood stars, had previously kept quiet for fear of being "attacked and ruined in the process of speaking." Time's Up has broken that silence.

We write on behalf of over 300 women who work in film, television and theater. A little more than two months ago, courageous individuals revealed the dark truth of ongoing sexual harassment and assault by powerful people in the entertainment industry. At one of our most difficult and vulnerable moments, Alianza Nacional de Campesinas (the National Farmworker Women's Alliance) sent us a powerful and compassionate message of solidarity for which we are deeply grateful.

To the members of Alianza and farmworker women across the country, we see you, we thank you, and we acknowledge the heavy weight of our common experience of being preyed upon, harassed, and exploited by those who abuse their power and threaten our physical and economic security. We have similarly suppressed the violence and demeaning harassment for fear that we will be attacked and ruined in the process of speaking out. We share your feelings of anger and shame. We harbor fear that no one will believe us, that we will look weak or that we will be dismissed; and we are terrified that we will be fired or never hired again in retaliation.

JANUARY 1, 2018

Dear Sisters,

We also recognize our privilege and the fact that we have access to enormous platforms to amplify our voices. Both of which have drawn and driven widespread attention to the existence of this problem in our industry that farmworker women and countless individuals employed in other industries have not been afforded.

To every woman employed in agriculture who has had to fend off unwanted sexual advances from her boss, every housekeeper who has tried to escape an assaultive guest, every janitor trapped nightly in a building with a predatory supervisor, every waitress grabbed by a customer and expected to take it with a smile, every garment and factory worker forced to trade sexual acts for more shifts, every domestic worker or home health aide forcibly touched by a client, every immigrant woman silenced by the threat of her undocumented status being reported in retaliation for speaking up and to women in every industry who are subjected to indignities and offensive behavior that they are expected to tolerate in order to make a living: We stand with you. We support you.

Now, unlike ever before, our access to the media and to important decision makers has the potential of leading to real accountability and consequences. We want all survivors of sexual harassment, everywhere, to be heard, to be believed, and to know that accountability is possible.

We also want all victims and survivors to be able to access justice and support for the wrongdoing they have endured. We particularly want to lift up the voices, power, and strength of women working in low-wage industries where the lack of financial stability makes them vulnerable to high rates of gender-based violence and exploitation.

Unfortunately, too many centers of power — from legislatures to boardrooms to executive suites and management to academia — lack gender parity and women do not have equal decision-making authority. This systemic gender-inequality and imbalance of power fosters an environment that is ripe for abuse and harassment against women. Therefore, we call for a significant increase of women in positions of leadership and power across industries. In addition, we seek equal representation, opportunities, benefits and pay for all women workers, not to mention greater representation of women of color, immigrant women, disabled women, and lesbian, bisexual, and transgender women, whose experiences in the workforce are often significantly worse than their white, cisgender, straight peers. The struggle for women to break in, to rise up the ranks and to simply be heard and acknowledged in male-dominated workplaces must end; time's up on this impenetrable monopoly.

We are grateful to the many individuals — survivors and allies — who are speaking out and forcing the conversation about sexual harassment, sexual assault, and gender bias out of the shadows and into the spotlight. We fervently urge the media covering the disclosures by people in Hollywood to spend equal time on the myriad experiences of individuals working in less glamorized and valorized trades.

Harassment too often persists because perpetrators and employers never face any consequences. This is often because survivors, particularly those working in low-wage industries, don't have the resources to fight back. As a first step towards helping women and men across the country seek justice, the signatories of this letter will be seeding a legal fund to help survivors of sexual assault and harassment across all industries challenge those responsible for the harm against them and give voice to their experiences.

We remain committed to holding our own workplaces accountable, pushing for swift and effective change to make the entertainment industry a safe and equitable place for everyone, and telling women's stories through our eyes and voices with the goal of shifting our society's perception and treatment of women.

In Solidarity

ABOVE: The groundbreaking open letter published in the New York Times.

Letter from Greta Thunberg to Indian premier

Dear Mr Modi,

You need to take action now against the climate crisis, not just talking about it, because if you keep on going like this, doing business as usual, and just talking about and bragging about the little victories, you are going to fail. And if you fail, you are going to be seen as one of the worst villains in the human history of the future. And you don't want that.

LEFT: Greta Thunberg on one of her Friday protests in Stockholm.

BELOW: Despite snow in the Swedish capital, Thunberg would turn out, often joined by her classmates and other teenage activists.

Greta Thunberg reads a letter to the Indian Prime Minister

(2019)

With the fearlessness of youth, Swedish schoolgirl Greta Thunberg has confronted governments with her call for action on climate change. In 2019 she called on Prime Minister Narendra Modi of India to do more about his country's record on the environment.

Greta Thunberg came to global attention during her one-woman "Skolstrejk för Klimatet"—School Strike for Climate. She was shocked when her teachers showed images of emaciated polar bears and islands of plastic in the oceans. She could not understand why so little was being done to protect the Earth's climate and environment.

In August 2018, at the age of fifteen, she decided to cut school every Friday in protest. Instead she spent the day on the steps of the Swedish Parliament handing out leaflets to politicians, which declared: "I am doing this because you adults are shitting on my future." After a Swedish TV news crew reported on her stand, others began to join her there, and in time the idea crossed borders. By the end of 2018, similar strikes were taking place in over 250 cities and towns around the globe.

Ms. Thunberg has appeared at demonstrations all over the world, while still maintaining her Friday vigil in Stockholm. In April 2019, she joined the mass demonstration in London organized by Extinction Rebellion, at which she spoke. "We're facing an immediate unprecedented crisis that has never been treated as a crisis and our leaders are all acting like children."

Addressing a room full of such leaders at a United Nations convention on climate change, she told them, "You are not mature enough to tell it like it is. Even that burden you leave to us children." And speaking at the World Economic Forum in Davos in January 2019 she said, "Some people, some companies, some decision makers in particular have known exactly what priceless values they have been sacrificing to continue making unimaginable amounts of money. I think many of you here today belong to that group of people."

Indian Prime Minister Narendra Modi has come in for particular criticism from Thunberg, and she addressed him directly during an interview on February 15, 2019. Turning directly to camera, Greta Thunberg delivered her video letter to Modi and pulled no punches. "Dear Mr Modi," she began, "You need to take action now against the climate crisis, not just talking about it."

Modi was doing worse than "just talking." On taking power in 2014, he halved the budget of his government's Ministry of Environment, Forests, and Climate Change and greatly diluted its powers to protect wildlife and monitor pollution. He froze Greenpeace's bank accounts for their opposition to GM crops, which he has encouraged. Planning regulations were relaxed and industries were free to renew activity in highly polluted areas and required only to report their own pollution voluntarily.

"If you keep on going like this," Greta told Modi, her gaze never wavering, "doing business as usual, and just talking about and bragging about the little victories, you are going to fail. And if you fail, you are going to be seen as one of the worst villains in the human history of the future. And you don't want that."

What Malala Yousafzai did for children's right to education in 2014, Greta Thunberg is doing for their right to an environmentally sustainable future. Yousafzai became the youngest ever recipient of the Nobel Peace Prize in 2014 at the age of seventeen. Walking in her footsteps, the fearless Thunberg was nominated for the 2019 award.

Addendum

(A lifelong correspondence)

Alexander Graham Bell was the friend and benefactor of one of the world's most extraordinary women, Helen Keller. At first he corresponded with her teacher, Anne Sullivan (Macy), but eventually, Helen could construct her own letters with the aid of a Braille typewriter. These two letters touch upon a lifetime of friendship and letters between the two as Keller tries to persuade the elderly Scot to appear in a motion picture of her life story.

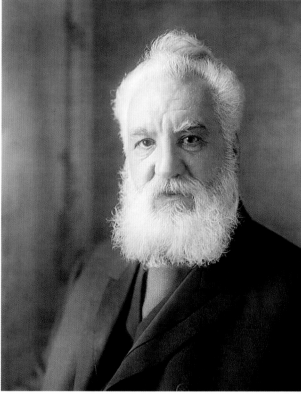

ABOVE: Helen Keller in her graduation robes, and Alexander Graham Bell.

LEFT: Helen Keller's early remark about a "submarine chaser" was in reference to Alexander Graham Bell's experiments with hydrofoils. He spent eleven years working with Casey Baldwin on different craft until in 1919 their HD-4 traveled at 70mph (113kph) across Bras d'Or Lake in Nova Scotia.

July 5, 1918.

Dear Dr. Bell:

Will you sit down on the edge of one of those wonderful submarine-chasers you told me about--if such a swift thing can be sat on with perfect safety--and read this letter? Mind, you are to read it through, and you are not to get what you read mixed up with charts and things! What I am going to write about is most important, it is about you and me--and my teacher.

When we saw you in New York several weeks ago, we told you that the story of my life was to be dramatized for a motion picture, and we asked you if you would be willing to appear in it. You laughed and said, "Do you expect me to go to California to have my picture taken?" Well, it is not as bad as that--not quite. The present plan is to have several pictures made here and in Boston and vicinity before we start West where the main part of the picture will be made. The idea of the picture is to represent my development, education, ambitions, aspirations and friendships faithfully. The intention is, as far as possible, to show distinguished people who have been important in my life. The producers are very desirous to have you appear with Caruso and my teacher and me in the opening scene of the drama.

I feel the greatest hesitation in asking you to come a

thousand leagues for a "snap-shot". If I had not had so many
proofs of your love and forbearance, I should not dare even to
consider making the request. I realize the effort it will cost
to make the journey to New York or Boston. I know how uncomfortable it is to travel in summer. But I hope you may agree with me
that the enterprise may have sufficient value and importance for
humanity to be worth the sacrifice. For a lifetime you have had
steadily before you the vision of service to others. If the picture should fulfil our expectations, it will be a permanent contribution to education.

I believe it has been suggested that if you cannot come,
some one might be "made up" to represent you, provided you would
consent to such a substitute. But that would be only an imitation
of you, not your dear self, and I should not know how to behave
towards a mere substitute of you.

Dear Dr. Bell, it would be such a happiness to have you
beside me in my picture-travels! As in real journeys you have
often made the hours short and free from ennui, so in the drama
of my life, your eloquent hand in mine, you make the way bright
and full of interest, give to misfortune an undertone of hope
and courage that will assist many others beside myself to the
very end. You know that Gibbon has told us how, when he wrote
the last lines of the last page of "The Decline and Fall," he

went out into the garden and paced up and down in his acacia walk overlooking Lausanne and the mountains. He says the silver orb of the moon was reflected from the waters, and all nature was silent. I conceive of the picture-drama as my walk under the acacias. I mean, in a sense it will be the finish of the story of my life. It should carry a message of hope and fulfilment. It should emphasize the significance of courage, faith and devotion. You can readily see, if the people taking part in the drama are not the real people who have walked with me under the acacias, this message will lose something of its force and genuineness. A number of the friends whose love and devotion have enriched my life are gone. Phillips Brooks, Oliver Wendell Holmes, Edward Everett Hale, Henry Rogers, Samuel Clemens and many others would have a place in the picture if they were living. You and Mrs. William Thaw are almost the only ones left who entered the acacia walk with me where it begins in the sweet dawn of childhood.

Even before my teacher came, you held out a warm hand to me in the dark. Indeed, it was through you that she came to me. How vividly it all comes back! How plainly I see the vanquished little child, and the young girl God sent to liberate her! Untrained, alone, almost blind, she journeyed swiftly to me. I still feel her strong, tender, quivering touch, her kisses upon my face. Sometimes I feel that in that supreme moment she thought me into being. Certainly she forestalled and defeated a cruel fate. O the waking rapture! O the shining joy of feet approaching light, of eager, inquisitive hands grasping knowledge! My fingers still glow with the "feel" of the first word that opened its golden heart to me. How everything seemed to think, to live! Shall I, in all the years of eternity, forget the torrent of wonders that rushed upon me out of the darkness and silence? And you are part of that wonder, that joy! I have not forgotten how you followed step by step my teacher's efforts to free my mind, my life, my heart from the tyranny of circumstance. From the first you understood the stupendous task of the young teacher. You were quick to recognize her ability, her tireless energy, enthusiasm and originality. I love you for the generous way in which you have always upheld her work. When others who had little faith in the power of spirit to conquer blindness doubted and faltered, it was you who heartened us for the struggle. When I made up my mind to learn to speak, you cheered us on with a faith that outran our own. How closely I felt your sympathy and forward-looking faith in me when I fought my way through college! Again and again you said to me, "Helen, let no sense of limitations hold you back. You can do anything you think you can. Remember that

25 SEMINOLE AVENUE
FOREST HILLS
L. I., N.Y.

many will be brave in your courage." You have always shown a
father's joy in my successes and a father's tenderness when things
have not gone right. After all these years you still take us both
up in your great heart.

How can I ever express what all this means to us? Words are
not eloquent enough to declare all the good fortune, the pride, the
joy, the inspiration we feel in your friendship. That is why we
want so very much to have you appear in our picture. Your name
alone is a rich harvest from which come high thoughts and desires.
It is as a deep, sweet chime ringing in our hearts and telling us
of a life beautiful in its boundless generosity, in its consecra-
tion to the service of humanity. As Praxiteles animated stone, so
you have quickened dumb lips with living speech. You have poured
the sweet waters of language into the deserts where the ear hears
not, and you have given might to man's thought, so that on auda-
cious wings of sound it pours over land and sea at his bidding.
Will you not let the thousands who know your name and have given
you their hearts look upon your face and be glad?

With dear love from us both, I am,

Affectionately your friend,

Helen Keller

P.S. They would like to make the picture of you about the middle
of this month.

Helen Keller,
Drawer 25

Beinn Bhreagh
Near Baddeck
Nova Scotia

1918 July 18

My dear Helen:

I have the greatest aversion to appearing in a moving-picture, and I had just written to Dr. Francis Trevelyan Miller declining positively, when your letter of July 5 arrived. It is a letter which would move a heart of stone and it has touched me deeply. It brings back recollections of the little girl I met in Washington so long ago, and you are still that little girl to me. I can only say that anything you want me to do I will do for your sake, but I can't go down to the States before you go to California, and we will have to wait till you come back.

You must remember that when I met you first I wasn't seventy-one years old and didn't have white hair, and you were only a little girl of seven, so it is obvious that any historical picture will have to be made with substitutes for both of us. You will have to find someone with dark hair to impersonate the Alexander Graham Bell of your childhood, and then perhaps your appearance with me in a later scene when we both are as we are now may be interesting by contrast. I have no doubt that when you return from California we can arrange a meeting to suit both of us.

With much love to you and Teacher,

Your loving friend,

(signed) Alexander Graham Bell

Miss Helen Keller
25 Seminole Avenue,
Forest Hills, Long Island, N.Y.

Index

Acknowledgments

The publisher wishes to thank the following for kindly supplying the images and letters that appear in this book:

African Studies Center (University of Pennsylvania), Alamy, Archives National (France), Art-vanGogh.com, Associated Press, *Atlantic Monthly*, AtomicArchive.com, Beatrix Potter Gallery, Beinecke Rare Book and Manuscript Library, BlackPast.org, Bletchley Park, Bonhams, British Library, British Online Archives, Cambridge University Library, Christie's London, *Daily Mail*, Digital National Security Archives, Dwight D. Eisenhower Library and Museum, Eddie Jordan Racing, English Heritage, Franklin D. Roosevelt Presidential Library and Museum, Founders Archives.org, FriendsOfDarwin.com, General Register Office, Getty Images, *The Guardian*, *The Independent*, International Institute of Social History, JewishVirtual Library, John F. Kennedy Presidential Library and Museum, The Karl Marx House, Karpels Manuscript Library, Lambeth Palace Archives, Library of Congress, Mary Evans Picture Library, Massachusetts Historical Society, Metropolitan Museum of Art (New York), Motorsport News, National Air and Space Museum (Smithsonian), National Archives (Kew), National Gallery (London), National Maritime Museum (Greenwich), National Museum of Capodimonte, Nelson Mandela Centre of Memory, Newport Historical Society, *New York Times*, Ohio State University, Oxford Institute, Parliamentary Archives (London), Pavilion Image Library, Perkins School for the Blind, Portal de Archivos Españoles, Presidential Library (Moscow), The Postal Museum (London), Sackett Family Association, Simon Wiesenthal Center, Sotheby's, Thomas Fisher Rare Book Archive, Times Up, University of Michigan Library, University of Nebraska-Lincoln, Venganza.org

Publisher's note: Unusual, outdated, or erroneous spelling and terminology have been retained in the featured transcripts in order to accurately reflect the source material.